Android Espresso Revealed

Writing Automated UI Tests

Denys Zelenchuk

Apress®

Android Espresso Revealed: Writing Automated UI Tests

Denys Zelenchuk
Zürich, Switzerland

ISBN-13 (pbk): 978-1-4842-4314-5　　　　ISBN-13 (electronic): 978-1-4842-4315-2
https://doi.org/10.1007/978-1-4842-4315-2

Library of Congress Control Number: 2019933720

Managing Director, Apress Media LLC: Welmoed Spahr
Acquisitions Editor: Steve Anglin
Development Editor: Matthew Moodie
Coordinating Editor: Mark Powers

Cover designed by eStudioCalamar

Distributed to the book trade worldwide by Springer Science+Business Media New York, 233 Spring Street, 6th Floor, New York, NY 10013. Phone 1-800-SPRINGER, fax (201) 348-4505, e-mail orders-ny@springer-sbm.com, or visit www.springeronline.com. Apress Media, LLC is a California LLC and the sole member (owner) is Springer Science + Business Media Finance Inc (SSBM Finance Inc). SSBM Finance Inc is a **Delaware** corporation.

For information on translations, please e-mail editorial@apress.com; for reprint, paperback, or audio rights, please email bookpermissions@springernature.com.

Apress titles may be purchased in bulk for academic, corporate, or promotional use. eBook versions and licenses are also available for most titles. For more information, reference our Print and eBook Bulk Sales web page at http://www.apress.com/bulk-sales.

Any source code or other supplementary material referenced by the author in this book is available to readers on GitHub via the book's product page, located at www.apress.com/9781484243145. For more detailed information, please visit http://www.apress.com/source-code.

Printed on acid-free paper

Table of Contents

About the Author

Denys Zelenchuk's professional career as a test engineer started in Poland in 2010. Since 2011, he has been involved in testing mobile applications. He has worked at companies such as Tieto Poland and XING (Hamburg, Germany) and currently works and lives in Zurich, Switzerland for Numbrs Personal Finance AG as Senior Quality Assurance Engineer. As of October 2013, he's been using the Espresso for Android test automation framework to write automated tests.

About the Technical Reviewer

Massimo Nardone has more than 24 years of experience in security, web/mobile development, and cloud and IT architecture. His true IT passions are security and Android.

He has been programming and teaching others how to program using Android, Perl, PHP, Java, VB, Python, C/C++, and MySQL for more than 20 years.

He holds a Master of Science degree in Computing Science from the University of Salerno, Italy.

He has worked as a project manager, software engineer, research engineer, chief security architect, information security manager, PCI/SCADA auditor, and senior lead IT security/Cloud/SCADA architect for many years.

His technical skills include security, Android, cloud, Java, MySQL, Drupal, Cobol, Perl, web and mobile development, MongoDB, D3, Joomla, Couchbase, C/C++, WebGL, Python, Pro Rails, Django CMS, Jekyll, Scratch, and more.

He worked as a visiting lecturer and supervisor for exercises at the Networking Laboratory of the Helsinki University of Technology (Aalto University). He holds four international patents (in the PKI, SIP, SAML, and Proxy areas).

He currently works as the Chief Information Security Officer (CISO) for Cargotec Oyj and he is member of the ISACA Finland Chapter Board.

Massimo has reviewed more than 45 IT books for different publishers and has coauthored *Pro JPA in Java EE 8* (Apress, 2018), *Beginning EJB in Java EE 8* (Apress, 2018), and *Pro Android Games* (Apress, 2015).

Introduction

Who This Book Is For

This book is a guideline on how to write Android user interface tests for quality assurance engineers and test automation engineers who are interested in Android test automation using Espresso for Android (Espresso). It can also be valuable to Android developers involved in writing UI or integration tests.

This book was written mostly for software or test engineers with medium to advanced knowledge in Android test automation; however, engineers with basic development and test automation experience will benefit from it as well.

What This Book Covers

There is a lot of good official Android testing documentation out there, including GitHub projects with source code, but it is sometimes hard to find the needed portion of information, especially when it comes to plain automated UI end-to-end testing, which Android Espresso users face on a daily basis.

I tried to cover all the major topics of writing functional UI automated tests using the Espresso testing framework, including different ways of running automated tests, architecting test projects in easy and maintainable ways, and using tools that help to implement automated tests with the less effort.

Source Code and Sample Project

To demonstrate all the code examples throughout the book, the Google samples Android architecture TO-DO application project (`https://github.com/googlesamples/ android-architecture`) was forked and modified so it was possible to showcase the majority of the Android UI test automation samples using the Espresso for Android and UI Automator testing frameworks.

The sample TO-DO application project contains two branches, where one uses Android Testing Support library dependencies and the other covers AndroidX Test library usage. Readers are free to select the one they prefer.

The source code is also accessible via the Download Source Code link located at www.apress.com/9781484243145.

Chapter Overview

Chapter 1: Getting Started with Espresso for Android

This chapter describes the basics of Espresso. It defines goals and approaches of user interface testing and provides examples for setting up tests inside the Android Studio IDE project. It also explains how to identify Android application UI elements, perform actions and assertions, and apply matchers to them. At the end of this chapter, you will be able to write simple tests and execute them from inside the Android Studio IDE on the device or emulator. It also includes examples for how to run tests using Gradle or shell commands.

Chapter 2: Customizing Espresso for Our Needs

With more advanced examples, you will learn how to implement a custom ViewAction, including clicks and swiping actions; and a ViewMatcher, such as matching complex views as RecyclerView matchers. You will learn how to use custom actions and matchers, implement a custom FailureHandler with the possibility to take and save screenshots upon failure.

Chapter 3: Writing Espresso Tests with Kotlin

This chapter gives an overview of the benefits of using the Kotlin programming language in tests and explains how to migrate tests written in Java to Kotlin. It also provides an example of creating an Espresso domain specific language in Kotlin.

Chapter 4: Handling Network Operations and Asynchronous Actions

This chapter explains how to handle application network requests and long-lasting operations during test execution with the help of the `IdlingResource` interface. It provides an example of using `ConditionalWatcher` as an alternative to `IdlingResource`.

Chapter 5: Verifying and Stubbing Intents with IntentMatchers

This chapter explains using `IntentMatchers` inside an application as well as how to stub external intents and provide extras. A good example of an external intent is selecting an image from the photo gallery, which then can be used by the application you're testing.

Chapter 6: Testing Web Views

This chapter covers testing `WebViews` inside an application. Implemented `WebViews` showcase different UI elements that the Espresso-Web API is able to operate on. You will be provided an Espresso-Web cheat sheet as part of the book's content.

Chapter 7: Accessibility Testing

This chapter unleashes the topic of how to test application accessibility using Espresso for Android. It raises awareness about the importance of accessibility testing and provides an overview of manual tools that can be used to test application accessibility.

Chapter 8: Espresso and UI Automator: The Perfect Tandem

This chapter explains one of the most powerful test automation setups for Android, which combines the Espresso test framework with the UI Automator testing tool. Examples show how to test notifications or operate on third-party apps during Espresso tests execution.

Chapter 9: Dealing with Runtime System Actions and Permissions

This chapter explains different ways that you can deal with system actions like permission request dialogs and describes possible solutions for changing the Android emulator system language programmatically.

Chapter 10: Android Test Automation Tooling

After reading this chapter, you will understand how to use the Espresso test recorder, set up a test device or emulator to minimize test flakiness, and run tests in the Firebase cloud.

Chapter 11: Screen Object Design Pattern in Android UI Tests

This chapter shows you how to apply the screen object (the same as page object) architecture approach to the test project, which allows you to reduce the maintenance effort spent on reworking tests after changes in the application's source code.

Chapter 12: Testing the Robot Pattern with Espresso and Kotlin

In this chapter, you learn how to apply a testing robot pattern that splits the test implementation from the business logic to the Espresso UI tests.

Chapter 13: Supervised Monkey Tests with Espresso and UI Automator

This chapter shows how to implement supervised pseudo-monkey tests using Espresso and UI Automator, which can be applicable to applications whose source code you have access to as well as to third-party applications.

Chapter 14: AndroidX Test Library

This chapter demonstrates how to migrate test code from Android support to the AndroidX Test library. You will find information about new APIs introduced in the AndroidX Test library and see how they can be applied to UI tests.

Chapter 15: Improving Productivity and Testing Unusual Components

This chapter contains code samples that were not covered in the other chapters and Espresso testing tips that may increase your daily test writing productivity. This includes creating parameterized tests, aggregating tests into test suites, using AndroidStudio Live templates in UI tests, setting SeekBar progress in Espresso UI tests, and Espresso Drawable matchers topics.

What This Book Doesn't Cover

The goal of the book is to create a guide for how to write end-to-end UI automated tests for Android applications without mocking or stubbing application dependencies. From my point of view, this is the closest way to reproduce end user behavior. The book does not explain how to mock application data and network connection requests or bypass some states in the application workflow.

Tools Requirements

To be able to work with this book, you need to have at least a basic knowledge in working with such tools and platforms as Android Studio IDE, Gradle, GitHub, and shell/bash. In most cases, I explain how to configure your IDE and note which commands should be used to run the specific scripts.

Legal Notice

This book contains code, documentation, and images taken from the Android developers page at https://developer.android.com. They are covered by the Apache 2.0 License (http://www.apache.org/licenses/) mentioned in Appendix C.

CHAPTER 1

Getting Started with Espresso for Android

Espresso for Android is a lightweight, fast, and customizable Android testing framework, designed to provide concise and reliable automated UI tests. At the end of October 2013, Espresso was open sourced by Google after it was announced at the Google Test Automation Conference. From that moment it has been gaining popularity across Android software and test engineers. Now it is the most popular testing framework for the Android platform because its features and development are driven by Google and the Android Open Source community.

This chapter describes Espresso's basics—the core components of the Espresso testing framework that are used in test automation to replicate the end user behavior. This includes locating application UI elements on the screen and operating on them.

Espresso includes the following packages:

- `espresso-core`—Contains core and basic view matchers, actions, and assertions.

- `espresso-contrib`—External contributions that contain DatePicker, RecyclerView, and Drawer actions, accessibility checks, and the `CountingIdlingResource`.

- `espresso-intents`—Extensions to validate and stub intents for hermetic testing.

- `espresso-idling-resource`—Espresso's mechanism for synchronizing background jobs.

- `espresso-remote`—Location of Espresso's multi-process functionality.

- `espresso-web`—Contains resources for WebView support.

© Denys Zelenchuk 2019
D. Zelenchuk, *Android Espresso Revealed*, https://doi.org/10.1007/978-1-4842-4315-2_1

User Interface Testing: Goals and Approach

As mentioned, this book focuses on writing functional end-to-end UI tests, which is the closest way to replicate end user behavior and catch potential issues before a product goes live. Despite the fact that such tests can be much slower than unit or integration tests, they usually discover issues that were not caught during the unit and integration testing stages.

I would like to emphasize the fact that all the test examples in the book do not contain any conditional logic. Conditional logic in test automation is a bad practice because the same test can be executed in different ways, which eliminates easy ways of bug reproduction, reduces the trust in the tests, and increases the test maintenance effort.

Tests should be written in a simple and plain way, so everyone who looks at them will understand what step led to the issue.

Setting Up the Sample Project

The Espresso for Android testing framework supports devices running Android 2.3.3 (API level 10) and higher. It was developed for writing UI tests within a single target application. In this book, all the examples were developed and tested with the following environment:

- Device—Nexus 5X, Android 8.1.0 (API level 27)

- IDE—AndroidStudio 3.2.1

Let's start setting up our sample project. It is a simple TO-DO application forked from the googlesamples/android-architecture GitHub repository (https://github.com/googlesamples/android-architecture) and modified in a way to show you most of the Espresso use cases.

Here is the link to the GitHub page where you can download the source code or check out the project directly in your AndroidStudio IDE—https://github.com/Apress/android-espresso-revealed. The sample application allows us to add, edit, and delete TO-DO tasks. It contains different types of UI elements without functional load but the variety of the components used there allows us to see Espresso in action.

After the repository is pulled into the AndroidStudio IDE, you will see a todoapp project with one app module. This sample project already contains a test package. Espresso dependencies are added to the build.gradle file. See Figure 1-1. In general, for every test project where Espresso is used, the following steps should be done (this example is based on the TO-DO application):

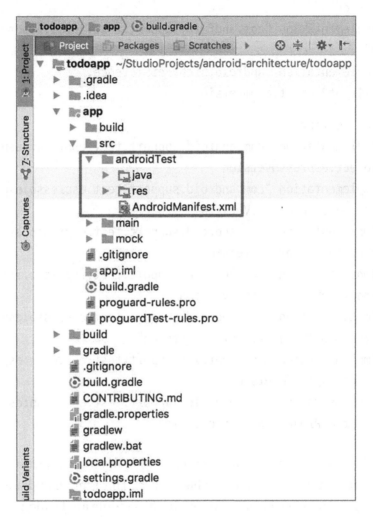

Figure 1-1. *Sample project structure*

1. Add an `androidTest` package inside the application module.

2. Set up the Espresso dependencies in the `todoapp/app/build.gradle` file inside the application module. Put them in the `dependencies{...}` section.

```
// Android Testing Support Library's runner and rules
androidTestImplementation "com.android.support.test:runner:$rootProject.
ext.runnerVersion"
androidTestImplementation "com.android.support.test:rules:$rootProject.ext.
rulesVersion"
androidTestImplementation "android.arch.persistence.
room:testing:$rootProject.roomVersion"

// Espresso UI Testing
androidTestImplementation "com.android.support.test.espresso:espresso-
core:$rootProject.espressoVersion"
androidTestImplementation "com.android.support.test.espresso:espresso-
contrib:$rootProject.espressoVersion"
androidTestImplementation "com.android.support.test.espresso:espresso-
intents:$rootProject.espressoVersion"
androidTestImplementation "com.android.support.test.espresso.idling:idling-
concurrent:$rootProject.espressoVersion"
androidTestImplementation "com.android.support.test.espresso:espresso-
idling-resource:$rootProject.espressoVersion"
androidTestImplementation "com.android.support.test.espresso:espresso-
web:$rootProject.espressoVersion"
androidTestImplementation "com.android.support.test.espresso:espresso-
accessibility:$rootProject.espressoVersion"
```

3. Put the Espresso dependency versions inside the root project
   todoapp/build.gradle file (see Figure 1-2). This is not mandatory
   but is good practice in case there's a multi-module application
   structure. Later, instead of updating dependency versions in
   multiple gradle files, we would only need to update them in
   one place.

```
// Define versions in a single place
ext {
    // Sdk and tools
    minSdkVersion = 26
    targetSdkVersion = 28
    compileSdkVersion = 28
    buildToolsVersion = '27.0.3'

    // App dependencies
    supportLibraryVersion = '28.0.0'
    guavaVersion = '18.0'
    runnerVersion = '1.0.2'
    rulesVersion = '1.0.2'
    espressoVersion = '3.0.2'
    accessibilityFramework = '2.1'
    uiautomatorVersion = '2.1.3'
    roomVersion = "1.1.1"
}
```

Figure 1-2. *todoapp/build.gradle: keeping dependency versions in one place*

In most cases, after dependencies have been added, changed, or deleted, we must synchronize the project in AndroidStudio by clicking on the Gradle Sync icon ⊚. You need an Internet connection to download any changed dependencies.

4. Add a test package inside the `todoapp/app/src/androidTest/ java` directory. Usually the test package will have the same name as the application being tested, but with a `.test` postfix.

Starting from this moment, you can add your first test class and begin writing tests.

Understanding Android Instrumentation

On Android UI tests, we use the instrumentation mechanism to execute tests. Unlike unit tests, which can run on the JVM directly, instrumented tests run on a real device or emulator. Such tests have access to the Instrumentation API, which enables us to control the test application from our test code, provides access to the context of the application, and allows us to replicate user behavior through different UI actions, like click, swipe, etc. This is achieved because the instrumented test application runs in the same process as the application being tested. Instrumentation will be instantiated before any of the application code, allowing it to monitor the interactions that the system has with the application.

5

Instrumentation is usually declared in test application Android manifest file using the `instrumentation` XML tag. Here is the example of instrumentation declaration with the `AndroidJUnitRunner` from the Android Support library:

```
<instrumentation
    android:name="android.support.test.runner.AndroidJUnitRunner"
    android:targetPackage="com.example.android.architecture.blueprints.
    todoapp" />
```

Here is the same sample for the AndroidX Test library:

```
<instrumentation
    android:name="androidx.test.runner.AndroidJUnitRunner"
    android:targetPackage="com.example.android.architecture.blueprints.
    todoapp" />
```

This also can be achieved by declaring it in the application module `build.gradle` file:

```
android {
...
    defaultConfig {
        ...
        applicationId "com.example.android.architecture.blueprints.todoapp"
        testInstrumentationRunner 'android.support.test.runner.AndroidJUnitRunner'
    }
...
}

android {
...
    defaultConfig {
        ...
        applicationId "com.example.android.architecture.blueprints.todoapp"
        testInstrumentationRunner 'androidx.test.runner.AndroidJUnitRunner'
    }
...
}
```

In both cases, we provide the instrumentation test runner name and the target application package, which is the test application package. In the `build.gradle` file, it is called `applicationId`. `AndroidJUnitRunner` is the default Android JUnit test runner, starting from API level 8 (Android 2.2). It allows us to run JUnit3 or JUnit4 based tests.

The test runner handles loading your test package and the test app to a device, running your tests, and reporting the test results.

To access the information about the current test, we run the `InstrumentationRegistry` class. It holds a reference to the instrumentation object running in the process as well as to the target application context object, the test application context object, and the command-line arguments passed into your test.

A couple of words about annotations used with Espresso:

- Whenever we create a test class, it or its superclass should be annotated with a `@RunWith(AndroidJUnit4.class)` annotation. Otherwise, the default JUnit runner will take over the running process and the tests will fail.

- To execute code once before or after any test method inside the class, the `@BeforeClass` or `@AfterClass` JUnit annotations can be used.

- To execute code before or after each test method inside the class, the `@Before` or `@After` JUnit annotations can be used. This can be useful when several tests need similar objects created or deleted before/after they can run.

- The `@Rule` annotates fields that reference rules or methods that return a rule. Rules can be used for different purposes. For example, later in the book, we will talk about activity or `TestWatcher` rules.

Refer to the `BaseTest.java` class to see how some of the described annotations are used:

```
@RunWith(AndroidJUnit4.class)
public class BaseTest {

    @Before
    public void setUp() throws Exception {
        setFailureHandler(new CustomFailureHandler(
                InstrumentationRegistry.getInstrumentation().
                getTargetContext()));
    }
```

```
@Rule
public ActivityTestRule<TasksActivity> menuActivityTestRule =
    new ActivityTestRule<>(TasksActivity.class);
}
```

Espresso Basics

Every mobile application has some form of user interface (UI). In the Android world, this is accomplished through the use of View and ViewGroup objects. They are used for drawing UI elements on the Android device screen. From a testing point of view, we are interested in these UI elements to further perform actions or verifications on them. The first step we have to do is locate these views in the application UI.

Identifying Application UI Elements

Before jumping into the Espresso topic, let's think about the mobile application from the end user perspective. What do users do when they use the application? They:

1. Search for UI elements on the screen (buttons, lists, edit text fields, icons, etc.).

2. Perform actions on UI elements (click, double-click, swipe, type, etc.).

3. Check the result (text is typed, click led to expected result, list is scrolled, etc.).

So, our first task when we start writing automated tests is to find the UI elements in the application we would like to perform actions on. They can be easily located with the help of a couple of tools. The first possibility is to use Android Device Monitor.

To start the standalone Device Monitor application, enter the following on the command line inside the `android-sdk/tools/` directory:

```
monitor
```

After the Android Device Monitor starts, connect the device. Select it by tapping on the device name inside the Devices tab, open the screen you want to inspect, and click the Phone 📱 icon (see Figure 1-3). After following these steps, you will be able to inspect the application UI by just clicking on the available elements inside the Android Device Monitor. The details of the element are shown on the right side, including resource ID, text, content description, etc. This information is very important because it will become the base for views identification inside the application UI.

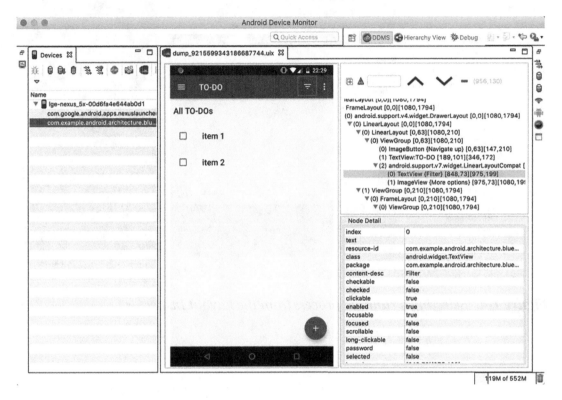

Figure 1-3. *Identifying UI elements by clicking on them*

The second option is to use Layout Inspector, which is available from the AndroidStudio Tools ➤ Layout Inspector menu. Select the needed activity or fragment and start to investigate the application layout (see Figures 1-4 and 1-5).

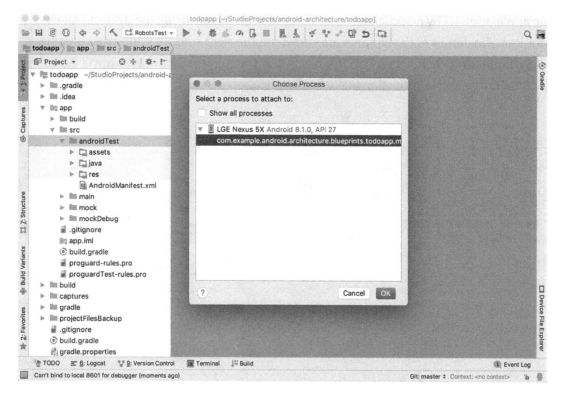

Figure 1-4. *Selecting a running process from the Layout Inspector*

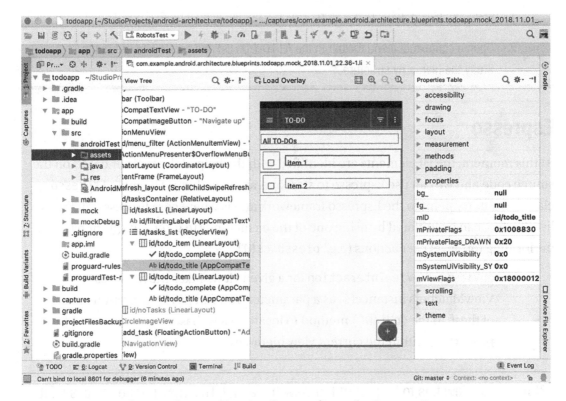

Figure 1-5. *Analyzing the application layout from the Layout Inspector*

As you can see in Figure 1-5, the Layout Inspector view is more detailed. It provides us with more data compared to the Android Device Monitor, which provides more possibilities for view identification and verification. Another benefit of the Layout Inspector is that it saves the layout dumps inside the /captures folder, which can be easily accessed without the need to start another tool. They can be committed into the source control system and used by multiple team members.

EXERCISE 1

Inspecting the Application Layout

Now it is time for the first exercise—to build and install the sample TO-DO application on an emulator or real device, launch it, and then make layout dumps with the Monitor and Layout Inspector tools in different application sections. You can then analyze the layouts and understand how these tools work and finally decide which one is better for you.

1. Make the layout dump in the All TO-DOs list and study the hierarchy structure.

2. Open a contextual menu toolbar in the All TO-DOs list and create a layout dump. Study the hierarchy structure.

Espresso

At this moment, the UI elements are identified with the help of the tools or based on the source code and we can use Espresso to start operating on them. The main Espresso class is the entry point to the Espresso framework and is where core Espresso methods live. Testing can be initiated by using one of the on methods (e.g., onView()) or by performing top-level user actions (e.g., pressBack()).

- onView()—A ViewInteraction for a given view. Takes the hamcrest ViewMatchers instance(s) as a parameter. You can pass one or more of these to the onView() method to locate a view, based on view properties, within the current view hierarchy.

Note   The view has to be part of the view hierarchy. This may not be the case if it is rendered as part of an AdapterView (e.g., a ListView). If this is the case, use Espresso.onData to load the view first.

- onData()—A DataInteraction for a data object (e.g., a ListView). Takes as a parameter a hamcrest matcher that matches the data object represented by the single item in the list.

- pressBack()—A press on the back button. Throws PerformException if the currently displayed activity is a root activity, since pressing the back button would result in the application closing.

- closeSoftKeyboard()—Closes the soft keyboard if it's open.

- openContextualActionModeOverflowMenu()—Opens the overflow menu displayed in the contextual options of an ActionMode.

- openActionBarOverflowOrOptionsMenu()—Opens the overflow menu displayed within an ActionBar.

We will start with the basic Espresso functionality. First we will see how operations on single views work with the onView() method. As a parameter, it takes a hamcrest matcher to match a view in the application UI. We will learn more about view matchers in the next section.

Espresso ViewMatchers

View matchers form a collection of hamcrest Java matchers that match views. The Espresso ViewMatchers are as follows (I have noted the most frequently used ones based on my experience):

- isAssignableFrom()—Matches a view based on an instance or subclass of the provided class. Normally used in combination with other ViewMatchers. Commonly used.

- withClassName()-Returns a matcher that matches views with class name matching the given matcher.

- isDisplayed()-Returns a matcher that matches views that are currently displayed on the screen to the user. Commonly used.

Note   isDisplayed() will select views that are partially displayed (e.g., the full height/width of the view is greater than the height/width of the visible rectangle). If you want to ensure the entire rectangle is displayed, use isCompletelyDisplayed().

- isCompletelyDisplayed()-Returns a matcher that only accepts a view whose height and width fit perfectly within the currently displayed region of this view.

Note   There exist views (such as ScrollViews) whose height and width are larger than the physical device screen by design. Such views will never be completely displayed.

- isDisplayingAtLeast()-Returns a matcher that accepts a view so long as a given percentage of that view's area is not obscured by any parent view and is thus visible to the user.

- isEnabled()-Returns a matcher that matches view(s) that are enabled. Commonly used.

- isFocusable()-Returns a matcher that matches view(s) that are focusable.

- hasFocus()-Returns a matcher that matches view(s) that currently have focus.

- isSelected()-Returns a matcher that matches view(s) that are selected.

- hasSibling()-Returns a matcher that matches view(s) based on their siblings. This may be particularly useful when a view cannot be uniquely selected on properties such as text or view ID. For example, a call button is repeated several times in a contact layout and the only way to differentiate the call button view is by what appears next to it (e.g., the unique name of the contact).

- withContentDescription()-Returns a matcher that matches view(s) based on the content description property value. Commonly used.

- withId()-Returns a matcher that matches view(s) based on content description's id. Commonly used.

Note   Android resource IDs are not guaranteed to be unique. You may have to pair this matcher with another one to guarantee a unique view selection.

- withResourceName()-Returns a matcher that matches view(s) based on resource ID names, (for instance, channel_avatar).

- withTagKey()-Returns a matcher that matches view(s) based on tag keys.

- withTagValue()-Returns a matcher that matches view(s) based on tag property values.

- `withText()`-Returns a matcher that matches view(s) based on its text property value.

- `withHint()`-Returns a matcher that matches view(s) based on its hint property value.

- `isChecked()`-Returns a matcher that accepts it only if the view is a `CompoundButton` (or a subtype of) and is in checked state. Commonly used.

- `isNotChecked()`-Returns a matcher that accepts it only if the view is a `CompoundButton` (or subtype of) and is not in the checked state. Commonly used.

- `hasContentDescription()`-Returns a matcher that matches view(s) with any content description.

- `hasDescendant()`-Returns a matcher that matches view(s) based on the presence of a descendant in its view hierarchy.

- `isClickable()`-Returns a matcher that matches view(s) that are clickable.

- `isDescendantOfA()`-Returns a matcher that matches view(s) based on the given ancestor type.

- `withEffectiveVisibility()`-Returns a matcher that matches view(s) that have "effective" visibility set to the given value.

- `withAlpha()`-Matches view(s) with the specified alpha value. Alpha is a view property value from 0 to 1, where 0 means the view is completely transparent and 1 means the view is completely opaque.

- `withParent()`-A matcher that accepts a view only if the view's parent is accepted by the provided matcher.

- `withChild()`-Matches view(s) whose child is accepted by the provided matcher.

- `hasChildCount()`-Matches a `ViewGroup` (e.g., a `ListView`) if it has exactly the specified number of children.

- `hasMinimumChildCount()`-Matches a `ViewGroup` (e.g., a `ListView`) if it has at least the specified number of children.

- `isRoot()`-Returns a matcher that matches the root view.

- `hasImeAction()`-Returns a matcher that matches views that support input methods.

- `hasLinks()`-Returns a matcher that matches TextView(s) that have links.

- `withSpinnerText()`-Returns a matcher that matches a descendant of a spinner that is displaying the string of the selected item associated with the given resource ID.

- `isJavascriptEnabled()`-Returns a matcher that matches web view(s) if they are evaluating JavaScript.

- `hasErrorText()`-Returns a matcher that matches `EditText` based on the edit text error string value.

- `withInputType()`-Returns a matcher that matches `android.text.InputType`.

- `withParentIndex()`-Returns a matcher that matches the child index inside the `ViewParent`.

As an example, here is the `withText()` ViewMatcher that is passed to the `onView()` method to match the view, shown in Figure 1-6, based on its text:

```
onView(withText("item 1"));    // locating view with todo "item 1"
```

A similar approach is used to locate the filter view in Figure 1-3 based on the view ID and using the `withId()` ViewMatcher. You probably know that all Android application assets, from views to strings, are stored in dynamically created `R.java` files. Therefore, if the target view has an ID value defined by a developer, we are able to locate it by referencing the ID value from the `R.java` class-`R.id.view_id`:

```
onView(withId(R.id.menu_filter));    //locating the filter menu item
```

It is time to look at the official Espresso cheat sheet, available from the following link-`https://developer.android.com/training/testing/espresso/cheat-sheet`. (See Figure 1-6) At this moment we are interested in ViewMatchers section. You can see that ViewMatchers are grouped into the following focus areas:

- User properties

- UI properties

- Object matchers

- Hierarchy

- Input

- Class

- Root matchers

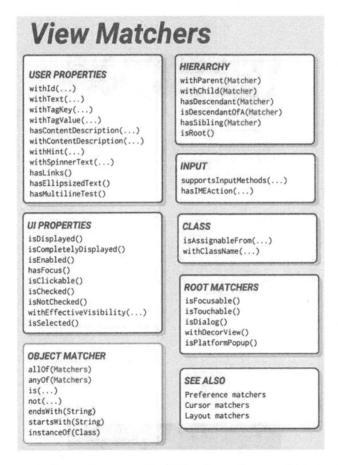

Figure 1-6. *Espresso cheat sheet 2.1-ViewMatchers (source* https://developer. android.com/training/testing/espresso/cheat-sheet)

Let's look at some examples of how these ViewMatchers can be used with our sample application. Open the ViewMatchersExampleTest.java class and look at the test methods. All of them are listed in Figure 1-7.

```
@Test
public void userProperties() {
    onView(withId(R.id.fab_add_task));
    onView(withText("All TO-DOs"));
    onView(withContentDescription(R.string.menu_filter));
    onView(hasContentDescription());
    onView(withHint(R.string.name_hint));
}
```

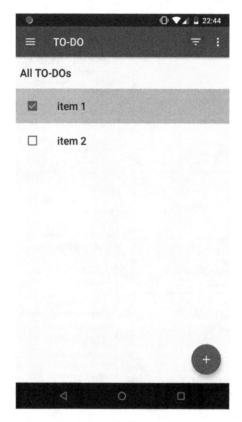

Figure 1-7. *List of TO-DOs in the TO-DO application*

In the test case, you can see that we identify views on the screen shown in Figure 1-7. The floating action button is identified by its ID-onView(withId(R.id.fab_add_task)). The TO-DO items list title is identified based on its text-onView(withText("All TO-DOs")). The filter icon in the toolbar is located by the content description text-onVie w(withContentDescription(R.string.menu_filter)). The presence of the content description is in a view or based on a view hint.

```
@Test
public void uiProperties() {
    onView(isDisplayed());
    onView(isEnabled());
    onView(isChecked());
}
```

In this test case, there are examples of identifying views by their UI appearance. Based on the screen in Figure 1-7, we see that most of the views are displayed and enabled. That means onView(isDisplayed()) or onView(isEnabled()) can't be used without additional matchers, because the tests will fail with ambiguous matching exceptions. In the following test case, you can see how two matchers are combined into a sequence of matchers with the help of the allOf() hamcrest logical matcher. It will return the matched object only when all the matchers inside it successfully execute. See Figures 1-8 through 1-10. In a later section, you will learn more about the hamcrest matchers.

```
@Test
public void objectMatcher() {
    onView(not(isChecked()));
    onView(allOf(withText("item 1"), isChecked()));
}

@Test
public void hierarchy() {
    onView(withParent(withId(R.id.todo_item)));
    onView(withChild(withText("item 2")));
    onView(isDescendantOfA(withId(R.id.todo_item)));
    onView(hasDescendant(isChecked()));
```

```
    onView(hasSibling(withContentDescription(R.string.menu_filter)));
}

@Test
public void input() {
    onView(supportsInputMethods());
    onView(hasImeAction(EditorInfo.IME_ACTION_SEND));
}

@Test
public void classMatchers() {
    onView(isAssignableFrom(CheckBox.class));
    onView(withClassName(is(FloatingActionButton.class.
getCanonicalName())));
}

@Test
public void rootMatchers() {
    onView(isFocusable());
    onView(withText(R.string.name_hint)).inRoot(isTouchable());
    onView(withText(R.string.name_hint)).inRoot(isDialog());
    onView(withText(R.string.name_hint)).inRoot(isPlatformPopup());
}

@Test
public void preferenceMatchers() {
    onData(withSummaryText("3 days"));
    onData(withTitle("Send notification"));
    onData(withKey("example_switch"));
    onView(isEnabled());
}

@Test
public void layoutMatchers() {
    onView(hasEllipsizedText());
    onView(hasMultilineText());
}
```

Figure 1-8. *EditText example from the General preferences in the application settings*

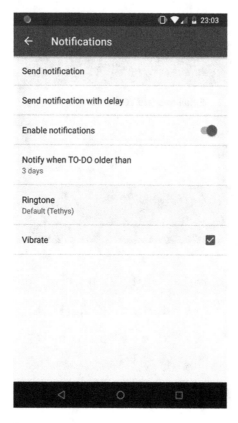

Figure 1-9. *General preferences section in the application settings*

Figure 1-10. *The TO-DO task detail view*

We will not discuss the cursor matchers shown in the ViewMatchers section of the Espresso spreadsheet, because their goal is to operate at a database level, which is used in unit and integration tests and is therefore out of this book's scope.

Now let's take a step aside from our sample application and look at some examples of hamcrest string matchers. For simplicity, the string "XXYYZZ" will be used as an expected text pattern. The Espresso ViewMatcher class implements two string-matcher methods— withText() and withContentDescription(). They match a view with text that's equal to the expected text or the expected content description:

```
onView(withText("XXYYZZ")).perform(click());
onView(withContentDescription("XXYYZZ")).perform(click());
```

Using Hamcrest string matchers, we can create more flexible matcher combinations. We can match a view with text that starts with the "XXYY" pattern:

```
onView(withText(startsWith("XXYY"))).perform(click());
```

We can match a view with text that ends with a "YYZZ" pattern:

```
onView(withText(endsWith("YYZZ"))).perform(click());
```

We can assert that the text of a particular view with specified R.id has a content description that contains the "YYZZ" string anywhere:

```
onView(withId(R.id.viewId)).check(matches(withContentDescription(contains
String("YYZZ"))));
```

We can match a view with text that's equal to the specified string, ignoring case:

```
onView(withText(equalToIgnoringCase("xxYY"))).perform(click());
```

We can match a view with text that's equal to the specified text when whitespace differences are (mostly) ignored:

```
onView(withText(equalToIgnoringWhiteSpace("XX YY ZZ"))).perform(click());
```

We can assert that the text of a particular view with specified R.id does not contain the "YYZZ" string:

```
onView(withId(R.id.viewId)).check(matches(withText(not(containsString
("YYZZ")))));
```

Adding the allOf() or anyOf() hamcrest core matchers gives us even more power. We can assert that the text of a particular view with a specified R.id doesn't start with the "ZZ" string and contains the "YYZZ" string anywhere:

```
onView(withId(R.id.viewId))
    .check(matches(allOf(withText(not(startsWith("ZZ"))),
        withText(containsString("YYZZ")))));
```

We can also assert that the text of a particular view with a specified R.id ends with the "ZZ" string or contains the "YYZZ" string anywhere:

```
onView(withId(R.id.viewId))
    .check(matches(anyOf(withText(endsWith("ZZ")),
        withText(containsString("YYZZ")))));
```

To get a full overview of the hamcrest matchers, refer to their official documentation at http://hamcrest.org/JavaHamcrest.

So, now we have an understanding of ViewMatchers. We also understand that they play one of the most important roles in the Espresso testing framework. Their task is to locate the matched view inside the application layout or fail if the match did not happen.

Espresso's ViewInteraction Class

In the previous examples, we were doing new `perform()` and `check()` operations on the views. These methods are representatives of the `ViewInteraction` class. Interactions act like glue between the ViewMatcher and the ViewAssertion or ViewAction.

Each interaction is tied to the view that was previously located by the ViewMatcher. You probably guessed based on the method names that the `perform()` method takes an action and the `check()` method asserts some condition provided as a parameter. There is one more ViewInteraction we haven't used yet-`inRoot()`.

- `perform()`-Receives a view action or a set of view actions as a parameter and performs them on the view selected by the current ViewMatcher.

- `check()`-Receives a view action or a set of view actions as a parameter and checks it on the the view selected by the current ViewMatcher.

So, what about the `inRoot()` method then? With this view interaction, we are targeting the multi-window states in our application. For example, the AutoComplete window layout that is drawn over the test application. In this case, we should explicitly indicate which window Espresso should operate on by matching the proper window with the `RootMatcher`.

- `inRoot()`-Receives a root matcher as a parameter and sets the scope of the view interaction to the root view, identified by the root matcher.

Note   Espresso performs all the actions on the UI thread, which means that it will first wait for the application UI to render and only after that perform the required steps. This ensures that the application UI elements are fully loaded and displayed on the screen, which increases test reliability and robustness. It will also eliminate the need of having waits and sleeps in the tests.

In the following section, you will see examples of how perform() and check() view interactions can be used.

Espresso's ViewActions Class

As you may guess, a ViewAction is responsible for performing actions on a required view. The target is to replicate the end user behavior by interacting with the UI elements on the screen. Here are examples of the type of actions we can perform (see Figure 1-11):

- clearText()-Returns an action that clears text on the view. The view must be displayed on the screen.

- click()-Returns an action that clicks the view. At least 90% of the view must be displayed on the screen.

- swipeLeft()-Returns an action that performs a swipe right-to-left across the vertical center of the view. The swipe doesn't start at the very edge of the view, but is a bit offset, since swiping from the exact edge may cause unexpected behavior (e.g., it may open a navigation drawer). Other swipe actions defined by Espresso are swipeRight(), swipeDown(), and swipeUp(). For all the swipe actions, at least 90% of the views must be displayed onscreen.

- closeSoftKeyboard()-Returns an action that closes the soft keyboard. If the keyboard is already closed, it is non-operational.

- pressImeActionButton()-Returns an action that presses the current action button (Next, Done, Search, etc.) on the IME (Input Method Editor).

- pressBack()-Returns an action that clicks the hardware back button.

- pressMenuKey()-Returns an action that presses the hardware menu key. Most modern devices on the market no longer support the hardware menu key, so this method is rarely used.

- pressKey()-Returns an action that presses the key specified by the key code (e.g., KeyEvent.KEYCODE_BACK). There is a huge list of all possible key codes declared in the andrid.view.KeyEvent.java class.

- doubleClick()-Similar to the click() action, this returns an
  action that double-clicks the view. At least 90% of the view must be
  displayed onscreen.

- longClick()-Returns an action that long-clicks the view. At least 90%
  of the view must be displayed onscreen.

- scrollTo()-Returns an action that scrolls to the view. Based on the
  current implementation, the view we would like to scroll to must be
  a descendant of one of the following classes: ScrollView.class,
  HorizontalScrollView.class, ListView.class. At least 90% of the
  view must be displayed onscreen.

Note   The scrollTo() action will have no effect if the view is already displayed.

- typeText()-Returns an action that selects the view (by clicking on
  it) and types the provided string into the view. Appending an '\n' to
  the end of the string translates to a Enter key event. The view must be
  displayed onscreen and must support input methods.

Note   The typeText() method performs a tap on the view before typing to force
the view into focus. If the view already contains text, this tap may place the cursor
at an arbitrary position within the text.

- replaceText()-Returns an action that updates the text attribute of a
  view.

- openLink()-Returns an action that opens a link matching the given link
  text and URI matchers. The action is performed by invoking the link's
  onClick method (as opposed to actually issuing a click on the screen).

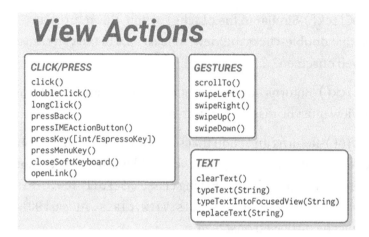

Figure 1-11. *Espresso cheat sheet 2.1—ViewActions (source https://developer. android.com/training/testing/espresso/cheat-sheet)*

The Espresso cheat sheet in Figure 1-11 shows that all the actions are split into three categories:

- Click/Press actions

- Gestures

- Text-related actions

From my point of view, we can add one more type here, which will probably come in the next cheat sheet version:

- Conditional actions

These types of actions are represented by one method at this time— `repeatedlyUntil()`. It enables performing a given action on a view until it reaches the desired state matched by the given ViewMatcher. This action is useful when you're performing the action repeatedly on a view and then it changes its state at runtime. A good use case to automate with this view action is going through the walkthrough or on-boarding screens from the beginning until the end.

As you can see, Espresso provides almost all the actions needed to cover the end user behavior, but still lacks some. The examples may be:

- Drag and drop actions

- Multi-gesture actions like pinch to zoom

Having in our hands the Espresso core methods—ViewInteractions, ViewMatchers, and ViewActions—we can start to automate simple use cases of our example TO-DO application. Let's come up with some:

- Add a new TO-DO that provides the title and description. Verify it is shown in the TO-DO list.

- Add a new TO-DO, mark it completed, and verify it is in the list of completed TO-DOs.

- Add a new TO-DO, edit it, and verify the changes.

Refer to the ViewActionsTest to see the example code. The first, second, and third use cases are shown in the addsNewToDo(), checksToDoStateChange(), and editsToDo() test cases, respectively. We will drill down into one of them to see some details:

```
@Test
public void checksToDoStateChange() {
    // adding new TO-DO
    onView(withId(R.id.fab_add_task)).perform(click());
    onView(withId(R.id.add_task_title))
            .perform(typeText(toDoTitle), closeSoftKeyboard());
    onView(withId(R.id.add_task_description))
            .perform(typeText(toDoDescription), closeSoftKeyboard());
    onView(withId(R.id.fab_edit_task_done)).perform(click());

    // marking our TO-DO as completed
    onView(withId(R.id.todo_complete)).perform(click());

    // filtering out the completed TO-DO
    onView(withId(R.id.menu_filter)).perform(click());
    onView(allOf(withId(android.R.id.title), withText(R.string.nav_completed)))
        .perform(click());
    onView(withId(R.id.todo_title))
        .check(matches(allOf(withText(toDoTitle), isDisplayed())));
}
```

Note that we introduced the TestData class to keep all the methods that generate input data. This helps reduce the test method boilerplate code. You may notice that we add a unique timestamp in milliseconds to each TO-DO item title and description.

This keeps our test data unique, which simplifies a lot of view identification and validation inside the application layout.

Now, regarding the Espresso test code. Note the single combination of ViewInteraction, ViewMatcher, and ViewAction, visible in the following line of code:

```
onView(withId(R.id.fab_add_task)).perform(click());
```

There are also examples of taking multiple view actions as parameters by the perform() view interaction:

```
onView(withId(R.id.add_task_title))
        .perform(typeText(toDoTitle), closeSoftKeyboard());
```

There are also examples of how multiple ViewMatchers can be combined to give us a stronger combination of conditions to match the desired view or validate its state, or to avoid extra lines of code. The maximum number of matchers that can be provided to the allOf() matcher is six:

```
onView(allOf(withId(android.R.id.title), withText(R.string.nav_completed)))
        .perform(click());
onView(withId(R.id.todo_title))
        .check(matches(allOf(withText(toDoTitle), isDisplayed())));
```

Notice how the Espresso notation is flexible—allOf() matcher can be used both inside the onView() method and inside the check(matches()) view interaction.

EXERCISE 2

Writing Your First Espresso Test Cases

Based on the examples in ViewActionsTest, write test cases for the following application functionality:

1. Add a TO-DO and mark it as completed. Verify that the checkbox of the completed TO-DO is checked.

2. Add a new TO-DO, open the TO-DO details by clicking on it (hint: use withText() matcher), and delete it by clicking the Delete Task button. Verify the the All TO-DOs list is empty (i.e., verify that the text "You have no TO-DOs!" and that the ID R.id.noTasksIcon are displayed onscreen).

Espresso's DataInteraction Class

As mentioned in the "Understanding Android Instrumentation" section, the Android application represents its elements via the View or ViewGroup. Single UI elements are drawn inside the View. The ViewGroup is used to represent a set of views or another view group. Think about ViewGroup as a container of UI elements. To represent a list of objects in Android, you can use a class called AdapterView, which extends the ViewGroup class and whose child views are determined by the Adapter. Another possibility to represent a list of objects is to use the RecyclerView, but we discuss it in later chapters.

Thus, Adapter is responsible for transforming the data from an external source into the View that's bound to AdapterView. In the end, AdapterView contains many of views with the data produced by Adapter and forms a list of items, which is called the ListView (see Figure 1-12).

Figure 1-12. *ListView visualization (source* https://developer.android.com/ guide/topics/ui/layout/listview)

To operate on the such lists, Espresso provides the `DataInteraction` interface, which allows us to interact with elements displayed inside `AdapterViews`. Let's briefly go through the commonly used `DataInteraction` methods:

- `atPosition(Integer atPosition)`-Selects the view that matches the nth position on the adapter based on the data matcher.

- `inAdapterView(Matcher<View> adapterMatcher)`-Points to a specific adapter view on the screen to operate on. Should be used when we have two or more AdapterViews in one layout. An example may be the layout with a list view and a menu drawer list view.

- `inRoot(Matcher<Root> rootMatcher)`-Causes the data interaction to work within the root window specified by the given root matcher. May be useful when we have an AutoComplete list view popping up over the application window.

- `onChildView(Matcher<View> childMatcher)`-Redirects perform and check actions to the view inside the adapter item returned by `Adapter.getView()`.

Now, let's see how `DataInteraction` methods are used in a test case written for one of the setting functionalities. The Settings application was implemented using the Android Preference component—the UI building block displayed by a `PreferenceActivity` in the form of a `ListView`. This class provides the view to be displayed in the activity and associates with a SharedPreferences to store/retrieve the preference data. When specifying a preference hierarchy in XML, each element can point to a subclass of Preference, similar to the view hierarchy and layouts. This class contains a key that will be used as the key into the SharedPreferences.

As you can see in Figure 1-13, the main Settings section contains a list with four preference headers (General, Notifications, Data&Sync and WebView sample), where each header contains subsections with lists of preferences.

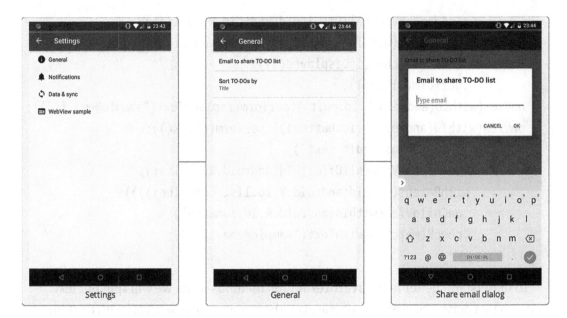

Figure 1-13. The dataInteraction() test case flow, starting from the Settings section

Open the DataInteractionsTest class to see the code examples.

```
@Test
public void dataInteraction() {
    openDrawer();
    onView(allOf(withId(R.id.design_menu_item_text),
            withText(R.string.settings_title))).perform(click());
    // start of the flow as shown in Figure 1-13
    onData(instanceOf(PreferenceActivity.Header.class))
            .inAdapterView(withId(android.R.id.list))
            .atPosition(0)
            .onChildView(withId(android.R.id.title))
            .check(matches(withText("General")))
            .perform(click());
    onData(withKey("email_edit_text"))
            /*we have to point explicitly to the parent of the General
            prefs list
            because there are two {@ListView}s with id android.R.id.list in
            the hierarchy*/
```

```
            .inAdapterView(allOf(withId(android.R.id.list),
            withParent(withId(android.R.id.list_container))))
            .check(matches(isDisplayed()))
            .perform(click());
    onView(withId(android.R.id.edit)).perform(replaceText("sample@ema.il"));
    onView(withId(android.R.id.button1)).perform(click());
    onData(withKey("email_edit_text"))
            .inAdapterView(allOf(withId(android.R.id.list),
            withParent(withId(android.R.id.list_container))))
            .onChildView(withId(android.R.id.summary))
            .check(matches(withText("sample@ema.il")));
}
```

To understand better how DataInteraction methods work, we will split our test case into two parts. The first part operates on the main Settings sections with the four headers:

```
onData(instanceOf(PreferenceActivity.Header.class))
        .inAdapterView(withId(android.R.id.list))
        .atPosition(0)
        .onChildView(withId(android.R.id.title))
        .check(matches(withText("General")))
        .perform(click());
```

First, we explicitly point out that the object we should operate on is its instance of PreferenceActivity.Header.class:

```
instanceOf(PreferenceActivity.Header.class)
```

Second, we point out which adapter contains our object. Inside an adapter of the Android default ListView component, with an ID of android.R.id.list, at position "0". This is the first row in our list:

```
inAdapterView(withId(android.R.id.list)).atPosition(0)
```

Third, we point out that we would like to operate on the child view of our list item with ID android.R.id.title that matches the text "General" and perform a click on it:

```
onChildView(withId(android.R.id.title)).check(matches(withText("General"))).
perform(click())
```

Moving on to the second part of our test case, which operates on the subsection of the General Settings section:

```
onData(withKey("email_edit_text"))
        .inAdapterView(allOf(withId(android.R.id.list),
        withParent(withId(android.R.id.list_container))))
        .check(matches(isDisplayed()))
        .perform(click());
onView(withId(android.R.id.edit)).perform(replaceText("sample@ema.il"));
onView(withId(android.R.id.button1)).perform(click());
onData(withKey("email_edit_text"))
        .inAdapterView(allOf(withId(android.R.id.list),
        withParent(withId(android.R.id.list_container))))
        .onChildView(withId(android.R.id.summary))
        .check(matches(withText("sample@ema.il")));
```

Here, you may observe the preference matcher withKey("email_edit_text") pointing to the EditTextPreference component by its key, which is set in the pref_general.xml file:

```
withKey("email_edit_text")
```

We again point to the ID of the adapter view our entry belongs to, combining it with additional matcher to avoid multiple view matching. We check that such an object is displayed on the screen and click on it:

```
.inAdapterView(allOf(
    withId(android.R.id.list),
    withParent(withId(android.R.id.list_container))))
.check(matches(isDisplayed()))
.perform(click())
```

At the very end, after the email is typed into the edit text field, we validate that the summary of the list item matches the email we provided:

```
.inAdapterView(allOf(
    withId(android.R.id.list),
    withParent(withId(android.R.id.list_container))))
.onChildView(withId(android.R.id.summary))
.check(matches(withText("sample@ema.il")))
```

Let's summarize what we have learned about DataInteractions with the help of the Espresso cheat sheet shown in Figure 1-14. The Espresso onData() method is used to operate on the object inside the list view. The list view item is identified by one or by a combination of data options. After an object is identified and located, we can perform actions or do assertions on it.

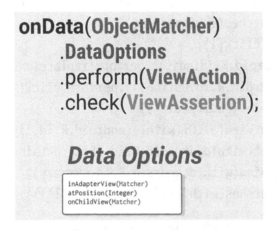

onData(ObjectMatcher)
.DataOptions
.perform(**ViewAction**)
.check(**ViewAssertion**);

Data Options

```
inAdapterView(Matcher)
atPosition(Integer)
onChildView(Matcher)
```

Figure 1-14. *Espresso cheat sheet—DataInteraction (source* $https://developer.$ *android.com/training/testing/espresso/cheat-sheet)*

EXERCISE 3

<u>Writing a Test Case that Operates on a ListView</u>

Based on examples in the DataInteractionsTest:

1. Write a test case that navigates to the Notifications Settings section and clicks the Enable Notifications toggle by text or by ID. Use the Layout Inspector tool to analyze the Notifications Section layout

2. Expand the case from Step 1 and verify that after Enable Notification toggle is switched on, the other notification settings are displayed on the screen.

Operating on RecyclerView Using Espresso

RecyclerView is one of the most commonly used views in Android development. It is a more advanced version of the ListView. Whether your application is an image gallery, a news app, or a messenger, a RecyclerView is usually the best tool to implement it. That is why understanding how to properly write automated tests for this component is so important.

Similar to the simple view, Espresso has a `RecyclerViewActions` class that contains all the actions you can perform on a RecyclerView, but unfortunately Espresso doesn't provide RecyclerView matchers. For now, we will look at the `RecyclerViewActions` examples and in Chapter 2 you will see how to create your own RecyclerView matchers.

We will again refer to our sample TO-DO application, where a list of TO-DOs is represented by a `RecyclerView` component.

RecyclerViewActions

The current class represents view actions that can interact on a RecyclerView. At first look, you may think that we can apply the `onData()` method here because a RecyclerView is used to display the list of items, but in fact a RecyclerView is not an AdapterView, hence it cannot be used with it. So, to operate on a RecyclerView, we use `onView()` with a RecyclerView matcher to match the item or its child inside the RecyclerView list. Then we have to perform a `RecyclerViewAction` or a simple `ViewAction` on it.

- `actionOnItem(final Matcher<View> itemViewMatcher, final ViewAction viewAction)`-Returns a ViewAction that scrolls a RecyclerView to the view matched by `viewHolderMatcher`.

- `actionOnHolderItem(final Matcher<VH> viewHolderMatcher, final ViewAction viewAction)`-Performs a ViewAction on a view matched by `viewHolderMatcher`. First it scrolls a RecyclerView to the view matched by `itemViewMatcher` and then performs an action on the matched view.

- `actionOnItemAtPosition(final int position, final ViewAction viewAction)`-First it scrolls a RecyclerView to the view matched by `itemViewMatcher` and then performs an action on the view at position.

- scrollToHolder(final Matcher<VH> viewHolderMatcher)-Returns
  a ViewAction that scrolls a RecyclerView to the view matched by
  viewHolderMatcher.

- scrollTo(final Matcher<View> itemViewMatcher)-ViewAction that
  scrolls a RecyclerView to the view matched by itemViewMatcher.

- scrollToPosition(final int position)-ViewAction that scrolls
  a RecyclerView to a given position. The view we operate on must be
  assignable from a RecyclerView class and should be displayed on the
  screen.

The following code shows how RecyclerViewActions are used in real tests (the same
test case is present in the RecyclerViewActionsTest.java class):

```
@Test
public void addNewToDos() throws Exception {
    generateToDos(12);
    onView(withId(R.id.tasks_list))
            .perform(actionOnItemAtPosition(10, scrollTo()));
    onView(withId(R.id.tasks_list))
            .perform(scrollToPosition(1));
    onView(withId(R.id.tasks_list))
            .perform(scrollToPosition(12));
    onView(withId(R.id.tasks_list))
            .perform(actionOnItemAtPosition(12, click()));
    Espresso.pressBack();
    onView(withId(R.id.tasks_list))
            .perform(scrollToPosition(2));
}
```

You can omit for now the generateToDos() method and methods that take view
holder matchers as parameters (like scrollToHolder() and actionOnHolderItem()).
They will be discussed in Chapter 2. These tests add 12 TO-DOs, so that some of them
are not visible on the device screen. The important information here is that RecyclerView
adapter knows about all the 12 TO-DO items, but ViewActions can be performed only
on items that are displayed to the user. Here, the scrollToPosition() view holder

ViewAction helps us do the scrolling and make the needed TO-DO item visible on the screen. Then, the view action can be performed without issues.

You may notice that both cases can perform the same actions and they are both valid:

```
onView(withId(R.id.tasks_list))
          .perform(actionOnItemAtPosition(12, scrollTo()));
```

and

```
onView(withId(R.id.tasks_list))
          .perform(scrollToPosition(12));
```

As a side note, the current test case is a good example of how can we chain perform() actions if the same view is used in the onView() method-R.id.tasks_list. This test case may look like this:

```
@Test
public void addNewToDosChained() throws Exception {
    generateToDos(12);
    onView(withId(R.id.tasks_list))
          .perform(actionOnItemAtPosition(10, scrollTo()))
          .perform(scrollToPosition(1))
          .perform(scrollToPosition(12))
          .perform(actionOnItemAtPosition(12, click()))
          .perform(pressBack())
          .perform(scrollToPosition(2));
}
```

The chained test case required only one change—the ViewActions.pressBack() method was used instead of Espresso.pressBack().

EXERCISE 4

Experimenting with RecyclerView Actions

1. Based on the examples here, experiment with actions in a RecyclerView. Try to perform actions on the non-visible TO-DO items without scrolling to them and observe the results.

Running Espresso Tests from AndroidStudio

At this moment, we have a basic understanding on how to write automated tests with Espresso. Let's see how our Espresso tests can be run. This is achievable in two ways–via AndroidStudio or from the command line.

Before jumping into running tests, we should understand the concept of the Gradle BuildVariant in AndroidStudio. The BuildVariant represents the process that converts the project into an Android Application Package (APK). The Android build process is very flexible and enables you to create a custom build configuration without modifying the application source code. The flexibility is achieved by BuildVariants, which are the the combined product of build type and product flavor.

Build types define certain properties that Gradle uses when building and packaging your application and are typically configured for different stages of your development lifecycle. For example, the *debug* build type enables debug options and signs the APK with the debug key, while the *release* build type may shrink, obfuscate, and sign your APK with a release key for distribution.

The *product flavor* represents different versions of your app that you may release to users, such as free and paid versions of your app. You can customize product flavors to use different code and resources, while sharing and reusing the parts that are common to all versions of your app.

Figure 1-15 shows the Android build process.

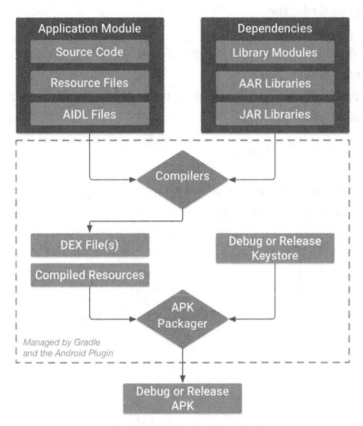

Figure 1-15. *Android build process (source* https://developer.android.com/ *studio/build)*

In short, unlike the release APK, the debug APK will contain debug or test dependencies (such as Espresso dependencies) and test resources needed for our UI tests to run. Therefore, it is important first to have the debug build type, as shown in the following build.gradle file:

```
buildTypes {
    debug {
        minifyEnabled true
        useProguard false
        proguardFiles getDefaultProguardFile('proguard-android.txt'),
        'proguard-rules.pro'
        testProguardFiles getDefaultProguardFile('proguard-android.txt'),
        'proguardTest-rules.pro'
    }
```

```
release {
    minifyEnabled true
    useProguard true
    proguardFiles getDefaultProguardFile('proguard-android.txt'),
    'proguard-rules.pro'
    testProguardFiles getDefaultProguardFile('proguard-android.txt'),
    'proguardTest-rules.pro'
  }
}
```

Second, we must select the proper BuildVariant for our application module in AndroidStudio, as shown in Figure 1-16.

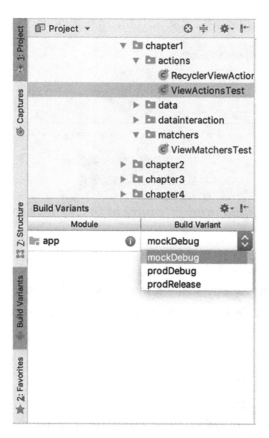

Figure 1-16. *Select a BuildVariant in AndroidStudio*

When the proper build type is selected, we can right-click on the test class or test method and create the run configuration for the UI test, as shown in Figure 1-17.

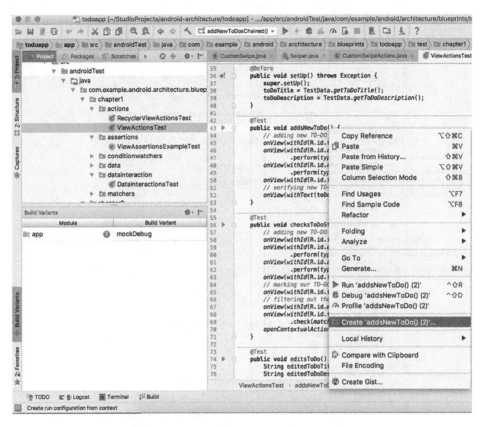

Figure 1-17. *Creating an instrumentation test configuration*

Then we select Create from the popup menu and confirm it with the OK button. See Figure 1-18.

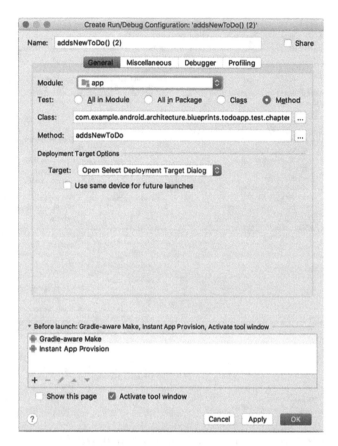

Figure 1-18. *Creating an instrumentation test run configuration*

When these steps are done, we are ready to run the selected test. We do so by clicking the arrow ▶ button in the AndroidStudio toolbar.

Running Espresso Tests from the Terminal

There are different ways to run Espresso and Android Instrumentation tests from the terminal. Among them are:

- Running Instrumentation tests using shell commands
- Running Instrumentation tests using Gradle commands

Running Instrumentation Tests Using Shell Commands

The following shell command can be used to run tests located in the app module.

Running App Module Tests with the Android Testing Support Library.

```
adb shell am instrument -w com.example.android.architecture.blueprints.
todoapp.mock.test/android.support.test.runner.AndroidJUnitRunner
```

Running App Module Tests with the AndroidX Test Library.

```
adb shell am instrument -w com.example.android.architecture.blueprints.
todoapp.test/androidx.test.runner.AndroidJUnitRunner
```

If you want to run tests from specific test classes, you would add the -e class <Class> parameter to the previous command.

Running Tests from the chapter1.actions.ViewActionsTest.java Class with the Android Testing Support Library.

```
adb shell am instrument -w -r -e debug false -e class com.example.android.
architecture.blueprints.todoapp.test.chapter1.actions.ViewActionsTest com.
example.android.architecture.blueprints.todoapp.test/android.support.test.
runner.AndroidJUnitRunner
```

Running Tests from the chapter1.actions.ViewActionsTest.java Class with the AndroidX Test Library.

```
adb shell am instrument -w -r -e debug false -e class com.example.
android.architecture.blueprints.todoapp.test.chapter1.actions.
ViewActionsTest#addsNewToDo com.example.android.architecture.blueprints.
todoapp.mock.test/androidx.test.runner.AndroidJUnitRunner
```

In order to run specific test methods or functions, the class parameter can be extended with the #<testMethod> value, as shown next.

Running Tests from the chapter1.actions.ViewActionsTest.addsNewToDo() Test with the Android Testing Support Library.

```
adb shell am instrument -w -r -e debug false -e class com.example.
android.architecture.blueprints.todoapp.test.chapter1.actions.
ViewActionsTest#addsNewToDo com.example.android.architecture.blueprints.
todoapp.test/android.support.test.runner.AndroidJUnitRunner
```

Running Tests from the chapter1.actions.ViewActionsTest.addsNewToDo() Test with the AndroidX Test Library.

```
adb shell am instrument -w -r -e debug false -e class com.example.
android.architecture.blueprints.todoapp.test.chapter1.actions.
ViewActionsTest#addsNewToDo com.example.android.architecture.blueprints.
todoapp.mock.test/androidx.test.runner.AndroidJUnitRunner
```

If you want to run tests configured to use the Android Test Orchestrator, the following shell command should be used.

Running the chapter1.actions.ViewActionsTest.addsNewToDo() Test with the Android Testing Support Library.

```
adb shell CLASSPATH=$(adb shell pm path android.support.test.
services) app_process / android.support.test.services.shellexecutor.
ShellMain am instrument -r -w -e targetInstrumentation com.example.
android.architecture.blueprints.todoapp.mock.test/android.support.
test.runner.AndroidJUnitRunner   -e debug false -e class 'com.example.
android.architecture.blueprints.todoapp.test.chapter1.actions.
```

```
ViewActionsTest#addsNewToDo' -e clearPackageData true android.support.test.
orchestrator/android.support.test.orchestrator.AndroidTestOrchestrator
```

*Running the chapter1.actions.ViewActionsTest.addsNewToDo() Test with the
AndroidX Test Library.*

```
adb shell CLASSPATH=$(adb shell pm path androidx.test.services) app_process
/ androidx.test.services.shellexecutor.ShellMain am instrument -r -w -e
targetInstrumentation com.example.android.architecture.blueprints.todoapp.
mock.test/androidx.test.runner.AndroidJUnitRunner  -e debug false -e class
'com.example.android.architecture.blueprints.todoapp.test.chapter1.actions.
ViewActionsTest#addsNewToDo' -e clearPackageData true androidx.test.
orchestrator/androidx.test.orchestrator.AndroidTestOrchestrator
```

Running Instrumentation Tests Using Gradle Commands

The following Gradle command should be used in order to run all the tests from the app
project module (the current directory must be the project's root directory):

```
./gradlew app:connectedAndroidTest
```

Note that for our sample application project (and for many other projects you may
work with), in order to test the application, it should be built with the debug build type.
On top of this, we have different flavors—mock and prod—as stated in the build.gradle
file. That means that the command to run all the tests from the app module will change
to reflect the build type and flavor, as shown here:

```
./gradlew app:connectedMockDebugAndroidTest
```

As is the case with shell commands, Gradle commands also can accept additional
arguments in order to run a specific test class or test method. Here is an example of
running the tests from a specific test class:

```
./gradlew app:connectedMockDebugAndroidTest -Pandroid.
testInstrumentationRunnerArguments.class=com.example.android.architecture.
blueprints.todoapp.test.chapter1.actions.ViewActionsTest
```

Similar to the shell commands, the class parameter in Gradle can be extended with
the #<testMethod> value.

Running the chapter1.actions.ViewActionsTest.checksToDoStateChange() Test.

```
./gradlew app:connectedMockDebugAndroidTest -Pandroid.testInstrumentation
RunnerArguments.class=com.example.android.architecture.blueprints.todoapp.
test.chapter1.actions.ViewActionsTest#checksToDoStateChange
```

EXERCISE 5

Creating a Test Run Configuration

1. Create a test run configuration for a test method, a test class, and a package. Run the tests.

2. Edit one of the configurations by navigating to the AndroidStudio menu Run ➤ Edit Configurations.... Remove one of the configurations.

3. Practice running a test class or a specific test method using the `shell` terminal commands.

4. Practice running a test class or a specific test method using the `gradle` terminal commands.

Summary

In this first chapter, you learned all about the Espresso basics, starting from the dependencies declaration to writing a simple test, which will be the foundation for more advanced examples described later in this book. In addition to that, you received information about how the application layout should be inspected using the Monitor and Layout Inspector tools, how the build process looks, and how Espresso tests are configured and run from the AndroidStudio IDE.

CHAPTER 2

Customizing Espresso for Our Needs

Espresso is a really good testing framework, but it is not possible to cover all the test automation cases with a predefined set of methods and classes. In the same way that Android's fundamental components can be customized during application development, Espresso enables us to customize its components. Engineers are free do create their own actions, matchers, and failure handlers and plug them into the tests. In this chapter, we learn how to create our custom view, swipe, and recycler view actions; understand how to build different types of matchers; handle test failures in a customized way, and take the proper screenshots on failure.

Writing Custom ViewActions

ViewActions are one of the most commonly used Espresso functionalities. Espresso provides a big list of them, but we need more just because they may not suit our specific needs. In my practice, most of the time, the following view action types require customization:

- Swipe actions
- Recycler view actions
- ViewActions

We also discuss examples of customizing a simple click action for specific cases in this chapter.

© Denys Zelenchuk 2019
D. Zelenchuk, *Android Espresso Revealed*, https://doi.org/10.1007/978-1-4842-4315-2_2

Adapting Espresso Swipe Actions

In Chapter 1, we mentioned four swipe actions that Espresso provides—swipeUp(), swipeDown(), swipeLeft(), and swipeRight(). This is how the swipeUp() action is implemented:

```
public static ViewAction swipeUp() {
  return actionWithAssertions(new GeneralSwipeAction(Swipe.FAST,
    GeneralLocation.translate(GeneralLocation.BOTTOM_CENTER, 0, -EDGE_
    FUZZ_FACTOR),
    GeneralLocation.TOP_CENTER, Press.FINGER));
}
```

As you may guess, GeneralLocation.BOTTOM_CENTER and GeneralLocation.TOP_
CENTER represent the from and to coordinates inside the view we would like to swipe.
The full positions list, which can be used as from and to coordinates, are TOP_LEFT,
TOP_CENTER, TOP_RIGHT, CENTER_LEFT, CENTER, CENTER_RIGHT, BOTTOM_LEFT, and BOTTOM_
CENTER, BOTTOM_RIGHT.

Swipe.FAST represents the length of time a "fast" swipe should last, in milliseconds.
For now, Swipe has FAST (100 milliseconds) and SLOW (1500 milliseconds) swipe speeds.

The Press.FINGER returns a touch target with the size 16x16 mm. Other press
options are PINPOINT 1x1 mm and THUMB 25x25 mm press areas.

The -EDGE_FUZZ_FACTOR value defines the distance from the edge to the swipe
action's starting point in terms of the view's length. This is helpful when swiping from the
exact edge can lead to undesired behavior—for example, opening the navigation drawer.

The other three swipe actions happen in a similar way, with the difference only in the
from and to coordinates.

There may be cases when these four swipe actions are not enough. You may need
swiping left or right slowly or swiping up or down from the middle of the screen. In such
cases, you can create your own custom swipe action.

To implement our own action, we will follow the approach of how Espresso swipe
actions like swipeDown() are implemented. First, we add our own CustomSwipe type and
call it CUSTOM. This enum class should implement the Espresso Swiper interface like Swipe
enum does, where the FAST and SLOW swiping types are declared.

chapter2.customswipe.CustomSwipe.java.

```java
public enum CustomSwipe implements Swiper {

    CUSTOM{
        @Override
        public Status sendSwipe(UiController uiController,
                                float[] startCoordinates,
                                float[] endCoordinates,
                                float[] precision) {
            return sendLinearSwipe(
                    uiController,
                    startCoordinates,
                    endCoordinates,
                    precision,
                    swipeCustomDuration);
        }
    };

    /** The number of motion events to send for each swipe. */
    private static final int SWIPE_EVENT_COUNT = 10;
    /** The duration of a swipe */
    private static int swipeCustomDuration = 0;

    /**
     * Setting duration to our custom swipe action
     * @param duration length of time a custom swipe should last for in
     * milliseconds.
     */
    public void setSwipeDuration(int duration) {
        swipeCustomDuration = duration;
    }

    private static Swiper.Status sendLinearSwipe(UiController uiController,
                                                 float[] startCoordinates,
                                                 float[] endCoordinates,
                                                 float[] precision,
                                                 int duration) {
```

```
        ...
    }

    private static float[][] interpolate(float[] start, float[] end, int steps) {
        ...
        return res;
    }
}
```

In our implementation, we can control the swipe duration by setting it in the setSwipeDuration() method, which modifies the swipeCustomDuration static variable. We also have to paste the interpolate() and sendLinearSwipe() methods from the Espresso Swipe enum because they are not public. The full source code is available in the chapter2.customswipe.CustomSwipe.java class.

So, at this moment, we already have a fully customizable swipe type. Now we add the swipeCustom() view action.

chapter2.customactions.CustomSwipeActions.java.

```
public class CustomSwipeActions {
    /**
     * Fully customizable Swipe action for any need
     * @param duration length of time a custom swipe should last for, in
     milliseconds.
     * @param from for example [GeneralLocation.CENTER]
     * @param to for example [GeneralLocation.BOTTOM_CENTER]
     */
    public ViewAction swipeCustom(int duration, GeneralLocation from,
    GeneralLocation to) {
        CustomSwipe.CUSTOM.setSwipeDuration(duration);
        return actionWithAssertions(new GeneralSwipeAction(
                CustomSwipe.CUSTOM,
                translate(from, 0f, 0f),
                to, Press.FINGER)
        );
    }
```

```java
/**
 * Translates the given coordinates by the given distances.
 * The distances are given in term of the view's size
 * -- 1.0 means to translate by an amount equivalent
 * to the view's length.
 */
private static CoordinatesProvider translate(final CoordinatesProvider
coords, final float dx, final float dy) {
    return new CoordinatesProvider() {
        @Override
        public float[] calculateCoordinates(View view) {
            float xy[] = coords.calculateCoordinates(view);
            xy[0] += dx * view.getWidth();
            xy[1] += dy * view.getHeight();
            return xy;
        }
    };
}
}
```

The swipeCustom() method first sets the swipe duration and then performs GeneralSwipeAction with our CUSTOM swipe type. Again, we have to paste the translate() method from inside the GeneralSwipeAction class, as it cannot be accessed from outside of the class.

EXERCISE 6

Writing a Test Case with a Custom Swipe Action

1. Write a test case that refreshes the TO-DO list by performing the swipeDown() action on the TO-DO list view with ID R.id.tasks_list.

2. Replace the swipeDown() action from the first task with the swipeCustom() view action.

Creating Custom RecyclerView Actions

The RecyclerViewActions class provides a limited amount of actions that can be used inside a recycler view or recycler view item. For example, clicking on the whole TO-DO item in the TO-DO recycler view is useful and can be used to open item details. But what if we need to click on the checkbox to mark a TO-DO item as done. Of course, we can do this based on position. As an engineer who owns the test data, I have the full control over each TO-DO name and I can make all the names unique. This enables me to identify each TO-DO item based on its name and then narrow down the focus to the specific element inside the TO-DO item. In our case, we want to click on the checkbox. Take a look at how this custom recycler view action may look on the clickTodoCheckBoxWithTitle() method from the CustomRecyclerViewActions.java class.

chapter2.customactions.CustomRecyclerViewActions.java.

```java
class ClickTodoCheckBoxWithTitleViewAction implements
CustomRecyclerViewActions {

    private String toDoTitle;

    public ClickTodoCheckBoxWithTitleViewAction(String toDoTitle) {
        this.toDoTitle = toDoTitle;
    }

    public static ViewAction clickTodoCheckBoxWithTitle(final String
    toDoTitle) {
        return actionWithAssertions(new ClickTodoCheckBoxWithTitleViewAction
        (toDoTitle));
    }

    @Override
    public Matcher<View> getConstraints() {
        return allOf(isAssignableFrom(RecyclerView.class), isDisplayed());
    }

    @Override
    public String getDescription() {
        return "Completes the task by clicking its checkbox.";
    }
```

```java
@Override
public void perform(UiController uiController, View view) {
    try {
        RecyclerView recyclerView = (RecyclerView) view;
        RecyclerView.Adapter adapter = recyclerView.getAdapter();
        if (adapter instanceof TasksFragment.TasksAdapter) {
            int itemCount = adapter.getItemCount();
            for (int i = 0; i < itemCount; i++) {
                View taskItemView = recyclerView.getLayoutManager().
                findViewByPosition(i);
                TextView textView = taskItemView.findViewById(R.id.title);
                if (textView != null && textView.getText() != null) {
                    if (textView.getText().toString().equals(toDoTitle)) {
                        CheckBox completeCheckBox = taskItemView.
                        findViewById(R.id.todo_complete);
                        completeCheckBox.performClick();
                    }
                } else {
                    throw new RuntimeException(
                            "Unable to find view with ID R.id.todo_title
                            as child of TO-DO item at position " + i);
                }
            }
        }
        uiController.loopMainThreadForAtLeast(ViewConfiguration.
        getTapTimeout());
    } catch (RuntimeException e) {
        throw new PerformException.Builder().
        withActionDescription(this.getDescription())
                .withViewDescription(HumanReadables.describe(view)).
                withCause(e).build();
    }
}
```

The clickTodoCheckBoxWithTitle() view action returns a new
ClickTodoCheckBoxWithTitleViewAction class where the getConstraints() method
filters out views that are assignable from the RecyclerView.class and are visible on the
screen:

```
public Matcher<View> getConstraints() {
    return allOf(isAssignableFrom(RecyclerView.class), isDisplayed())

}
```

The getDescription() method describes our ViewAction. This is what you will see if
the test fails in the Espresso exception trace.

```
public String getDescription() {
    return "Completes the task by clicking its checkbox.";
}
```

The perform() method is doing the heavy work here—we already can rely on the
fact that our view is RecyclerView. Then we get the adapter from it and ensure that the
adapter is an instance of the TasksFragment.TasksAdapter class. After that, we iterate
through each item inside the adapter and fetch an item title from TextView with an ID
of R.id.title. If the item's title is equal to the title from TaskItem, we search for the
CheckBox element with a R.id.todo_complete ID and call a click action on it. In the
end, we loop the main thread for a short period of time to let the application handle
our tap event. If a TO-DO with the expected title doesn't exist in the list, it will throw an
exception with the help of Espresso's PerformException class.

chapter2.customactions.CustomRecyclerViewActions.java.

```
public void perform(UiController uiController, View view) {
    try {
        RecyclerView recyclerView = (RecyclerView) view;
        RecyclerView.Adapter adapter = recyclerView.getAdapter();
        if (adapter instanceof TasksFragment.TasksAdapter) {
```

```java
            int itemCount = adapter.getItemCount();
            for (int i = 0; i < itemCount; i++) {
                View taskItemView = recyclerView.getLayoutManager().
                findViewByPosition(i);
                TextView textView = taskItemView.findViewById(R.id.title);
                if (textView != null && textView.getText() != null) {
                    if (textView.getText().toString().equals(toDoTitle)) {
                        CheckBox completeCheckBox = taskItemView.
                        findViewById(R.id.todo_complete);
                        completeCheckBox.performClick();
                    }
                } else {
                    throw new RuntimeException(
                            "Unable to find TO-DO item with title " +
                            toDoTitle);
                }
            }
        }
        uiController.loopMainThreadForAtLeast(ViewConfiguration.
        getTapTimeout());
    } catch (RuntimeException e) {
        throw new PerformException.Builder().withActionDescription(this.
        getDescription())
                .withViewDescription(HumanReadables.describe(view)).
                withCause(e).build();
    }
}
```

Another example of RecyclerViewAction is shown in the same
CustomRecyclerViewActions.java class inside the scrollToLastHolder() method and
it explains how to implement the scroll action on RecyclerView. We will not discuss the
getConstraints() and getDescription() methods since they are the same. As for the
perform() method, you can see that it retrieves the items count from the RecyclerView
adapter and scrolls to the last item using the scrollToPosition() RecyclerView
method:

```
public void perform(UiController uiController, View view) {
    RecyclerView recyclerView = (RecyclerView) view;
    int itemCount = recyclerView.getAdapter().getItemCount();
    try {
        recyclerView.scrollToPosition(itemCount - 1);
        uiController.loopMainThreadUntilIdle();
    } catch (RuntimeException e) {
        throw new PerformException.Builder().withActionDescription(this.
        getDescription())
                .withViewDescription(HumanReadables.describe(view)).
                withCause(e).build();
    }
}
```

EXERCISE 7

Writing a Custom RecyclerView Action

1. Based on the `clickTodoCheckBoxWithTitle()` action, implement a
   RecyclerView action that verifies that the TO-DO item is not present in the
   list. Hint: Use one of the `JUnit` `assert` methods inside the `perform()`
   method. The final use may look like the following:

```
onView(withId(R.id.tasks_list)).perform(assertNotInTheListTodoWithTitle("title"))
```

Writing Custom Matchers

Espresso matchers are powerful tools that help locate or validate elements in the
application layout. Espresso view matchers may not fully fit your use cases or needs. In
that case, you can create custom matchers.

Creating Custom Matchers for Simple UI Elements

We will start using the simple matchers as an introduction. The following use case will be used as an example:

> Add a new TO-DO without a title and description, and as a result,
> the TO-DO title field's hint color should become red.

In this case, BoundedMatcher is the perfect candidate since it returns the Matcher<View> type but will operate only on elements with EditText type. Refer to the CustomViewMatchers.java class, which contains the withHintColor() matcher implementation that matches the color of the EditText hint.

chapter2.custommatchers.CustomViewMatchers.java.

```java
public static Matcher<View> withHintColor(final int expectedColor) {
    return new BoundedMatcher<View, EditText>(EditText.class) {

        @Override
        protected boolean matchesSafely(EditText editText) {
            return expectedColor == editText.getCurrentHintTextColor();
        }

        @Override
        public void describeTo(Description description) {
            description.appendText("with TO-DO title: " + expectedColor);
        }
    };
}
```

Here, BoundedMatcher enables us to match the EditText view that's the subtype of the Android View type and return to the end object of the Matcher<View> type. When the EditText element is identified on the screen, its hint color is compared to the expected color, returning a true or false value. Whenever a true value is returned, it means that EditText with the expected hint color was found.

Here is how the usage of the withHintColor() matcher looks in a real test case (refer to the CustomViewMatchers.java class for more details).

chapter2.custommatchers.CustomViewMatchersTest.java.

```
@Test
public void addsNewToDoError() {
    // adding new TO-DO
    onView(withId(R.id.fab_add_task)).perform(click());
    onView(withId(R.id.fab_edit_task_done)).perform(click());
    onView(withId(R.id.add_task_title))
            .check(matches(hasErrorText("Title cannot be empty!")))
            .check(matches(withHintColor(Color.RED)));
}
```

Implementing Custom RecyclerView Matchers

From my point of view, the RecyclerView matchers are the most hidden part in Espresso. The Android documentation does not explain how to implement them but, based on the past examples from this book, you may guess that the BoundedMatcher class can be used to create them.

We will refer to our sample application and create the RecyclerView matcher that matches the TO-DO item in the TO-DO list based on its title. Again, the title is assumed to be unique since we have the full control over the test data.

chapter2.custommatchers.RecyclerViewMatchers.java.

```
public static Matcher<RecyclerView.ViewHolder> withTitle(final String
taskTitle) {
    Checks.checkNotNull(taskTitle);

    return new BoundedMatcher<RecyclerView.ViewHolder, TasksFragment.
    TasksAdapter.ViewHolder>(
            TasksAdapter.ViewHolder.class) {
        @Override
        protected boolean matchesSafely(TasksAdapter.ViewHolder holder) {
            final String holderTaskTitle = holder.getHolderTask().
            getTitle();
            return taskTitle.equals(holderTaskTitle);
        }
```

```
    @Override
    public void describeTo(Description description) {
        description.appendText("with task title: " + taskTitle);
    }
    };
}
```

Here it is important to understand the application under test and know which ViewHolder to use. In the sample, we put TasksFragment.TasksAdapter.ViewHolder as the second parameter into BoundedMatcher. Whenever our matcher identifies elements on the screen with the type, we retrieve the title from the holder and compare it to the title we provided as a matcher parameter.

chapter2.custommatchers.RecyclerViewMatchers.java.

```
public static Matcher<RecyclerView.ViewHolder> withTask(final TaskItem
taskItem) {
        Checks.checkNotNull(taskItem);

        return new BoundedMatcher<RecyclerView.ViewHolder, TasksFragment.
        TasksAdapter.ViewHolder>(
                TasksAdapter.ViewHolder.class) {
            @Override
            protected boolean matchesSafely(TasksAdapter.ViewHolder holder)
{

                final String holderTaskTitle = holder.getHolderTask().
                getTitle();
                final String holderTaskDesc = holder.getHolderTask().
                getDescription();
                return taskItem.getTitle().equals(holderTaskTitle)
                        && taskItem.getDescription().
                        equals(holderTaskDesc);
            }

            @Override
            public void describeTo(Description description) {
                description.appendText("task with title: " + taskItem.getTitle()
                        + " and description: " + taskItem.
                        getDescription());
```

```java
            }
        };
    }

    public static Matcher<RecyclerView.ViewHolder>
    withTaskTitleFromTextView(final String taskTitle) {
        Checks.checkNotNull(taskTitle);

        return new BoundedMatcher<RecyclerView.ViewHolder, TasksFragment.
        TasksAdapter.ViewHolder>(
                TasksAdapter.ViewHolder.class) {
            @Override
            protected boolean matchesSafely(TasksAdapter.ViewHolder holder)
{

                final TextView titleTextView = (TextView) holder.itemView.
                findViewById(R.id.title);
                return taskTitle.equals(titleTextView.getText().
toString());
            }

            @Override
            public void describeTo(Description description) {
                description.appendText("with task title: " + taskTitle);
            }
        };
    }
}
```

Handling Errors with a Custom FailureHandler

The Espresso testing framework is very flexible and customizable, and error handling is no exception. Espresso provides an interface called FailureHandler that can be implemented in a custom failure handler to manage failures that happen during test execution.

The reason to implement a custom FailureHandler may be to reduce the exception text or to save on screenshots or other application data, such as saving device dumps, etc.

As an example, the sample TO-DO application codebase contains a CustomFailureHandler.

chapter2.customfailurehandler.CustomFailureHandler.java.

```java
public class CustomFailureHandler implements FailureHandler{

    private final FailureHandler delegate;

    public CustomFailureHandler(Context targetContext) {
        delegate = new DefaultFailureHandler(targetContext);
    }

    @Override
    public void handle(Throwable error, Matcher<View> viewMatcher) {
        try {
            delegate.handle(error, viewMatcher);
        } catch (NoMatchingViewException e) {
            // For example save device dump, take screenshot, etc.
            throw e;
        }
    }
}
```

You can see the try...catch block in the handle() method. That's where we catch the error and can do whatever we want with it. Usually the exception is propagated further after all needed steps are complete.

To let Espresso intercept each test failure with a CustomFailureHandler, it is important to register it inside the test class or inside the base test class, as shown in the BaseTest.java class:

```java
@Before
public void setUp() throws Exception {
    setFailureHandler(new CustomFailureHandler(
            InstrumentationRegistry.getInstrumentation().
getTargetContext()));
}
```

If you register it in a base test class, don't forget to call `super.setUp()` from inside your test class:

```
@Before
public void setUp() throws Exception {
    super.setUp();
}
```

EXERCISE 8

Applying a CustomFailureHandler to a New Test Class

1. Create a new test class with a test method that will fail on every run. Apply `CustomFailureHandler` to it.

Taking and Saving Screenshots Upon Test Failure

Running tests is important, but it is also important to get proper and descriptive test results, especially when you have a test failure, so they can be easily analyzed. The JUnit reporter that is used by `AndroidJUnitRunner` reports test results in old, simple raw text format. Engineers then have to adapt it to their needs. Of course, one of those needs is to create a screenshot when a test fails. There are many third-party libraries and tools that can take screenshots upon test failure. A good example is Spoon from Square. But here we will talk about the native solution that comes with JUnit and Espresso.

Let's identify what we want to achieve in the test run flow:

1. Identify the moment when the test fails.

2. Take a screenshot and name it appropriately.

3. Save the screenshot on the given device or emulator.

The JUnit Library starting with version 4.9 provides a `TestWatcher` mechanism that allows us to monitor and log passing and failing tests. It is an abstract class that extends `TestRule` and enables us to react to the following test states:

- `succeeded(Description description)`—Invoked when a test succeeds.

- `failed(Throwable e, Description description)`—Invoked when a test fails.

- skipped(AssumptionViolatedException e, Description description)—Invoked when a test is skipped due to a failed assumption.

- starting(Description description)—Invoked when a test is about to start.

- finished(Description description)—Invoked when a test method finishes (whether passing or failing).

Here we are interested in the failed() method, which we will override the BaseTest class (however, other methods can be also helpful in many cases). This addresses our first point (identify the moment when the test fails).

The Android Testing support library provides the Screenshot and ScreenshotCapture classes, which capture the screenshot in bitmap format during instrumentation tests on an Android device or an emulator:

```
private void captureScreenshot(final String name) throws IOException {
    ScreenCapture capture = Screenshot.capture();
    capture.setFormat(Bitmap.CompressFormat.PNG);
    capture.setName(name);
    capture.process();
}
```

As to the screenshot name, we need help from the TestName() JUnit rule available from JUnit version 4.7. The TestName rule makes the current test name available from inside the test. It returns the currently-running test method name via the getMethodName() function:

```
@Rule
public TestName testName = new TestName();
```

The second point has also been addressed (take a screenshot and name it appropriately).

Actually, it's almost solved since we need the following permissions to be granted in order to let the Screenshot class save screenshots to an external storage location:

- android.Manifest.permission.READ_EXTERNAL_STORAGE

- android.Manifest.permission.WRITE_EXTERNAL_STORAGE

Luckily, the Android Testing support library provides `GrantPermissionRule` to do this at runtime. The only limitation is that it can be used only from Android M (API level 23):

```
@Rule
public GrantPermissionRule mRuntimePermissionRule = GrantPermissionRule
        .grant(android.Manifest.permission.WRITE_EXTERNAL_STORAGE,
                android.Manifest.permission.READ_EXTERNAL_STORAGE);
```

At this moment, all three points have been addressed (the final one being to save the screenshot on a given device or emulator), and this is how it looks in the `BaseTest.class`.

com.example.android.architecture.blueprints.todoapp.test.BaseTest.java.

```
@RunWith(AndroidJUnit4.class)
public class BaseTest {

    ......

    @Rule
    public GrantPermissionRule mRuntimePermissionRule = GrantPermissionRule
            .grant(android.Manifest.permission.WRITE_EXTERNAL_STORAGE,
                    android.Manifest.permission.READ_EXTERNAL_STORAGE);

    @Rule
    public TestName testName = new TestName();

    public class ScreenshotWatcher extends TestWatcher {

        @Override
        protected void succeeded(Description description) {
            // all good, tell everyone
        }

        @Override
        protected void failed(Throwable e, Description desc) {
            try {
                captureScreenshot(testName.getMethodName());
            } catch (IOException e1) {
                e1.printStackTrace();
            }
        }
```

```
private void captureScreenshot(final String name) throws
IOException {
    ScreenCapture capture = Screenshot.capture();
    capture.setFormat(Bitmap.CompressFormat.PNG);
    capture.setName(name);
    capture.process();
    }
  }
}
```

One last note—screenshots will be saved in the sdcard/Pictures/screenshots directory. On Android emulator, it is /storage/emulated/0/Pictures/screenshots.

EXERCISE 9

Failing One of the Tests and Observing the Screenshots

1. Modify one of the tests so that it will fail. Run the test. After the test runs, with the help of the adb command, start the shell session on the device or emulator and navigate to the folder that contains the screenshot.

2. Pull the screenshot taken in Step 1 from your device to your hard disk.

Summary

As you can see, Espresso for Android is a flexible and customizable framework that allows us to create custom classes and methods to meet specific testing needs. There are, of course, some limitations, such as the missing RecyclerView matchers. These limitations can be mitigated by using a custom ViewAction. Creating custom ViewActions, ViewMatchers, and other methods and classes is essential knowledge, sometimes even a must-have for an experienced Espresso user. In addition to that, you can fully customize UI error handling and perform desired actions on each test error.

CHAPTER 3

Writing Espresso Tests with Kotlin

The Google I/O event in May 2017 announced official Kotlin support. From that moment, Kotlin popularity skyrocketed among Android developers. Keeping in mind the current trends and considering Google's announcements about shifting the Android toward Kotlin, which is reflected in the Android documentation and the code examples, we can assume that in two to three years, Kotlin will displace Java.

Figure 3-1 shows Java vs. Kotlin usage prediction, which indicates that Kotlin will soon overtake Java in the Android development world.

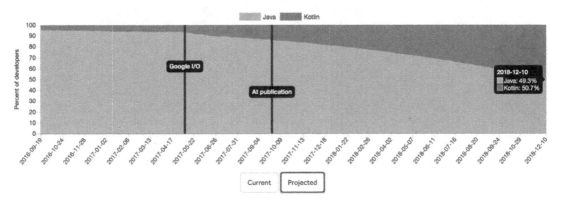

Figure 3-1. *Kotlin vs. Java usage on Android (source:* `https://realm.io/realm-report/`*)*

This chapter explains how to migrate existing Espresso Java tests to Kotlin, lists the possible benefits of writing UI tests in Kotlin, and provides an example of creating Espresso DSL with practical examples and tasks.

© Denys Zelenchuk 2019
D. Zelenchuk, *Android Espresso Revealed*, https://doi.org/10.1007/978-1-4842-4315-2_3

Migrating Espresso Java Tests to Kotlin

Kotlin works side-by-side with Java on Android, meaning that you can add Kotlin code to your existing projects and can call Java code from Kotlin and vice versa.

The first step is to tell the Android Studio IDE that the project uses Kotlin by adding the `kotlin-gradle-plugin` dependency to the project `build.gradle` file, as shown:

```
dependencies {
    classpath "com.android.tools.build:gradle:3.1.4"
    classpath "org.jetbrains.kotlin:kotlin-gradle-plugin:1.2.61"
    ...
}
```

After the project is synched, you can start converting Java classes to Kotlin. This can easily be achieved by selecting a Java file or a package, opening the Code menu, and choosing the Convert Java File to Kotlin File option. You can also right-click the file or package and select this option from the pop-up menu (see Figure 3-2).

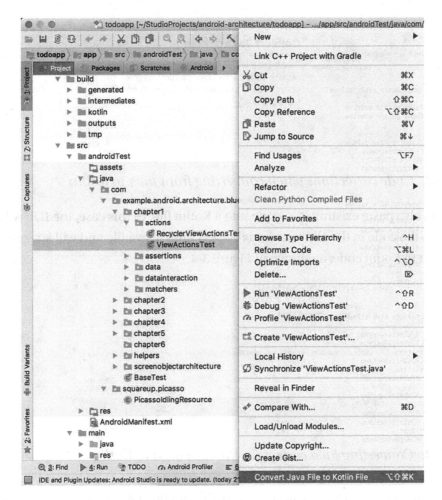

Figure 3-2. *Converting a Java file to Kotlin*

Things can look simple for the test classes files, but can be complicated for complex ViewActions or ViewMatchers. When the IDE convertor can't handle the code complexity, it will require developer interaction. The dialog box in Figure 3-3 alerts the developer to this fact.

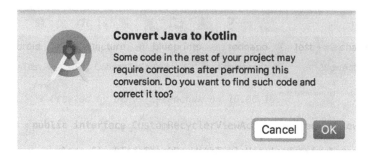

Figure 3-3. *Code corrections when converting from Java to Kotlin*

You can also paste existing Java code into a Kotlin file. In this case, the IDE will identify that the code in the clipboard was copied from a Java file and will suggest converting it to Kotlin code, as shown in Figure 3-4.

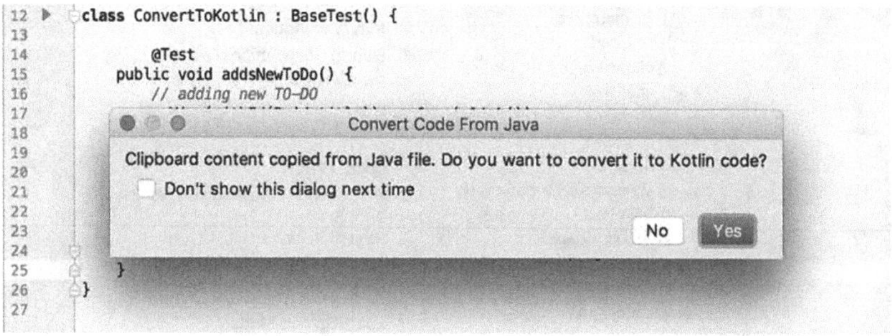

Figure 3-4. *Converting Java code from the clipboard to Kotlin*

You will be asked to add new imports to the Kotlin file if they are not present, as shown in Figure 3-5.

Figure 3-5. *Adding new imports to a file after conversion to Kotlin*

The conversion cannot handle methods with multiple imports. This requires manual interaction from the developer as well (see Figure 3-6).

```
60        @Test
61  ▶   ⊖ fun checksToDoStateChange() {
62            // adding new TO-DO
63            onView(withId(R.id.fab_add_task)).perform(click())
64            onView(withId(R.id.add_task_title))
65                .perform(typeText(toDoTitle), closeSoftKeyboard())
66            onView(withId(R.id.add_task_description))
67                .perform(typeText(toDoDescription), closeSoftKeyboard())
68            onView(withId(R.id.fab_edit_task_done)).perform(click())
69            // marking our TO-DO as completed
70            onView(withId(R.id.todo_complete)).perform(click())
71            // filtering out the completed TO-DO
72            onView(v  ? android.view.View? (multiple choices...) ⌄⏎
73            onView(withId(R.id.todo_title))
74                .check(matches(allOf<View>(withText(toDoTitle), isDisplayed())))
75            openContextualActionModeOverflowMenu()
76        }
77
```

Figure 3-6. *Multiple choices when converting from Java to Kotlin*

The following shows an example of an Espresso UI test method conversion from Java to Kotlin. As you may notice, there is almost no difference except for the function declaration and semicolons at the end of the lines.

Adding a New TO-DO Test in the Java and Kotlin Languages, Respectively.

```java
@Test
public void addsNewToDo() {
    // adding new TO-DO
    onView(withId(R.id.title)).perform(click());
    onView(withId(R.id.add_task_title))
            .perform(typeText(toDoTitle), closeSoftKeyboard());
    onView(withId(R.id.add_task_description))
            .perform(typeText(toDoDescription), closeSoftKeyboard());
    onView(withId(R.id.fab_edit_task_done)).perform(click());
    // verifying new TO-DO with title is shown in the TO-DO list
    onView(withText(toDoTitle)).check(matches(isDisplayed()));
}
```

```kotlin
@Test
fun addsNewToDo() {
    // adding new TO-DO
    onView(withId(R.id.title)).perform(click())
    onView(withId(R.id.add_task_title))
            .perform(typeText(toDoTitle), closeSoftKeyboard())
    onView(withId(R.id.add_task_description))
            .perform(typeText(toDoDescription), closeSoftKeyboard())
    onView(withId(R.id.fab_edit_task_done)).perform(click())
    // verifying new TO-DO with title is shown in the TO-DO list
    onView(withText(toDoTitle)).check(matches(isDisplayed()))
}
```

You can see more examples of converting Java files to Kotlin—based on the examples implemented in the ViewActionsTest.kt, RecyclerViewActionsTest.kt, and DataInteractionsTest.kt classes—in the chapter3/testsamples package.

EXERCISE 10

Converting Java Code to Kotlin

1. Convert an existing Java file to Kotlin.

2. Convert a package containing multiple Java files to Kotlin.

3. Copy a Java code sample and paste it into a Kotlin file. See what happens if you paste only half of the Java method. Will the conversion be correct?

Benefits of Writing Tests in Kotlin

Bringing Kotlin into your test codebase has many advantages. Among them are these:

- Function as a type support

- Extension functions

- String templates

- Ability to import R.class resources

- Much cleaner code

Function as a Type

This process saves a function in a variable and then uses it as another function argument or returns a function by another function. In the following example, you can see how the Espresso ViewMatchers.withText() function is returned as a value of the viewWithText() function:

```
fun viewWithText(text: String): ViewInteraction =
            Espresso.onView(ViewMatchers.withText(text))
```

Extension Functions

Extensions do not actually modify the classes they extend. By defining an extension, you do not add new members into a class, but only make new functions callable with the dot-notation on instances of this type. With the help of extension functions, the Espresso perform(ViewAction.typeText()) function can be represented in the following way:

```kotlin
fun ViewInteraction.type(text: String): ViewInteraction =
                perform(ViewActions.typeText(text))
```

In this example, we extended the ViewInteraction class with an additional type() method.

String Templates

Strings may contain template expressions, i.e. pieces of code that are evaluated and whose results are concatenated into the string. A template expression starts with a dollar sign ($) and contains a simple name. Take a look at this example:

```kotlin
fun main(args: Array<String>) {
    val i = 10
    println("i = $i") // prints "i = 10"
}
```

Or consider an arbitrary expression in curly braces:

```kotlin
 fun main(args: Array<String>) {
    val s = "abc"
    println("$s.length is ${s.length}") // prints "abc.length is 3"
}
```

Import R.class Resources

Kotlin—together with the Kotlin Android Gradle plugin—simplifies the way that project resources (including string values, IDs, and drawables) can be accessed. In the following listing, based on the addsNewToDo() test implementation from the chapter3/testsamples/ViewActionsKotlinTest.kt file, you can see how Kotlin allows us to import application resources.

chapter3.testsamples.ViewActionsKotlinTest.kt.

```
... // other imports and package
import com.example.android.architecture.blueprints.todoapp.R.id.*

class ViewActionsKotlinTest : BaseTest() {

    private var toDoTitle = ""
    private var toDoDescription = ""

    @Before
    override fun setUp() {
        super.setUp()
        toDoTitle = TestData.getToDoTitle()
        toDoDescription = TestData.getToDoDescription()
    }

    @Test
    fun addsNewToDo() {
        // adding new TO-DO
        onView(withId(fab_add_task)).perform(click())
        onView(withId(add_task_title))
                .perform(typeText(toDoTitle), closeSoftKeyboard())
        onView(withId(add_task_description))
                .perform(typeText(toDoDescription), closeSoftKeyboard())
        onView(withId(fab_edit_task_done)).perform(click())
        // verifying new TO-DO with title is shown in the TO-DO list
        onView(withText(toDoTitle)).check(matches(isDisplayed()))
    }
}
```

Instead of the whole R.class, Android Studio IDE allows you to import only one or several resources (see Figure 3-7).

Figure 3-7. *Importing R class resources with Kotlin*

Espresso Domain-Specific Language in Kotlin

With the help of the Kotlin extension functions and function as a type support, we can drastically reduce the boilerplate of the test code by implementing Espresso domain-specific language (DSL). The goal of our Espresso DSL is to simplify our test codebase, make it more legible and, most importantly, make our tests easy to write and maintain.

First, we must determine which Espresso functions or expressions we use the most in our UI test codebase:

- View or data interactions represented by the `Espresso.onView()` and `Espresso.onData()` methods—The starting point of every line of Espresso test code.

- Different view actions, like `ViewActions.click()`, `ViewActions.typeText()`, `ViewActions.swipeDown()`, `ViewActions.closeSoftKeyboard()`, etc.

- Plenty of view matchers, which are the most used functions inside the test codebase, since they are used not only to locate elements on the page but also in combination with view assertions check view properties: `ViewMatchers.withId()`, `ViewMatchers.withText()`, `check(matches(ViewMatchers.isDisplayed()))`, and so on.

- Aggregated Hamcrest matchers like `Matchers.allOf()` or `Matchers.anyOf()`.

- Recycler view actions such as `RecyclerViewActions.scrollToHolder()` and `RecyclerViewActions.actionOnItem()`.

Of course, this list can be extended or reduced based on your needs. It is worth it to highlight that the aim of this paragraph is not to standardize the Espresso DSL with Kotlin, but to provide an example of how it can be done, so that you can apply it to your test projects.

The core `Espresso.onView()` and `Espresso.onData()` methods are the first functions we going to work with. Seeing that they always take a parameter view matcher or object matcher, we can convert the whole expression into one single Kotlin function, as follows:

```
fun viewWithText(text: String): ViewInteraction = Espresso.
onView(ViewMatchers.withText(text))
```

Or in case of `onData()`:

```
fun onAnyData(): DataInteraction = Espresso.onData(CoreMatchers.anything())
```

You may notice that the returning types are identical to those returned by the `onView()` and `onData()` methods—`ViewInteraction` and `DataInteraction`, respectively. Another thing is that it is possible to pass a parameter into the extension function that's used inside the original one. These examples are using Kotlin local functions (i.e., a function inside another function) to simplify the code and can be represented by the following more complex function declarations:

```
fun viewWithText(text: String): ViewInteraction {
    return  Espresso.onView(ViewMatchers.withText(text))
}
```

and

```
fun onAnyData(): DataInteraction {
    return Espresso.onData(CoreMatchers.anything())
}
```

Now moving to view actions. It is time to use Kotlin extension function support. Here is how the Espresso click action on a view with text looks:

```
onView(withText("item 1")).perform(ViewActions.click())
```

You already know that the onView() method returns a ViewInteraction type containing the perform() public method. Now we are going to declare another function that will replace perform(ViewActions.click()). In order to keep the dot notation for the ViewInteraction class, we are going to extend it with our new function, as follows:

```
fun ViewInteraction.click(): ViewInteraction = perform(ViewActions.click())
```

This way, we represent the perform(ViewActions.click()) expression by a simple click() function. This example, using the view with text, looks this way now:

```
viewWithText("item 1").click()
```

Here we also keep the right return ViewInteraction type. It's the same one that is returned by the original perform() method.

The same extension function can be added to the DataInteraction class. The only thing we need to do is replace the ViewInteraction extension class with DataInteraction:

```
fun DataInteraction.click(): ViewInteraction = perform(ViewActions.click())
```

That is it. Looking good so far.

Moving forward to view matchers and view assertions where the same approach with extension functions is used. Here is an example of an assertion of a view being displayed:

```
onView(withText("item 1")).check(matches(isDisplayed()))
```

The check part of the expression can be replaced with this extension function:

```
fun ViewInteraction.checkDisplayed(): ViewInteraction =
        check(ViewAssertions.matches(ViewMatchers.isDisplayed()))
```

This, in combination with the viewWithText() extension function example, is transformed into the following simplified expression:

```
viewWithText("item 1").checkIsDisplayed()
```

Again, replacing ViewInteraction with the DataInteraction class adds the same extension function to DataInteraction.

```
fun DataInteraction.checkDisplayed(): ViewInteraction =
        check(ViewAssertions.matches(ViewMatchers.isDisplayed()))
```

Having DSL samples of the `Espresso.onView()`, `ViewActions`, and `ViewAssertions` methods allows us to compare one of the commonly used raw Espresso expressions with one written in DSL (also assuming that we imported all the Espresso static methods):

```
onView(withText("item 1")).check(matches(isDisplayed())).perform(click())
```

Here's the same line written using DSL:

```
viewWithText("item 1").checkIsDisplayed().click()
```

We can apply the same approach to an aggregated `allOf()` Hamcrest matcher:

```
check(matches(allOf(withText(), isDisplayed())))
```

This will turn into the `allOf()` function, as follows:

```
fun ViewInteraction.allOf(vararg matcher: Matcher<View>): ViewInteraction {
    return check(ViewAssertions.matches(Matchers.allOf(matcher.asIterable())))
}
```

And the usage will be as follows:

```
viewWithId(R.id.title).allOf(withText("item 1"), isDisplayed())
```

Next, we have the recycler view actions. Similar to the previous examples, we can handle recycler view actions. The following example is based on `RecyclerViewActions.actionOnItemAtPosition()` and looks the following way:

```
onView(withId(R.id.tasks_list)).perform(actionOnItemAtPosition(10, scrollTo()));
```

After applying the DSL to this method, we have the following expression:

```
fun ViewInteraction.actionAtPosition(position: Int, action: ViewAction):
ViewInteraction =
        perform(actionOnItemAtPosition<RecyclerView.ViewHolder>(position,
        action))
```

So, the final usage is:

```
viewWithId(R.id.tasks_list)).actionAtPosition(10, scrollTo())
```

These examples and even more are defined in the chapter3/EspressoDsl.kt file of our sample project for your reference.

Now it is time to apply our domain specific language to our tests and observe how converted Espresso Kotlin tests look compared to those written using DSL. First let's look at the ViewActions tests samples implemented in ViewActionsKotlinTest.kt.

The checksToDoStateChange() Test Method Implemented in chapter3.
testsamples.ViewActionsKotlinTest.kt.

```
@Test
fun checksToDoStateChange() {
    // adding new TO-DO
    onView(withId(R.id.fab_add_task)).perform(click())
    onView(withId(R.id.add_task_title))
            .perform(typeText(toDoTitle), closeSoftKeyboard())
    onView(withId(R.id.add_task_description))
            .perform(typeText(toDoDescription), closeSoftKeyboard())
    onView(withId(R.id.fab_edit_task_done)).perform(click())

    // marking our TO-DO as completed
    onView(withId(R.id.todo_complete)).perform(click())

    // filtering out the completed TO-DO
    onView(withId(R.id.menu_filter)).perform(click())
    onView(allOf(withId(R.id.title), withText("Active"))).perform(click())
    onView(withId(R.id.todo_title)).check(matches(not(isDisplayed())))
    onView(withId(R.id.menu_filter)).perform(click())
    onView(allOf(withId(R.id.title), withText("Completed"))).
    perform(click())
    onView(withId(R.id.todo_title))
            .check(matches(allOf(withText(toDoTitle), isDisplayed())))
}
```

Now we can compare this to the tests from `ViewActionsKotlinDslTest.kt`.

The checksToDoStateChange() Test Method Implemented in chapter3.
testsamples.ViewActionsKotlinDslTest.kt.

```kotlin
// ViewInteractions used in tests
private val addFab = viewWithId(fab_add_task)
private val taskTitleField = viewWithId(add_task_title)
private val taskDescriptionField = viewWithId(add_task_description)
private val editDoneFab = viewWithId(fab_edit_task_done)
private val todoCheckbox = viewWithId(todo_complete)
private val toolbarFilter = viewWithId(menu_filter)
private val todoTitle = viewWithId(todo_title)
private val allFilterOption = onView(allOf(withId(title), withText("All")))
private val activeFilterOption = onView(allOf(withId(title), withText("Active")))
private val completedFilterOption = onView(allOf(withId(title),
withText("Completed")))

@Test
fun checksToDoStateChangeDsl() {
    // adding new TO-DO
    addFab.click()
    taskTitleField.type(toDoTitle).closeKeyboard()
    taskDescriptionField.type(toDoDescription).closeKeyboard()
    editDoneFab.click()

    // marking our TO-DO as completed
    todoCheckbox.click()

    // filtering out the completed TO-DO
    toolbarFilter.click()
    activeFilterOption.click()
    todoTitle.checkNotDisplayed()
    toolbarFilter.click()
    completedFilterOption.click()
    todoTitle.checkMatches(allOf(withText(toDoTitle), isDisplayed()))
}
```

As you may notice, the test method implemented with DSL is much more legible and clean. For even more readability, we declared all used view interactions at the beginning of the test class. This makes the tests even smoother.

EXERCISE 11

Practicing Espresso DSL Usage

1. Look through the tests implemented in the `DataInteractionKotlinDslTest.kt` and `RecyclerViewActionsKotlinDslTest.kt` classes and understand how DSL was applied to these tests.

2. Based on the `editsToDo()` test method from `ViewActionsKotlinTest.kt`, finish implementation of the `editsToDoDsl()` test case located in `ViewActionsKotlinDslTest.kt` using DSL.

Summary

After many years of the Java language dominating the Android platform, Kotlin brings a fresh and progressive approach to its applications and to test development. Tests written in Kotlin are more legible, cleaner, and easier to maintain. Its extension functions support allows developers to easily create and test domain-specific language, which simplifies the test code even more. Migration from Java to Kotlin is painless and fast. In the end, it is clear that at some point Kotlin will replace Java in Android application development. You should be prepared to at least migrate to Kotlin and improve your test code.

CHAPTER 4

Handling Network Operations and Asynchronous Actions

One of the key benefits of the Espresso framework is its test robustness. It is achieved through automatic synchronization of most of the test actions. Espresso waits for the main application UI thread while it is busy and releases test actions after the UI thread becomes idle. Moreover, it also waits for `AsyncTask` operations to complete before it moves to the next test step. In this chapter, we will see how Espresso can handle network operations using the `IdlingResource` mechanism and become familiar with the `ConditionWatcher` mechanism as an alternative to `IdlingResource`.

IdlingResource Basics

Each time your test invokes `onView()` or `onData()`, Espresso waits to perform the corresponding UI action or assertion until the following synchronization conditions are met:

- The message queue is empty.

- There are no instances of `AsyncTask` currently executing a task.

- All developer-defined idling resources are idle.

By performing these checks, Espresso substantially increases the likelihood that only one UI action or assertion can occur at any given time. This capability gives you more reliable and dependable test results.

© Denys Zelenchuk 2019
D. Zelenchuk, *Android Espresso Revealed*, https://doi.org/10.1007/978-1-4842-4315-2_4

However, it is not possible in every case to rely on automatic synchronization, for instance when the application being tested executes network calls via ThreadPoolExecutor. In order to let Espresso handle these kinds of long-lasting asynchronous operations, the IdlingResource must be created and registered before the test is executed.

It is important to register IdlingResource when these operations update the application UI you would like to further validate.

The common use cases in which IdlingResource can be used are when your app is:

- Performing network calls.

- Establishing database connections.

At the moment, Espresso provides the following idling resources:

- CountingIdlingResource—Maintains a counter of active tasks. When the counter is zero, the associated resource is considered idle. This functionality closely resembles that of a semaphore. In most cases, this implementation is sufficient for managing your app's asynchronous work during testing.

- UriIdlingResource—Similar to CountingIdlingResource, but the counter needs to be zero for a specific period of time before the resource is considered idle. This additional waiting period takes consecutive network requests into account, where an app in your thread might make a new request immediately after receiving a response to a previous request.

- IdlingThreadPoolExecutor—A custom implementation of ThreadPoolExecutor that keeps track of the total number of running tasks within the created thread pools. This class uses a CountingIdlingResource to maintain the counter of active tasks.

- IdlingScheduledThreadPoolExecutor—A custom implementation of ScheduledThreadPoolExecutor. It provides the same functionality and capabilities as the IdlingThreadPoolExecutor class, but it can also keep track of tasks that are scheduled for the future or are scheduled to execute periodically.

To start using an idling resource mechanism in an application, the following dependency must be added to the application `buid.gradle` file (dependencies are mentioned for the Android Support and AndroidX Libraries).

IdlingResource Dependency in the Android Support Library.

```
androidTestImplementation "com.android.support.test.espresso.idling:idling-
concurrent:3.0.1"
```

IdlingResource Dependency in the AndroidX Library.

```
androidTestImplementation 'androidx.test.espresso.idling:idling-
concurrent:3.1.0'
```

These idling resource types use `CountingIdlingResource` in their implementation, so we will focus on `CountingIdlingResource` as a reference.

The `IdlingResource` interface contains three methods:

- `getName()`—Returns the name of the resources.

Note The `IdlingResource` name is represented by a `String` class and is used when logging, and for registration/unregistration purposes. Therefore, the name of the resource should be unique.

- `isIdleNow()`—Returns `true` if the resource is currently idle. Espresso will always call this method from the main thread; therefore, it should be non-blocking and return immediately.

- `registerIdleTransitionCallback()`—Registers the given resource callback with the idling resource. The registered callback is then used in the `isIdleNow()` method.

Note The `IdlingResource` class contains a `ResourceCallback` interface that is used in the `registerTransitionCallback()` method. Whenever the application is going to switch states from busy to idle, the `callback. onTransitionToIdle()` method should be called to notify Espresso about it.

CountingIdlingResource is an implementation of IdlingResource that determines idleness by maintaining an internal counter. When the counter is zero, it is considered to be idle; when it is non-zero, it is not idle. This is very similar to the way a java.util. concurrent.Semaphore behaves.

The counter may be incremented or decremented from any thread. If it reaches an illogical state (like a counter that's less than zero), it will throw an IllegalStateException. This class can then be used to wrap operations that, while in progress, block tests from accessing the UI.

Writing the Code

This is how the simple CountingIdlingResource looks in our application (see the util/ SimpleCountingIdlingResource.java file from the main application source code):

```java
public final class SimpleCountingIdlingResource implements IdlingResource {

    private final String mResourceName;

    private final AtomicInteger counter = new AtomicInteger(0);

    // written from main thread, read from any thread.
    private volatile ResourceCallback resourceCallback;

    /**
     * Creates a SimpleCountingIdlingResource
     *
     * @param resourceName the name of the resource to report to Espresso.
     */
    public SimpleCountingIdlingResource(String resourceName) {
        mResourceName = checkNotNull(resourceName);
    }

    @Override
    public String getName() {
        return mResourceName;
    }
```

```java
@Override
public boolean isIdleNow() {
    return counter.get() == 0;
}

@Override
public void registerIdleTransitionCallback(ResourceCallback
resourceCallback) {
    this.resourceCallback = resourceCallback;
}

/**
 * Increments the count of in-flight transactions to the resource being
   monitored.
 */
public void increment() {
    counter.getAndIncrement();
}

/**
 * Decrements the count of in-flight transactions to the resource being
   monitored.
 *
 * If this operation results in the counter falling below 0 - an
   exception is raised.
 *
 * @throws IllegalStateException if the counter is below 0.
 */
public void decrement() {
    int counterVal = counter.decrementAndGet();
    if (counterVal == 0) {
        // we've gone from non-zero to zero. That means we're idle now!
            Tell espresso.
        if (null != resourceCallback) {
            resourceCallback.onTransitionToIdle();
        }
    }
```

```
    if (counterVal < 0) {
        throw new IllegalArgumentException("Counter has been corrupted!");
    }
  }
}
```

The SimpleCountingIdlingResource class is used by the EspressoIdlingResource class in the same location that contains a static reference to it (see the util/ EspressoIdlingResource.java file) and it uses its increment() and decrement() methods:

```
public class EspressoIdlingResource {

    private static final String RESOURCE = "GLOBAL";

    private static SimpleCountingIdlingResource mCountingIdlingResource =
            new SimpleCountingIdlingResource(RESOURCE);

    public static void increment() {
        mCountingIdlingResource.increment();
    }

    public static void decrement() {
        mCountingIdlingResource.decrement();
    }

    public static IdlingResource getIdlingResource() {
        return mCountingIdlingResource;
    }
}
```

Now let's take a look at the tasks/TasksPresenter.java class from the main application source code where EspressoIdlingResource is used. This class is responsible for loading TO-DOs and presenting them in the TO-DO list. You can see how the EspressoIdlingResource.increment() method is called when the task load process starts to pause the tests. When the task is loaded, EspressoIdlingResource. decrement() is called to notify Espresso about the upcoming idling state:

```java
private void loadTasks(boolean forceUpdate, final boolean showLoadingUI) {
    if (showLoadingUI) {
        mTasksView.setLoadingIndicator(true);
    }
    if (forceUpdate) {
        mTasksRepository.refreshTasks();
    }

    // The network request might be handled in a different thread so make
        sure Espresso
    // knows that the app is busy until the response is handled.
    EspressoIdlingResource.increment(); // App is busy until further notice

    mTasksRepository.getTasks(new TasksDataSource.LoadTasksCallback() {
            @Override
            public void onTasksLoaded(List<Task> tasks) {
                List<Task> tasksToShow = new ArrayList<Task>();

                // This callback may be called twice, once for the cache and
                    once for loading
                // the data from the server API, so we check before
                    decrementing, otherwise
                // it throws "Counter has been corrupted!" exception.
                if (!EspressoIdlingResource.getIdlingResource().isIdleNow()) {
                    EspressoIdlingResource.decrement(); // Set app as idle.
                }
            ... // other code here
            }
    }
}
```

Running the First Test

To see EspressoIdlingResource in action, we add some logging to the increment() and decrement() methods in the SimpleCountingIdlingResource.java class and run the addNewToDosChained() test:

```
@Override
public boolean isIdleNow() {
    Log.d(getName(), "Counter value is " + counter.get());
    return counter.get() == 0;
}
```

and

```
public void decrement() {
    int counterVal = counter.decrementAndGet();
    Log.d(getName(), "Counter decremented. Value is " + counterVal);
    if (counterVal == 0) {
        // we've gone from non-zero to zero. That means we're idle now!
            Tell espresso.
        if (null != resourceCallback) {
            resourceCallback.onTransitionToIdle();
        }
    }

    if (counterVal < 0) {
        throw new IllegalArgumentException("Counter has been corrupted!");
    }
}
```

During the test run, observe the logcat logs of our application, which can be filtered out by the GLOBAL tag. Figure 4-1 shows what you will see; each time a TO-DO is added, a TO-DO list is displayed to the user and the counter is incremented and decremented just after the load is done.

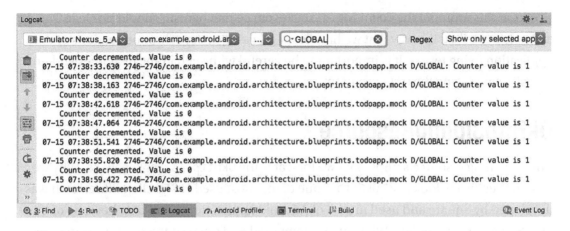

Figure 4-1. *Idling resource counter logging*

IdlingResource should be registered before usage. IdlingRegistry handles registering and unregistering IdlingResource.

Registering and Unregistering IdlingResource Instances.

```
@Before
fun registerResources() {
    val idlingRegistry = IdlingRegistry.getInstance()
    val okHttp3IdlingResource = OkHttp3IdlingResource(client)
    val picassoIdlingResource = PicassoIdlingResource()

    idlingRegistry.register(okHttp3IdlingResource)
    idlingRegistry.register(picassoIdlingResource)
}

@After
fun unregisterResources() {
    val idlingRegistry = IdlingRegistry.getInstance()
    for (idlingResource in idlingRegistry.resources) {
        if (idlingResource == null) {
            continue
        }
        idlingRegistry.unregister(idlingResource)
    }
}
```

So, at this moment the CountingIdlingResource mechanism should be clear. This example described the way that we handle long-lasting or asynchronous actions of the application being tested. It is important to be careful with such idling resources and not to lock them during the test execution.

OkHttp3IdlingResource

Another idling resource sample that we look at is the OkHttp3IdlingResource. Why we should specifically look at it? OkHttp is one of the most used HTTP client libraries. It was developed by Square and used in a lot of Android applications. Probably because of this one, Square developer Jake Wharton implemented and open sourced this resource. See https://github.com/JakeWharton/okhttp-idling-resource. Here is how it looks.

chapter4.idlingresources.OkHttp3IdlingResource.kt.

```
public final class OkHttp3IdlingResource implements IdlingResource {

    @CheckResult
    @NonNull
    @SuppressWarnings("ConstantConditions") // Extra guards as a library.
    public static OkHttp3IdlingResource create(@NonNull String name,
    @NonNull OkHttpClient client) {
        if (name == null) throw new NullPointerException("name == null");
        if (client == null) throw new NullPointerException("client == null");
        return new OkHttp3IdlingResource(name, client.dispatcher());
    }

    private final String name;
    private final Dispatcher dispatcher;
    volatile ResourceCallback callback;

    private OkHttp3IdlingResource(String name, Dispatcher dispatcher) {
        this.name = name;
        this.dispatcher = dispatcher;
        dispatcher.setIdleCallback(new Runnable() {
            @Override public void run() {
                ResourceCallback callback = OkHttp3IdlingResource.this.
                callback;
```

```
            if (callback != null) {
                callback.onTransitionToIdle();
            }
        }
    });
}

@Override public String getName() {
    return name;
}

@Override public boolean isIdleNow() {
    return dispatcher.runningCallsCount() == 0;
}

@Override public void registerIdleTransitionCallback(ResourceCallback
callback) {
    this.callback = callback;
}
}
```

Basically, this resource works out-of-the-box and almost everything is done for us here. The `dispatcher.runningCallsCount()` method call from the `iSIdleNow()` method returns both running synchronous and asynchronous requests counts, which are compared to zero. When the result is true, the resource is idle. There are, however, some steps we still have to take in order to use it:

1. Add a dependency in the `build.gradle` file:

```
androidTestCompile 'com.jakewharton.espresso:okhttp3-idling-resource:1.0.0'
```

2. In your test code, obtain the `OkHttpClient` instance and create an idling resource:

```
OkHttpClient client = // ... get OkHttpClient instance
IdlingResource resource = OkHttp3IdlingResource.create("OkHttp", client);
```

3. Register the idling resource in the test code before running any Espresso tests:

```
IdlingRegistry.getInstance().register(resource);
```

By the way, don't use the deprecated `Espresso.registerIdlingResources()` method; instead use the `IdlingRegistry` implementation shown in this section.

Picasso IdlingResource

Picasso is a powerful image-downloading and caching library for Android from Square. Picasso allows for hassle-free image loading in your application—often in one line of code (`http://square.github.io/picasso/`):

```
Picasso.get().load("http://i.imgur.com/DvpvklR.png").into(imageView);
```

Picasso is the most popular image-downloading library for Android, which means it is a perfect candidate for another type of `IdlingResource`. The image-download idling resource can be used when we want to ensure that the whole application window layout is loaded together with the graphics. This can be extremely important in cases where graphical resources should be verified in tests. Here is the example of the `PicassoIdling` resource that's also implemented in the `androidTest/com.squareup.picasso` package.

androidTest/com.squareup.picasso.PicassoIdlingResource.java.

```java
public class PicassoIdlingResource implements IdlingResource,
ActivityLifecycleCallback {

    private static final int IDLE_POLL_DELAY_MILLIS = 100;
    private ResourceCallback mCallback;
    private WeakReference<Picasso> mPicassoWeakReference;
    private final Handler mHandler = new Handler(Looper.getMainLooper());

    @Override
    public String getName() {
        return "PicassoIdlingResource";
    }

    @Override
    public boolean isIdleNow() {
        if (isIdle()) {
            notifyDone();
            return true;
```

```
        } else {
      /* Force a re-check of the idle state in a little while.
       * If isIdleNow() returns false, Espresso only polls it every few
         seconds which can slow down our tests.
       */
            mHandler.postDelayed(new Runnable() {
                @Override
                public void run() {
                    isIdleNow();
                }
            }, IDLE_POLL_DELAY_MILLIS);
            return false;
        }
}

public boolean isIdle() {
    return mPicassoWeakReference == null
            || mPicassoWeakReference.get() == null
            || mPicassoWeakReference.get().targetToAction.isEmpty();
}

@Override
public void registerIdleTransitionCallback(ResourceCallback
resourceCallback) {
    mCallback = resourceCallback;
}

void notifyDone() {
    if (mCallback != null) {
        mCallback.onTransitionToIdle();
    }
}

@Override
public void onActivityLifecycleChanged(Activity activity, Stage stage)
{

    switch (stage) {
```

```
            case RESUMED:
                mPicassoWeakReference = new WeakReference<>(Picasso.
                with(activity));
                break;
            case PAUSED:
                // Clean up reference
                mPicassoWeakReference = null;
                break;
            default: // NOP
        }
    }
}
```

Note   The reason that the Picasso `IdlingResource` is in a separate package is because of the visibility of the `targetToAction` variable in the `Picasso` class, which is package protected.

ConditionWatcher as an Alternative to IdlingResource

As you may notice, the `IdlingResource` implementation is not trivial and requires continuous control over registering and unregistering. It is also not convenient to use `IdlingResource` in deep UI tests when a specific activity instance is needed to make it work.

As an alternative, you can try the `ConditionWatcher` class from AzimoLabs (`https://github.com/AzimoLabs/ConditionWatcher`). It is simple class that makes Android automation testing easier, faster, cleaner, and more intuitive. It synchronizes operations that might occur on any thread, with the test thread. `ConditionWatcher` can be used as a replacement to Espresso's `IdlingResources` or it can work in parallel with them.

This is how it works: `ConditionWatcher` receives an instance of the `Instruction` class that contains a logical expression. Tests are paused until the moment the condition returns true. After that, the tests are immediately released. If the condition is not met within a specified timeout, the exception will be thrown and the test will fail.

ConditionWatcher acts on the same thread it is requested, which is the test thread. By default, ConditionWatcher includes three methods:

- setWatchInterval()—Sets the interval for periodic check of the logical expression. By default, it is set to 250 milliseconds.

- setTimeoutLimit()—Sets the timeout for the ConditionWatcher to wait for a true value from the checkCondition() method. By default, it is set to 60 seconds.

- waitForCondition()—Takes instructions containing a logical expression as a parameter and calls its checkCondition() method with the currently set interval, until it returns value true or until the timeout is reached. During that time, the test code won't proceed to the next line. If timeout is reached, an Exception is thrown.

From the other side, the Instruction class happens to have a very similar structure to IdlingResource:

- checkCondition()—A core method that's equivalent to isIdleNow() of IdlingResource. It's a logical expression and its changes, along with the monitored dynamic resource status, should be implemented there.

- getDescription()—A string returned along with the timeout exception. The test author can include helpful information for the test crash debugging process.

- setDataContainer() and getDataContainer() —A bundle that can be added to the Instruction class to share primitive types (e.g., a universal instruction that waits for any kind of view to become visible can be created, and resId could be sent via the bundle).

The following dependency should be added to the build.gradle file in order to start using ConditionWatcher:

```
dependencies {
    androidTestCompile 'com.azimolabs.conditionwatcher:conditionwatcher:0.2'
}
```

Or just copy the source code of the two ConditionWatcher.java and Instruction.java classes into your test source code.

The simplest example of ConditionWatcher usage is a condition to wait for an element be displayed on the screen:

```
ConditionWatcher.waitForCondition(new Instruction() {

    @Override
    public String getDescription() {
        return "waitForElementIsDisplayed";
    }

    @Override
    public boolean checkCondition() {
        try {
            interaction.check(matches(isDisplayed()));
            return true;
        } catch (NoMatchingViewException ex) {
            return false;
        }
    }
});
```

I prefer to wrap the ConditionWatcher into a method instead of creating a class that extends the Instruction class. Next, you see an example of the waitForElementIsDisplayed(final ViewInteraction interaction, final int timeout) watcher from the ConditionWatchers.java class:

```
public static ViewInteraction waitForElementIsDisplayed(
        final ViewInteraction interaction,
        final int timeout) throws Exception {
    ConditionWatcher.setTimeoutLimit(timeout);
    ConditionWatcher.waitForCondition(new Instruction() {

        @Override
        public String getDescription() {
            return "waitForElementIsDisplayed";
        }
```

```
    @Override
    public boolean checkCondition() {
        try {
            interaction.check(matches(isDisplayed()));
            return true;
        } catch (NoMatchingViewException ex) {
            return false;
        }
    }
});
return interaction;
}
```

With this implementation of waitForElementIsDisplayed(), we receive one important benefit—if the watcher receives ViewInteraction as a parameter, the wrapper method can return the same ViewInteraction, which simplifies our test source code:

```
private ViewInteraction addTaskFab = onView(withId(R.id.fab_add_task));

@Test
public void waitForElementCondition() throws Exception {
    waitForElementIsDisplayed(addTaskFab, 4000).perform(click());
}
```

Now let's move to more complicated examples. In our sample application, we have a nasty snackbar that pops up every time a new TO-DO is added. It doesn't allow us to add multiple TO-DOs to our list without waiting until it disappears. Our task is to create a watcher that will wait for the snackbar view to be gone. This is how it can be done.

chapter4.conditionwatchers.ConditionWatchers.tasksListSnackbarGone().

```
public static void tasksListSnackbarGone() throws Exception {
    ConditionWatcher.waitForCondition(new Instruction() {
        @Override
        public String getDescription() {
            return "Condition tasksListSnackbarGone";
        }
```

```
    @Override
    public boolean checkCondition() {
        final FragmentActivity fragmentActivity = getCurrentActivity();
        if (fragmentActivity != null) {
            Fragment currentFragment = fragmentActivity
                    .getSupportFragmentManager()
                    .findFragmentById(R.id.contentFrame);
            if (currentFragment instanceof TasksFragment) {
                View contentView =
                fragmentActivity.getWindow().getDecorView().
                findViewById(android.R.id.content);
                if (contentView != null) {
                    TextView snackBarTextView =
                            contentView.findViewById(android.support.
                            design.R.id.snackbar_text);
                    return snackBarTextView == null;
                }
            }
        }
        return false;
    }
});
}
```

ConditionWatchers can be extremely helpful when we have to wait for the different view states, but we should not overuse them in terms of waiting time. A problem can occur in cases when we may wait too much for a specific state of the view to be reached. When this waiting time becomes too long, it can seem like an issue with the application being tested and it is better to raise a bug than handle it inside your tests. Ideally, in most situations, IdlingResources should handle the majority of time the application is not idle, so ConditionWatchers should be a small addition to the waiting mechanism and be used occasionally, like in our snackbar case.

EXERCISE 12

Using a ConditionWatcher in a Test

1. Implement a test that opens the menu drawer and navigates to another section. In this test, add a condition watcher that waits for a menu drawer to be shown or hidden. Use `ViewMatchers.isDisplayed()` for the shown state and hamcrest `CoreMatchers.not(ViewMatchers.isDisplayed())` for hidden.

2. Implement a `waitForElement()` `ConditionWatcher` that can be used with the `DataInteraction` type. Use the `ViewInteraction` `waitForElement()` function as a reference.

Making Condition Watchers Part of Espresso Kotlin DSL

Chapter 3 explained the Espresso Kotlin DSL as an example of much cleaner and compact test code. As you may notice, in the current implementation, all the functions from the `ConditionWatchers` class are not yet ready to be used in a similar way.

The thing is `ConditionWatchers`, as well as other Espresso methods, are implemented and executed in the same place and at the same time as the test code, which is the opposite to how `IdlingResources` are used—by registering them before the test run (usually in the `@Before` method).

So, `ConditionWatchers` should ideally become part of the Espresso Kotlin DSL and be used as one of the chains while writing the test code. This is how our `ConditionWatchers` can be declared as part of the DSL (see `EspressoDsl.kt` for the implementation details):

- `ConditionWatchers.waitForElement()`:

```
fun ViewInteraction.wait(): ViewInteraction =
        ConditionWatchers.waitForElement(this, FOUR_SECONDS)
```

- `ConditionWatchers.waitForElementFullyVisible()`:

```
fun ViewInteraction.waitFullyVisible(): ViewInteraction =
        ConditionWatchers.waitForElementFullyVisible(this, FOUR_SECONDS)
```

- `ConditionWatchers.waitForElementIsGone()`:

```
fun ViewInteraction.waitForGone(): ViewInteraction =
        ConditionWatchers.waitForElementIsGone(this, FOUR_SECONDS)
```

All of these examples have the `ViewInteraction` return type and can be chained to Espresso test code as follows.

chapter3.testsamples.ViewActionsKotlinDslTest.addsNewToDoWithWaiterDsl().

```
@Test
fun addsNewToDoWithWaiterDsl() {
    // adding new TO-DO
    addFab.click()
    taskTitleField.wait().type(toDoTitle).closeKeyboard()
    taskDescriptionField.type(toDoDescription).closeKeyboard()
    editDoneFab.click()
    snackbar.waitForGone()
    // verifying new TO-DO with title is shown in the TO-DO list
    viewWithText(toDoTitle).checkDisplayed()
}
```

EXERCISE 13

ConditionWatcher as Part of the DSL

1. Implement a test that opens a menu drawer and navigates to another section. In this test, add a condition watcher that waits for the menu drawer to be shown or hidden. Use `ViewMatchers.isDisplayed()` for the shown state and hamcrest `CoreMatchers.not(ViewMatchers.isDisplayed())` for hidden.

2. Make the `DataInteraction` `waitForElement()` function in the previous task part of the DSL.

Summary

Properly handling network operations and asynchronous actions is a must-have in your UI tests. Applying `IdlingResource` or `ConditionWatcher` makes your UI tests much more stable and reliable. After using them at least once, it will be clear that there is no need to use explicit `Thread.sleep()` methods all over the tests, which is a bad practice and error-prone.

CHAPTER 5

Verifying and Stubbing Intents with IntentMatchers

Throughout this chapter, we will discuss how to verify and stub application intents. An intent is a messaging object you can use to request an action from another app component. Intents facilitate communication between components in several ways. According to the Android Intent and Filters documentation (`https://developer.android.com/guide/components/intents-filters`), there are three fundamental use cases:

- *Starting an activity*—An activity represents a single screen in the Android application. An activity instance can be launched by passing an intent to `Context.startActivity(Intent)`. Passed intents should contain information about which activity will be started and may contain extra data. The `Context.startActivityForResult(Intent)` method is used when we expect to receive the result from a launched activity. The result is returned in the form of an intent object and can be handled in an `Activity.onActivityResult()` callback.

- *Starting a service*—A service in Android represents a mechanism that performs operations in the background. Similar to an activity, a service is started by passing an intent to `Context.startService(Intent)`. Provided intents define the service to start and may contain extra data.

- *Delivering a broadcast* —A broadcast represents a message that can be sent and received by any application or system. An example of a system broadcast can be a system bootup event. Broadcasts can be delivered to other apps by passing an intent to `Context.sendBroadcast(Intent)`.

© Denys Zelenchuk 2019
D. Zelenchuk, *Android Espresso Revealed*, https://doi.org/10.1007/978-1-4842-4315-2_5

Here are examples of intents that belong to these intent types:

- *Starting an activity intent*—Usually an intent to start an activity for a result. An example can be clicking the attachment button in Gmail, which opens the file browser so you can find and attach a file to the email.

- *Starting a service intent*—Used to trigger long-lasting processes that are running in the background, like file downloads or for listening for some system events like connectivity state changes.

- *Delivering a broadcast*—Used when there is a need to send a local intent, meaning that we would like to broadcast to receivers that are in the same app as the sender. Or just send our broadcast to all apps in the system that can handle it. An example is a broadcast to send an SMS.

As you may already know, Espresso cannot operate outside of the application being tested, which is the common case in starting an activity intent or delivering a broadcast. Therefore, to make Espresso tests isolated and hermetic, we need to use Espresso-Intents, which is an extension to Espresso that enables validation and stubbing of intents sent out by the application being tested.

Setting Up Dependencies

In order to use Espresso-Intents, the following line of code should be added inside the build.gradle file of your app module:

Android Testing Support Library Espresso-Intents Dependency.

```
androidTestImplementation 'com.android.support.test.espresso:espresso-
intents:3.0.2'
```

AndroidX Test Library Espresso-Intents Dependency.

```
androidTestImplementation 'androidx.test.espresso:espresso-intents:3.1.0'
```

Note   Espresso-Intents is only compatible with Espresso 2.1+ and the Testing Support library 0.3+ or AndroidX Test library.

So, to fulfill this compatibility requirement, the following dependencies must be updated as well.

Android Testing Support Library Dependencies.

```
androidTestImplementation 'com.android.support.test:runner:1.0.2'
androidTestImplementation 'com.android.support.test:rules:1.0.2'
androidTestImplementation 'com.android.support.test.espresso:espresso-core:3.0.2'
```

Or in case of AndroidX Test library usage, we need the following.

AndroidX Test library Dependencies.

```
androidTestImplementation 'androidx.test:runner:1.1.0'
androidTestImplementation 'androidx.test:rules:1.1.0'
androidTestImplementation 'androidx.test.espresso:espresso-core:3.1.0'
```

In Chapter 1, we discussed the purpose and role of `ActivityTestRule` in Espresso tests. Similar to `ActivityTestRule`, Espresso has the `IntentsTestRule`, which is the extension of `ActivityTestRule` and must be used when intents should be stubbed or validated. As in the case of `ActivityTestRule`, an `IntentsTestRule` initializes Espresso-Intents before each test is annotated with @Test and releases Espresso-Intents after each test run.

Here is an `IntentsTestRule` example:

```
@get:Rule
var intentsTestRule = IntentsTestRule(TasksActivity::class.java)
```

Our sample application contains functionality for attaching an image to the TO-DO item and is an example of an activity for a result intent that receives an image file from the system. Figure 5-1 shows the intent flow when the start activity intent is sent to a third-party application.

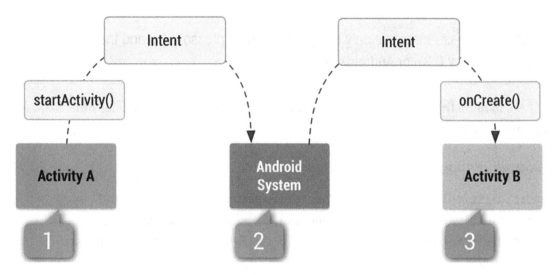

Figure 5-1. *Activity intent flow (image source:* `https://developer.android.`
`com/guide/components/intents-filters`*)*

Step 1 demonstrates sending a start activity intent from our application to notify the
system about the need to delegate some functionality to a third-party application. In
its order, the system knows what application(s) can be sent in Step 1 and, if at least one
application is found, it retransmits the same activity intent to it, which is shown in Step 2.
In Step 3, the selected application receives the intent and starts the appropriate activity.
In case of an intent that is sent with `startActivityForResult()`, the result of the started
activity (for example, the selected image link from the Gallery or Photos application) is
returned to the application that initially created the intent.

It is a time to look at how Espresso stubs intents sent to the third-party applications
outside of the application context.

Stubbing Activity Intents

As mentioned, Espresso does not support leaving applications under the text context,
i.e. leaving the tested application, in order to interact with third-party applications.
For this reason, Espresso provides the stubbing mechanism `intending()` method in the
`Intents` class.

This method enables stubbing intent responses and is particularly useful when the activity launching the intent expects data to be returned (and especially when the destination activity is external). In this case, the test author can call:

```
intending(intentMatcher).thenRespond(myResponse)
```

and validate that the launching activity handles the result correctly.

Note   The third-party application destination activity will not be launched in this code sample.

Stubbing Intents Without a Result

The first use case with intent stubbing can isolate our application from any action that can lead to the state when a third-party application is launched. To achieve this, the Espresso `intending()` mechanism enables stubbing intents that are not internal, i.e., that do not belong to our application. Here is how it can be implemented in the test class `@Before` method.

chapter5.StubAllIntentsTest.kt.

```
@Before
fun stubAllExternalIntents() {
    // By default Espresso Intents does not stub any Intents. Stubbing
needs to be setup before
    // every test run. In this case all external Intents will be blocked.
    intending(not(isInternal()))
            .respondWith(Instrumentation.ActivityResult(Activity.RESULT_OK,
            null))
}
```

Note   The method annotated with the `@Before` annotation will be executed for every test case before it's run.

You can observe two new methods in this code example:

- `isInternal()`—Intent matcher that matches an intent if its package is the same as the target package for the instrumentation test.

- `Instrumentation.ActivityResult(Activity.RESULT_OK, null)`—The `ActivityResult` class that allows us to create a new `ActivityResult`, which will be propagated back to the original activity with the specified result code. See the Android `Instrumentation.java` class and the `Activity.setResult()` method for more details.

We are already familiar with hamcrest matchers from Chapters 1 and 2. `IntentMatchers` have a similar functionality. Along with intent matchers, Espresso provides `BundleMatchers`, `ComponentNameMatchers`, and `UriMatchers`, which are used together with `IntentMatchers`. Here is a brief overview of all of them.

`IntentMatchers`:

- `anyIntent()`—Matches any intent.

- `hasAction()`—Matches an intent by intent action. The most common example is `Intent.ACTION_CALL` to perform the phone call action or `Intent.ACTION_SEND` to send an email or SMS. For more action types, refer to the Android `Intent.java` class.

- `hasCategories()`—Matches an intent category, which is the string containing additional information about the kind of component that should handle the intent. For example, the string value for `CATEGORY_LAUNCHER` is `android.intent.category.LAUNCHER` and is used to specify the initial application activity.

- `hasComponent()`—Can match an intent by class name, package name, or short class name. Uses `ComponentNameMatchers`.

- `hasData()`—Matches an intent that has specific data this intent is operating on. Often it uses the content: scheme, specifying data in a content provider. Other schemes may be handled by specific activities, such as http: by the web browser. Uses `UriMatchers`.

- `hasExtraWithKey()`—Matches an intent that has specific bundle attached to the intent. Uses a `hasExtras()` method that takes the bundle matcher as a parameter.

- `hasExtra()`—Same as `hasExtras()` but with extra data.

- `hasExtras()`—Matches an intent that has specific extended or extra data. This data is put into the intent in the form of a `<name, value>` pair by one of the overloaded `Intent.putExtra()` methods. The name of the extra parameter must include a package prefix. For example, the app `com.android.contacts` would use names like `com.android.contacts.ShowAll`.

- `hasType()`—Matches an intent with the explicit MIME type included in it.

- `hasPackage()`—Matches an intent that is limited to a specified application package name.

- `toPackage()`-Matches an intent based on the package of activity that can handle the intent.

- `hasFlag()`-Same as `getFlags()`.

- `hasFlags()`-Matches an intent with specified flag(s) associated with it. The list of flags can be found at `https://developer.android.com/reference/android/content/Intent#setFlags(int)`.

- `isInternal()`-Matches an intent if its package is the same as the target package for the instrumentation test.

The `BundleMatchers` class represents hamcrest matchers for intent bundles. Bundles are used for passing data between activities, usually in form of a `<key, value>` pair.

- `hasEntry()`-Matches a bundle object based on a `<key, value>` pair.

- `hasKey()`-Matches a bundle object based on a key.

- `hasValue()`-Matches a bundle object based on a value.

`ComponentNameMatchers:`

- `hasClassName()`-Matches a component based on a class name.

- `hasPackageName()`-Matches a component based on a provided package name.

- ***hasShortClassName()***-Matches a component based on the short class name.

- ***hasMyPackageName()***-Matches a component based on the target package name found through the Instrumentation Registry for the test.

`UriMatchers`-used for matching intents based on the URI object. For example, if the action is `ACTION_EDIT`, the data should contain the URI of the document to edit.

- `hasHost()`-Matches the URI object based on the host. For example, if the authority is "bob@google.com", this method will try to match the object based on "google.com".

- `hasParamWithName()`-Matches the URI object based on the parameter name.

- `hasParamWithValue()`-Matches the URI object based on the parameter value.

- `hasPath()`-Matches the URI object based on the path. Like mailto:nobody@google.com.

- `hasSchemeSpecificPart()`-Matches the URI object based on the specific scheme part. This is everything between the scheme separator `':'` and the fragment separator `'#'`. If this is a relative URI, this method returns the entire URI. For example, "`//www.google.com/search?q=android`".

Now let's return to the `chapter5.StubAllIntentsTest.kt` class and see how intent stubbing works. Here is the class implementation.

chapter5.StubAllIntentsTest.kt.

```kotlin
class StubAllIntents {

    @get:Rule
    var intentsTestRule = IntentsTestRule(TasksActivity::class.java)

    private var toDoTitle = ""
    private var toDoDescription = ""

    // ViewInteractions used in tests
    private val addFab = viewWithId(R.id.fab_add_task)
    private val taskTitleField = viewWithId(R.id.add_task_title)
    private val taskDescriptionField = viewWithId(R.id.add_task_description)
    private val editDoneFab = viewWithId(R.id.fab_edit_task_done)
    private val shareMenuItem =
            onView(allOf(withId(R.id.title), withText(R.string.share)))

    @Before
    fun setUp() {
        toDoTitle = TestData.getToDoTitle()
        toDoDescription = TestData.getToDoDescription()
    }

    @Before
    fun stubAllExternalIntents() {
        // By default Espresso Intents does not stub any Intents. Stubbing
        needs to be setup before
        // every test run. In this case all external Intents will be blocked.
        intending(not(isInternal()))
                .respondWith(Instrumentation.ActivityResult(Activity.
                RESULT_OK, null))
    }

    @Test
    fun stubsShareIntent() {
        // adding new TO-DO
        addFab.click()
        taskTitleField.type(toDoTitle).closeKeyboard()
```

```
        taskDescriptionField.type(toDoDescription).closeKeyboard()
        editDoneFab.click()
        // verifying new TO-DO with title is shown in the TO-DO list
        viewWithText(toDoTitle).checkDisplayed()
        openContextualActionModeOverflowMenu()
        shareMenuItem.click()
        //viewWithText(toDoTitle).click()
    }
}
```

Our class contains a simple test that adds a new TO-DO item and then clicks on the share button from the action bar menu. As you can see, we use the `IntentsTestRule` and `stubAllExternalIntents()` method.

The `stubsShareIntent()` test adds a new TO-DO item in the list, opens the action bar menu, and clicks on the Share option, which from its side, triggers the share intent to send it to the system. In a real use case, the system will redirect this intent to another application. If the system has more than one application that can handle the intent, a popup window showing the options will appear.

In our case, the `stubsAllExternalIntents()` method that is run before each test method will do its job and the intent will not go out of the application. Try to run the test and see the result. Figure 5-2 shows the end state of the application after the last test method step.

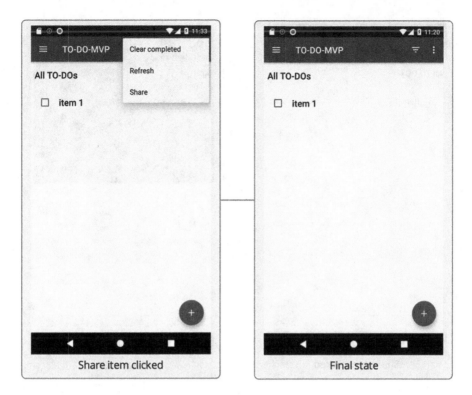

Figure 5-2. *The final state of the stubsShareIntent() test with stubbed external intents*

Let's see what happens when external intent stubbing is not in place-just comment out the `stubAllExternalIntents()` method and run the test again. Figure 5-3 shows the final application state.

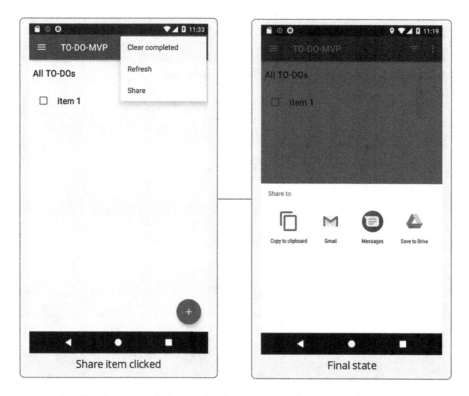

Figure 5-3. *The final state of the stubsShareIntent() test without stubbed external intents*

You see the difference and proof that intent stubbing works. The thing is that in both cases, the test passes. But in the second case, it passes just because we don't have any additional steps after the intent is sent. If you comment out this line of code, which follows the moment the intent is stubbed:

```
//viewWithText(toDoTitle).click()
```

and run the test again, you will see that the test fails. Uncommenting the `stubAllExternalIntents()` method will make the test green again.

Stubbing a Single Intent

We just saw how all external application intents are stubbed, but what if we want to stub just one intent? Then the only thing we have to do is replace the `intentMatcher` from the following expression with a specific one using the intent matchers:

```
intending(intentMatcher).thenRespond(myResponse)
```

The share TO-DOs intent implementation looks the following way.

Share Intent Java Implementation from the com.example.android.architecture. blueprints.todoapp.tasks.TasksFragment.java Class.

```
String email = PreferenceManager
        .getDefaultSharedPreferences(getContext())
        .getString("email_text", "");
Intent shareIntent = new Intent();
shareIntent.setAction(Intent.ACTION_SEND);
shareIntent.setType("text/plain");
shareIntent.putExtra(Intent.EXTRA_TEXT, getTaskListAsArray());
shareIntent.putExtra(Intent.EXTRA_EMAIL, email);
startActivity(Intent.createChooser(shareIntent,
getResources().getText(R.string.share_to)));
```

First, we will brake down the intent implementation and see what intent matchers can be applied to it:

- `shareIntent.setAction(Intent.ACTION_SEND)`-This intent property can be matched by an `hasAction()` intent matcher.

- `shareIntent.setType("text/plain")`-Can be matched by the `hasType()` intent matcher.

- `shareIntent.putExtra(Intent.EXTRA_TEXT, getTaskListAsArray())` and `shareIntent.putExtra(Intent. EXTRA_EMAIL, email)`-Can be matched by the `hasExtra()` or `hasExtras()` intent matchers.

It looks simple and clear, so to show how intent matchers can be implemented for each case, open the `chapter5.StubIntentTest.kt` class. Its implementation is similar to the `chapter5.StubAllIntentsTest.kt` class, but instead of applying external intents stubbing for each test method, we apply them on the method level, where specific intent matchers are applied.

chapter5.StubIntentTest.kt Class Shows How to Stub Intents Using Different Intent Matchers.

```kotlin
class StubIntentTest {

    private var toDoTitle = ""
    private var toDoDescription = ""

    // ViewInteractions used in tests
    private val addFab = viewWithId(R.id.fab_add_task)
    private val taskTitleField = viewWithId(R.id.add_task_title)
    private val taskDescriptionField = viewWithId(R.id.add_task_description)
    private val editDoneFab = viewWithId(R.id.fab_edit_task_done)
    private val shareMenuItem =
            onView(allOf(withId(R.id.title), withText(R.string.share)))

    @get:Rule
    var intentsTestRule = IntentsTestRule(TasksActivity::class.java)

    @Before
    fun setUp() {
        toDoTitle = TestData.getToDoTitle()
        toDoDescription = TestData.getToDoDescription()
    }

    @Test
    fun stubsShareIntentByAction() {
        Intents.intending(hasAction(equalTo(Intent.ACTION_SEND)))
                .respondWith(Instrumentation.ActivityResult(Activity.
                RESULT_OK, null))

        // adding new TO-DO
        addFab.click()
        taskTitleField.type(toDoTitle).closeKeyboard()
        taskDescriptionField.type(toDoDescription).closeKeyboard()
        editDoneFab.click()
        // verifying new TO-DO with title is shown in the TO-DO list
        viewWithText(toDoTitle).checkDisplayed()
        //open menu and click on Share item
```

```kotlin
    openContextualActionModeOverflowMenu()
    shareMenuItem.click()
    viewWithText(toDoTitle).click()
}

@Test
fun stubsShareIntentByType() {

    Intents.intending(hasType("text/plain"))
            .respondWith(Instrumentation.ActivityResult(Activity.
            RESULT_OK, null))

    // adding new TO-DO
    addFab.click()
    taskTitleField.type(toDoTitle).closeKeyboard()
    taskDescriptionField.type(toDoDescription).closeKeyboard()
    editDoneFab.click()
    // verifying new TO-DO with title is shown in the TO-DO list
    viewWithText(toDoTitle).checkDisplayed()
    //open menu and click on Share item
    openContextualActionModeOverflowMenu()
    shareMenuItem.click()
    viewWithText(toDoTitle).click()
}

@Test
fun stubsShareIntentByExtra() {

    Intents.intending(hasType("text/plain"))
            .respondWith(Instrumentation.ActivityResult(Activity.
            RESULT_OK, null))

    // adding new TO-DO
    addFab.click()
    taskTitleField.type(toDoTitle).closeKeyboard()
    taskDescriptionField.type(toDoDescription).closeKeyboard()
    editDoneFab.click()
```

```
    // verifying new TO-DO with title is shown in the TO-DO list
    viewWithText(toDoTitle).checkDisplayed()
    //open menu and click on Share item
    openContextualActionModeOverflowMenu()
    shareMenuItem.click()
    viewWithText(toDoTitle).click()
  }
}
```

And after running all these tests, you might be surprised to see that they fail. After starting to analyze the intent implementation from com.example.android. architecture.blueprints.todoapp.tasks.TasksFragment.java, we can clearly see what action, type, and extra parameters are set to our intent. Why then do they fail?

After debugging and drilling down to the implementation of how our share intent is launched, as follows:

```
startActivity(Intent.createChooser(
      shareIntent,
      getResources().getText(R.string.share_to)));
```

We can see that the Android Intent.createChooser() method was used to send this intent to the system with a custom title. This method wraps the provided intent parameter with a specified action, type, and extra parameters into another intent with a new action and adds our intent as part of its extra parameters. Figure 5-4 shows how it looks when you try to debug what is happening.

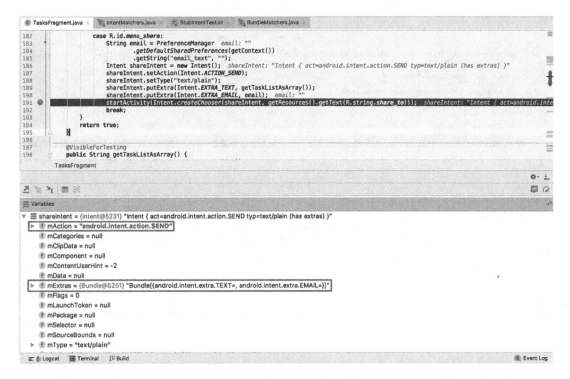

Figure 5-4. *ShareIntent instance implemented in the com.example.android. architecture.blueprints.todoapp.tasks.TasksFragment.java class*

The initial intent looks the same way we expect it to with the proper action (see the highlighted mAction variable) and proper extra parameters (see the highlighted mExtras variable). But if we put the debug breakpoint inside the IntentMatchers.hasExtras() matcher in the place where the intents are compared, we can see Figure 5-5.

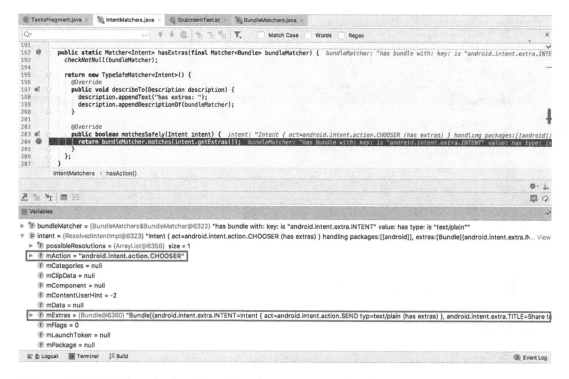

Figure 5-5. *Hitting the breakpoint when tapping the Share menu item during test execution*

At this moment in time, it is clear that the initial intent was added as an extra parameter inside the new intent (see the highlighted mExtras variable) with a modified action (see the highlighted mAction variable).

Now, to make our stubsShareIntentByAction() test green, we can change the action to ACTION_CHOOSER.

chapter5.StubChooserIntentTest.kt Class.

```
@Test
fun stubsShareIntentByAction() {
    Intents.intending(hasAction(equalTo(Intent. ACTION_CHOOSER)))
            .respondWith(Instrumentation.ActivityResult(Activity.
            RESULT_OK, null))

    // adding new TO-DO
    addFab.click()
    taskTitleField.type(toDoTitle).closeKeyboard()
```

```
    taskDescriptionField.type(toDoDescription).closeKeyboard()
    editDoneFab.click()
    // verifying new TO-DO with title is shown in the TO-DO list
    viewWithText(toDoTitle).checkDisplayed()
    //open menu and click on Share item
    openContextualActionModeOverflowMenu()
    shareMenuItem.click()
    viewWithText(toDoTitle).click()
}
```

Here are examples of working intent matchers when the `Intent.`
`createChooser()` method is used to start the intent implemented in the `chapter5.`
`StubChooserIntentTest.kt` class.

- Based on initial intent action:

```
Intents.intending(hasAction(equalTo(Intent.ACTION_CHOOSER)))
            .respondWith(Instrumentation.ActivityResult(Activity.
            RESULT_OK, null))
```

- Based on initial intent type:

```
Intents.intending(hasExtras(hasEntry(Intent.EXTRA_INTENT, hasType("text/
plain"))))
        .respondWith(Instrumentation.ActivityResult(Activity.RESULT_OK, null))
```

- Based on the EXTRA_TITLE parameter:

```
Intents.intending(hasExtras(hasEntry(Intent.EXTRA_TITLE, "Share to")))
        .respondWith(Instrumentation.ActivityResult(Activity.RESULT_OK, null))
```

And finally, to make the test from the `chapter5.StubIntentTest.kt` class pass,
we change the way that the share TO-DO intent starts by replacing line 192 of the `com.`
`example.android.architecture.blueprints.todoapp.tasks.TasksFragment.java` class:

```
startActivity(Intent.createChooser(shareIntent, getResources().getText(R.
string.share_to)));
```

with this:

```
startActivity(shareIntent);
```

This way, the intent is not modified, and we fully rely on the system to show the
popup to the user (see Figure 5-6).

125

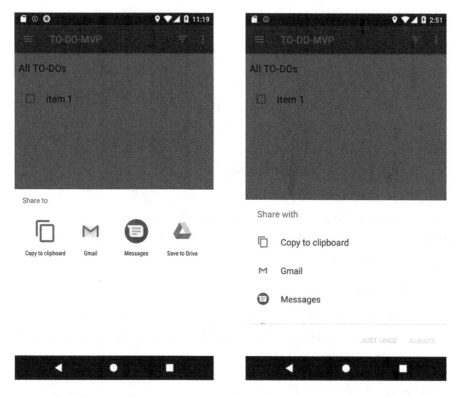

Figure 5-6. *The share todo intent sent with Intent.createChooser() (left) and without using the Intent.createChooser() method (right)*

EXERCISE 14

Stubbing intents

1. Put a breakpoint on line 191 of the `TaskFragment.java` file, as shown in Figure 5-4, and on line 204 of the `IntentMatchers.java` file, as shown in Figure 5-5. Run tests from the `StubIntentTest.kt` file in debug mode. When you reach the breakpoints, observe the `shareIntent` and `intent` variables.

2. Run all tests from the `StubIntentTest.kt` class and check the result. The test should fail. In the `TaskFragment.java` file, comment out line 191 and uncomment line 192. Run the test again and verify that they pass.

3. Revert to the changes done in Step 2 and run all the tests from the `StubChooserIntentTest.kt` class. The tests should all pass.

Stubbing Intents with the Result

In many cases, activity intents started by the application being tested have to return the results in the form of the image from a gallery or in form of a file from the device's filesystem. In Android, this is achieved by starting an activity using the startActivityForResult() method from inside the application's activity or fragment. When an activity is started, the user takes some action that generates the result and this result is returned to the activity or fragment that initially sent the intent. The onActivityResult() method from the Android activity class is responsible for receiving the result from a previous call to the startActivityForResult() method.

The sample TO-DO application contains an example of sending an intent with startActivityForResult() and handles the result in the onActivityResult() method implemented in the com.example.android.architecture.blueprints.todoapp. addedittask.AddEditTaskFragment.java class.

Starting and Handling Image Intents in AddEditTaskFragment.java

```
public void onImageButtonClick() {
    Intent intent = new Intent();
    intent.setType("image/*");
    intent.setAction(Intent.ACTION_GET_CONTENT);
    startActivityForResult(intent, SELECT_PICTURE);
}

public void onActivityResult(int requestCode, int resultCode, Intent data) {
    if (resultCode == RESULT_OK) {
        if (requestCode == SELECT_PICTURE) {
            Uri selectedImageUri = data.getData();
            BitmapDrawable bitmapDrawable =
                    ImageUtils.scaleAndSetImage(selectedImageUri,
                    getContext(), 200);

            // Apply the scaled bitmap
            imageView.setImageDrawable(bitmapDrawable);
```

```
            // Now change ImageView's dimensions to match the scaled image
            ConstraintLayout.LayoutParams params =
                    (ConstraintLayout.LayoutParams) imageView.
                    getLayoutParams();
            params.width = imageView.getWidth();
            params.height = imageView.getHeight();
            imageView.setLayoutParams(params);
        }
    }
}
```

You can observe that the intent from the onImageButtonClick() method has a preset type and action, which can be used in tests to match the intent and stub it.

The mechanism of starting an activity for a result should be clear now. The last thing we have to do is create the result used for stubbing. In the previous paragraph, we used the mechanism of returning the result, but we were setting it to null mainly because we were not expecting a result in the share intent case:

```
intending(not(isInternal()))
                .respondWith(Instrumentation.ActivityResult(Activity.
                RESULT_OK, null))
```

Now we need to implement the result on our own. We will discuss two ways of getting the result with stubbed images from an activity launched by the startActivityForResult() method:

- Providing the result with the image file stored in the test application drawables.

- Providing the result with the image file stored in the test application assets folder.

In Figure 5-7, you can observe the todo_image_drawable.png and todo_image_assets.png files stored in the test application res/drawable-xxxhdpi and assets folders, respectively.

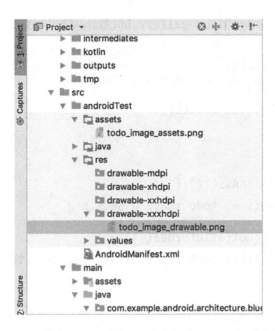

Figure 5-7. *The location of the .png files used in intents stubbing*

To showcase the implementation of both approaches, the sample application contains the chapter5.StubSelectImageIntentTest.kt class with test cases and the chapetr5.IntentHelper.kt object that holds methods responsible for generating the activity results used in intents stubbing.

Test Methods Implemented in the StubSelectImageIntentTest.kt Class

```
@Test
fun stubsImageIntentWithDrawable() {
    val toDoImage =
 com.example.android.architecture.blueprints.todoapp.mock.test.R.drawable.
 todo_image

    Intents.intending(not(isInternal()))
            .respondWith(IntentHelper.createImageResultFromDrawable(toDoImage))

    // Adding new TO-DO.
    addFab.click()
    taskTitleField.type(toDoTitle).closeKeyboard()
    taskDescriptionField.type(toDoDescription).closeKeyboard()
```

```kotlin
    // Click on Get image from gallery button. At this point stubbed image
    is returned.
    addImageButton.click()
    editDoneFab.click()
    viewWithText(toDoTitle).click()
}

@Test
fun stubsImageIntentWithAsset() {
    val imageFromAssets = "todo_image_assets.png"

    Intents.intending(not(isInternal()))
            .respondWith(IntentHelper.createImageResultFromAssets(imageFrom
            Assets))

    // Adding new TO-DO.
    addFab.click()
    taskTitleField.type(toDoTitle).closeKeyboard()
    taskDescriptionField.type(toDoDescription).closeKeyboard()

    // Click on Get image from gallery button. At this point stubbed image
    is returned.
    addImageButton.click()
    editDoneFab.click()
    viewWithText(toDoTitle).click()
}
```

IntentHelper.kt Objects That Provides Methods Responsible for Generating the
Activity Results Used in Intents Stubbing.

```kotlin
object IntentHelper {

    /**
     * Creates new activity result from an image stored in test
     application drawable.
     * See {@link Activity#setResult} for more information about the result.
     */
    fun createImageResultFromDrawable(drawable: Int): Instrumentation.
    ActivityResult {
```

```kotlin
    val resultIntent = Intent()
    val testResources = InstrumentationRegistry.getContext().resources

    // Build a stubbed result from drawable image.
    resultIntent.data = Uri.parse(ContentResolver.SCHEME_ANDROID_RESOURCE
            + "://${testResources.getResourcePackageName(drawable)}"
            + "/${testResources.getResourceTypeName(drawable)}"
            + "/${testResources.getResourceEntryName(drawable)}")
    return Instrumentation.ActivityResult(Activity.RESULT_OK, resultIntent)
}

/**
 * Creates new activity result from an image stored in test
 application assets.
 * See {@link Activity#setResult} for more information about the result.
 */
fun createImageResultFromAssets(imageName: String): Instrumentation.
ActivityResult {
    val resultIntent = Intent()

    // Declare variables for test and application context.
    val testContext = InstrumentationRegistry.getContext()
    val appContext = InstrumentationRegistry.getTargetContext()
    val file = File("${appContext.cacheDir}/todo_image_temp.png")

    // Read file from test assets and save it into main application
    cache todo_image_temp.png.
    if (!file.exists()) {
        try {
            val inputStream = testContext.assets.open(imageName)
            val fileOutputStream = FileOutputStream(file)
            val size = inputStream.available()
            val buffer = ByteArray(size)

            inputStream.read(buffer)
            inputStream.close()
```

```
            fileOutputStream.write(buffer)
            fileOutputStream.close()
        } catch (e: Exception) {
            throw RuntimeException(e)
        }
    }

    // Build a stubbed result from temp file.
    resultIntent.data = Uri.fromFile(file)
    return Instrumentation.ActivityResult(Activity.RESULT_OK, resultIntent)
    }
}
```

The stubsImageIntentWithDrawable() test case stubs the intent result with an image located in the test application drawables and stubsImageIntentWithAsset() does the intent stubbing with an image stored in the test application assets folder.

Storing all the test images and files inside the test application is really convenient because the main application does not store any unnecessary test data. In this same way, we can store all the file types that may be used in intents stubbing.

EXERCISE 15

Stubbing Intents with the Result

1. Run all the tests from the current section and observe them passing. Replace the images in the res/drawable-xxxhdpi and assets folders with different ones. Run the tests again.

2. Based on the image intent implemented in AddEditTaskFragment.java, change the Intents.intending(not(isInternal())) implementation and replace the not(isInternal()) part with a hasAction() IntentMatcher.

3. Do the same change as in Step 2, but instead of hasAction(), use a hasType() IntentMatcher.

Verifying Intents

As of now, we are armed with the knowledge of intent matchers and have used them in test examples. It is time to move to the topic of verifying intents.

Along with the `Intents.intending()` mechanism for intent stubbing, Espresso provides `Intents.indended()` for intent validation. This mechanism records all intents that attempt to launch activities from the application being tested. Using the `intended()` method, you can assert that a given intent has been seen. A lot of information and examples about intents matching was provided in previous section, so we provide the same intent matchers to the `intended()` method.

Note   Even if we stub intents, they can be further validated using the `intended()` method.

To see `intended()` in action, let's modify the existing `stubsImageIntentWithDrawable()` test as follows.

chapter5.StubSelectImageIntentTest.stubsImageIntentWithAsset().

```
@Test
fun stubsImageIntentWithAsset() {
    val imageFromAssets = "todo_image_assets.png"

    Intents.intending(not(isInternal()))
            .respondWith(IntentHelper.createImageResultFromAssets(imageFrom
            Assets))

    // Adding new TO-DO.
    addFab.click()
    taskTitleField.type(toDoTitle).closeKeyboard()
    taskDescriptionField.type(toDoDescription).closeKeyboard()

    // Click on Get image from gallery button. At this point stubbed image
    is returned.
    addImageButton.click()

    // Validate sent intent action.
    intended(hasAction(Intent.ACTION_GET_CONTENT))
```

```
    editDoneFab.click()
    viewWithText(toDoTitle).click()
}
```

In the current implementation, the tests pass because the image intent has set the ACTION_GET_CONTENT action. Of course, we can use the allOf() hamcrest matcher to combine different IntentMatchers and narrow down our validation.

Sometimes you may not see the intent implementation, but there is still a way to get all intents inside the Espresso failure stacktrace when the intended validation fails.

Part of Espresso Stacktrace from a Failed intended(intentMatcher) Validation.

```
IntentMatcher: has action: is "android.intent.action.ANSWER"
Matched intents:[]
Recorded intents:
-Intent { cmp=com.example.android.architecture.blueprints.todoapp.
mock/com.example.android.architecture.blueprints.todoapp.addedittask.
AddEditTaskActivity } handling packages:[[com.example.android.architecture.
blueprints.todoapp.mock]])
-Intent { act=android.intent.action.GET_CONTENT typ=image/* } handling
packages:[[com.android.documentsui, com.google.android.apps.docs, com.
google.android.apps.photos]])
```

This stacktrace was received after setting the wrong intent action in the previous test method to:

```
intended(hasAction(Intent.ACTION_ANSWER))
```

From the stacktrace, we can see that among the image intents:

```
 { act=android.intent.action.GET_CONTENT typ=image/* }
```

There is another one:

```
{ cmp=com.example.android.architecture.blueprints.todoapp.mock/com.example.
android.architecture.blueprints.todoapp.addedittask.AddEditTaskActivity }
```

To understand how intents appear in the stacktrace, let's take a closer look at the Espresso Intents.java class. This class is responsible for validating and stubbing intents sent out by the application being tested. It contains the init() method, which initializes intents and begins recording them. It must be called prior to triggering any actions that send out intents that need to be verified or stubbed. And it is because it is used by the IntentsTestRule that it's required to run intent tests.

Having this information, we can add modifications to the stubsImageIntentWithAsset() test case. We will also verify that after clicking the Add TO-DO floating action button, the AddEditTaskActivity is launched.

Modified stubsImageIntentWithAsset() Test Case.

```
@Test
fun stubsImageIntentWithAsset() {
    val imageFromAssets = "todo_image_assets.png"

    Intents.intending(not(isInternal()))
            .respondWith(IntentHelper.createImageResultFromAssets(imageFrom
            Assets))

    // Adding new TO-DO.
    addFab.click()

    // Validate that AddEditTaskActivity was launched.
    intended(hasComponent(AddEditTaskActivity::class.java.name))

    taskTitleField.type(toDoTitle).closeKeyboard()
    taskDescriptionField.type(toDoDescription).closeKeyboard()

    // Click on Get image from gallery button. At this point stubbed image
       is returned.
    addImageButton.click()

    // Validate sent intent action.
    intended(hasAction(Intent.ACTION_GET_CONTENT))

    editDoneFab.click()
    viewWithText(toDoTitle).click()
}
```

It is also important to pay attention to the stacktrace intent details and debug information, as shown in Figures 5-4 and 5-5. Both of these sources contain information about intents, like its action, type, or component. Let's take one more look at the stacktrace:

Recorded intents:

-Intent { **cmp**=com.example.android.architecture.blueprints.todoapp.
mock/com.example.android.architecture.blueprints.todoapp.addedittask.
AddEditTaskActivity } handling **packages**:[[com.example.android.architecture.
blueprints.todoapp.mock]])

-Intent { **act**=android.intent.action.GET_CONTENT **typ**=image/* } handling
packages:[[com.android.documentsui, com.google.android.apps.docs, com.
google.android.apps.photos]])

As you may guess:

- cmp-Stands for component. Applies hasComponent() IntentMatcher.

- packages-Stands for package. Applies hasPackage() or toPackage()
  IntentMatcher.

- act-Stands for action. Applies hasAction() IntentMatcher.

- typ-Stands for type. Applies hasType() IntentMatcher.

EXERCISE 16

<u>Verifying Intents</u>

1. Modify one of the intent tests and make it fail at the moment of intent validation
   with the intended() method. Observe the stacktrace.

2. Implement a test that verifies the share intent functionality discussed in the
   "Stubbing Intents Without Result" section. Make the verification based on the intent
   type and action. Use the allOf() hamcrest matcher to validate both of them.

Summary

Espresso-Intents enables you to keep your UI tests hermetic, without the need to
interact with third-party applications, and allows you to validate intents sent within or
outside of the application being tested. It is a powerful mechanism that helps you test
and stub application intents. After you get familiar with it, it will improve your overall
Android system knowledge since the majority of communication among application
components, applications, and the system is done through intents.

CHAPTER 6

Testing Web Views

Today we can find mobile applications for almost everything—gaming, social networking, banking, music, etc. Such a variety of applications developed by a single developer, small startup, or solid company means different development approaches. These approaches are represented by native and hybrid applications. Native applications are developed for a mobile operating system following platform standards, user interface, and user experience guidelines and access mobile device capabilities like the camera, GPS, etc. Hybrid applications typically use websites that are in a native wrapper or container. On Android, this container is called the *WebView*.

However, there is a gray area. Even when a developer selects the native application development, there are many places in an application that may use the integrated Android `WebView` component. This makes sense, because web views represent features that should be controlled remotely without the need to create redundant application releases. The common areas where `WebView` components can be used are as follows:

- Web browser applications
- Registration or login forms with Google, Facebook, or Twitter accounts
- Legal and privacy disclaimers
- Application FAQs
- Support contact forms

We already know that native Android applications can be tested by Espresso. This chapter presents Espresso-Web and shows how it can be used to test Android `WebView` UI components integrated into mobile applications. Both Espresso and Espresso-Web can be used in combination to fully interact with an application on its different levels.

© Denys Zelenchuk 2019
D. Zelenchuk, *Android Espresso Revealed*, https://doi.org/10.1007/978-1-4842-4315-2_6

Espresso-Web Basics

Similar to Espresso's `onData()` method, a `WebView` interaction is comprised of several *atoms*. `WebView` interactions use a combination of the Java programming language and a JavaScript bridge to do their work. Because there is no chance of introducing race conditions by exposing data from the JavaScript environment—everything Espresso sees on the Java-based side is an isolated copy—returning data from `Web.WebInteraction` objects is fully supported, allowing you to verify all the data that's returned from a request.

The WebDriver framework uses *atoms* to find and manipulate web elements programmatically. Atoms are used by WebDriver to accommodate browser manipulation. An atom is conceptually similar to a `ViewAction`. It's a self-contained unit that performs an action in your UI. You expose atoms using a list of defined methods, such as `findElement()` and `getElement()`, to drive the browser from the user's point of view. However, if you use the WebDriver framework directly, atoms need to be properly orchestrated, requiring logic that is quite verbose.

Within Espresso, the `Web` and `Web.WebInteraction` classes wrap this boilerplate and give an Espresso-like feel to interacting with `WebView` objects. So, in the context of a `WebView`, atoms are used as a substitution to traditional Espresso `ViewMatchers` and `ViewActions`.

The API then looks quite simple, as follows.

Espresso-Web API Usage Formula.

```
onWebView()
    .withElement(Atom)
    .perform(Atom)
    .check(WebAssertion)
```

To add Espresso-Web to a project, insert the following line of code into the application `build.gradle` file.

Espresso-Web Dependency in the Android Support Library.

```
androidTestImplementation 'com.android.support.test.espresso:espresso-web:3.0.2'
```

Or add the same dependency to the AndroidX Test Library.

Espresso-Web Dependency in the AndroidX Test Library.

```
androidTestImplementation 'androidx.test.espresso:espresso-web:3.1.0'
```

Espresso-Web Building Blocks

Espresso-Web contains the following API components:

- WebInteractions—An analogue to Espresso's ViewInteraction or DataInteraction. Used to perform actions and call validation methods, locate web elements, and set WebView properties.

- DriverAtoms—A collection of JavaScript atoms from the WebDriver project.

- WebAssertions—Asserts that the given atom's result is accepted by the provided matcher.

Web interactions:

- reset()—Deletes the Element and Window references from the web interaction.

- forceJavascriptEnabled()—Forces JavaScript usage on a WebView. Enabling JavaScript may reload the WebView under test.

- withNoTimeout()—Disables all timeouts on this WebInteraction.

- withTimelout()—Sets a defined timeout for current WebInteraction.

- inWindow()—Causes this WebInteraction to perform JavaScript evaluation in a specific DOM window.

- withElement()—Causes this WebInteraction to supply the given ElementReference to the atom prior to evaluation. After calling this method, it resets any previously selected ElementReference.

- withContextualElement()—Evaluates this WebInteraction on the subview of the selected element. Similar to the Espresso withChild() method.

- perform()—Executes the provided atom within the current context. This method blocks until the atom returns. Produces a new instance of WebInteraction that can be used in further interactions.

- `check()`—Evaluates the given `WebAssertion`. After this method completes, the result of the atom's evaluation is available via get.

- `get()`—Returns the result of a previous call to perform or check.

For better understanding, web interactions can be split into different groups where each group represents some functional load, as shown in Figure 6-1.

Driver atoms:

- `webClick()`—Simulates the JavaScript events to click on a particular element.

- `clearElement()`—Clears content from an editable element.

- `webKeys()`—Simulates JavaScript key events sent to a certain element.

- `findElement()`—Finds an element using the provided `locatorType` strategy.

- `selectActiveElement()`—Finds the currently active element in the document.

- `selectFrameByIndex()`—Selects a subframe of the currently selected window by its index.

- `selectFrameByIdOrName()`—Selects a subframe of the given window by its name or ID.

- `getText()`—Returns the visible text beneath a given DOM element.

- `webScrollIntoView()`—Returns true if the desired element is in view after scrolling.

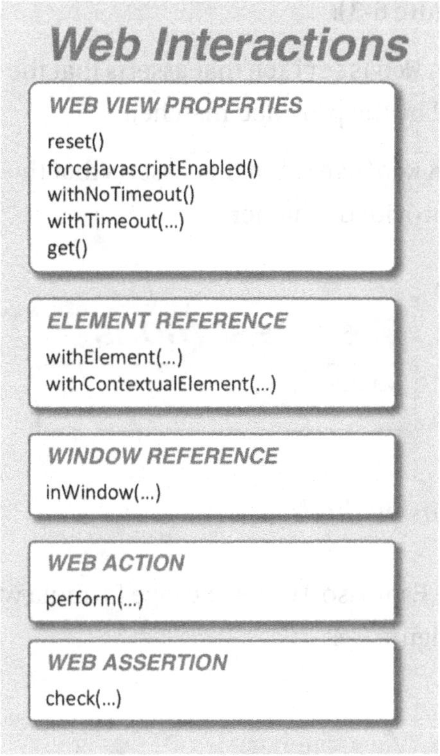

Web Interactions

WEB VIEW PROPERTIES

reset()
forceJavascriptEnabled()
withNoTimeout()
withTimeout(...)
get()

ELEMENT REFERENCE

withElement(...)
withContextualElement(...)

WINDOW REFERENCE

inWindow(...)

WEB ACTION

perform(...)

WEB ASSERTION

check(...)

Figure 6-1. *WebInteractions grouped by functional load*

DriverAtoms can be grouped by the return type, which determines where a specific method will be used. See Figure 6-2.

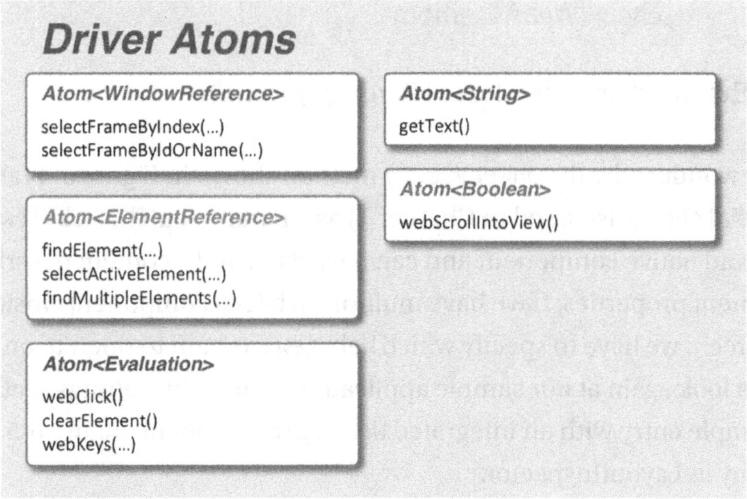

Driver Atoms

Atom<WindowReference>

selectFrameByIndex(...)
selectFrameByIdOrName(...)

Atom<ElementReference>

findElement(...)
selectActiveElement(...)
findMultipleElements(...)

Atom<Evaluation>

webClick()
clearElement()
webKeys(...)

Atom<String>

getText()

Atom<Boolean>

webScrollIntoView()

Figure 6-2. *DriverAtoms grouped by the return type*

141

Web assertions (see Figure 6-3):

- `webMatches()`—A `WebAssertion` that asserts that the given atom's result is accepted by the provided matcher.

- `webContent()`—A `WebAssertion` that asserts that the document is matched by the provided matcher.

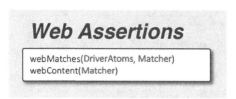

Figure 6-3. *WebAssertions methods*

Now we can extend the Espresso-Web API usage formula with more detailed information, as shown in Figure 6-4.

```
onWebView(ViewMatcher)
    .inWindow(Atom<WindowReference>)
    .withElement(Atom<ElementReference>)
    .withContextualElement(Atom<ElementReference>)
    .perform(Atom<Evaluation>)
    .check(WebAssertion)
```

Figure 6-4. *Extended Espresso-Web API usage formula*

You might wonder why the `onWebView()` method shown in Figure 6-4 takes the Espresso `ViewMatcher` (discussed in Chapter 1) as a parameter. The `WebView` UI element is still an Android native component and can have its own ID, content description, and other element properties. If we have multiple `WebView` components inside the application screen, we have to specify which `WebView` we want to operate on.

Let's take a look again at our sample application, where the Settings section contains a WebView sample entry with an integrated `WebView` component. Figure 6-5 shows the layout hierarchy in LayoutInspector.

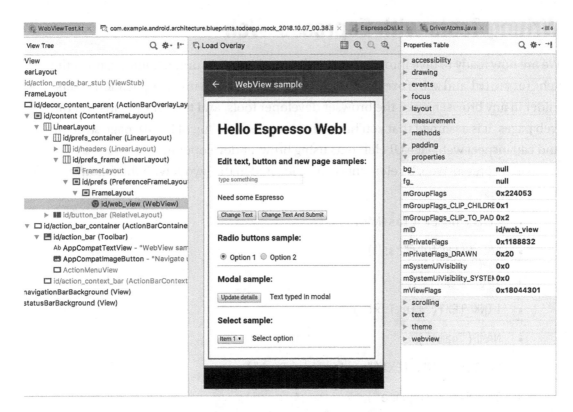

Figure 6-5. *Application Settings subsection layout of the WebView component*

As you can see, the WebView component can be identified using Espresso ViewMatcher based on the ID property web_view.

For your convenience, an Espresso-Web cheat sheet is included in Appendix A and as an addition to the sample application source code.

EXERCISE 17

<u>Verifying Intents</u>

1. Launch a sample application and navigate to Settings. Open the WebView sample section and do the layout dump with the LayoutInspector tool. Observe which WebView properties can be used in UI tests.

2. Similar to Step 1, do the layout dump using a monitor application. Observe which WebView properties can be analyzed using the monitor tool and compare it to the LayoutInspector results.

Writing Tests with Espresso-Web

We are now ready to dive into Espresso web tests. For better understanding, open the web_form.html and web_form_response.html files from the main application assets folder in any browser, open the browser developer tools, and then start to inspect the web pages. It is assumed that you have a basic understanding of HTML page structure and can inspect web page UI elements using browser developer tools.

With Espresso-Web, UI elements can be located in the layout with the following locator types:

- CLASS_NAME("className")
- CSS_SELECTOR("css")
- ID("id")
- LINK_TEXT("linkText")
- NAME("name")
- PARTIAL_LINK_TEXT("partialLinkText")
- TAG_NAME("tagName")
- XPATH("xpath")

Figure 6-6 shows the web_form.html page in the Chrome Developer Tools view.

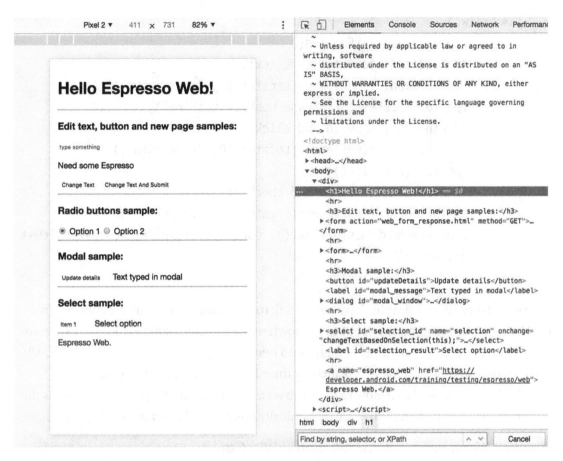

Figure 6-6. *Chrome browser developer tools view*

The web page is built in a way that allows you to showcase most of the Espresso-Web functionality. Open the chapter6.WebViewTest.kt class to see the implemented test cases. Here is the updatesLabelAndOpensNewPage() test case.

chapter6.WebViewTest.updatesLabelAndOpensNewPage().

```
@Test
fun updatesLabelAndOpensNewPage() {
    openDrawer()
    onView(allOf(withId(R.id.design_menu_item_text),
            withText(R.string.settings_title))).perform(click())
    onData(instanceOf(PreferenceActivity.Header::class.java))
            .inAdapterView(withId(android.R.id.list))
            .atPosition(3)
            .perform(click())
```

```
onWebView()
        .forceJavascriptEnabled()
        // Find edit text and type text.
        .withElement(findElement(Locator.ID, "text_input"))
        .perform(webKeys("Espresso WebView testing"))
        // Find button by id and click.
        .withElement(findElement(Locator.ID, "submitBtn"))
        .perform(webClick())
        // Find element by id and check its text.
        .withElement(findElement(Locator.ID, "response"))
        .check(webMatches(getText(), containsString("Espresso+WebView+t
        esting")))
}
```

Here, everything is simple. After navigating to the Settings section and clicking on the WebView sample item, the WebView is shown using Android WebViewClient. Espresso-Web handles web page loading, so there is no need to implement additional waiters. All the elements in this test case are located by their IDs, which is the ideal case.

The next test case shows how to find web elements by their CSS properties. This is the common case when element IDs are dynamically created and we cannot rely on them.

chapter6.WebViewTest.selectsRadioButtonWithCss().

```
@Test
fun selectsRadioButtonWithCss() {
    openDrawer()
    onView(allOf(withId(R.id.design_menu_item_text),
            withText(R.string.settings_title))).perform(click())
    onData(instanceOf(PreferenceActivity.Header::class.java))
            .inAdapterView(withId(android.R.id.list))
            .atPosition(3)
            .perform(click())
    onWebView()
            // Find radio button by CSS.
            .withElement(findElement(Locator.CSS_SELECTOR,
            "input[value=\"rb1\"]"))
            .perform(webClick())
}
```

Another way a web element can be located is by the XPATH selector, as follows.

chapter6.WebViewTest.findsElementsByXpath().

```
@Test
fun findsElementsByXpath() {
    openDrawer()
    onView(allOf(withId(R.id.design_menu_item_text),
            withText(R.string.settings_title))).perform(click())
    onData(instanceOf(PreferenceActivity.Header::class.java))
            .inAdapterView(withId(android.R.id.list))
            .atPosition(3)
            .perform(click())
    onWebView()
            // Find label XPATH and check its text.
            .withElement(findElement(Locator.XPATH, "//label[@
            id=\"selection_result\"]"))
            .perform(webScrollIntoView())
            .check(webMatches(getText(), equalTo("Select option")))
}
```

Note   Web browser developer tools can help locate elements by XPATH or CSS selectors. It is enough to use the CMD+F or CTRL+F shortcut and `try` expression on the search field. Elements are highlighted in the page layout.

The next sample test case shows how to operate on elements inside the dialog popup.

chapter6.WebViewTest.opensModal().

```
@Test
fun opensModal() {
    openDrawer()
    onView(allOf(withId(R.id.design_menu_item_text),
            withText(R.string.settings_title))).perform(click())
    onData(instanceOf(PreferenceActivity.Header::class.java))
            .inAdapterView(withId(android.R.id.list))
```

```
            .atPosition(3)
            .perform(click())
    onWebView()
            // Find button and click.
            .withElement(findElement(Locator.ID, "updateDetails"))
            .perform(webClick())
            // Find edit text field and input text in the popped up dialog.
            .withElement(findElement(Locator.ID, "modal_text_input"))
            .perform(webKeys("Text from modal"))
            // Find and click Confirm button.
            .withElement(findElement(Locator.ID, "confirm"))
            .perform(webClick())
            // Verify text from modal is set in label.
            .withElement(findElement(Locator.ID, "modal_message"))
            .check(webMatches(getText(), equalTo("Text from modal")))
}
```

In the current case, the dialog belongs to the HTML page and the elements inside can be easily found using the same onWebView() method, as shown in Figure 6-7.

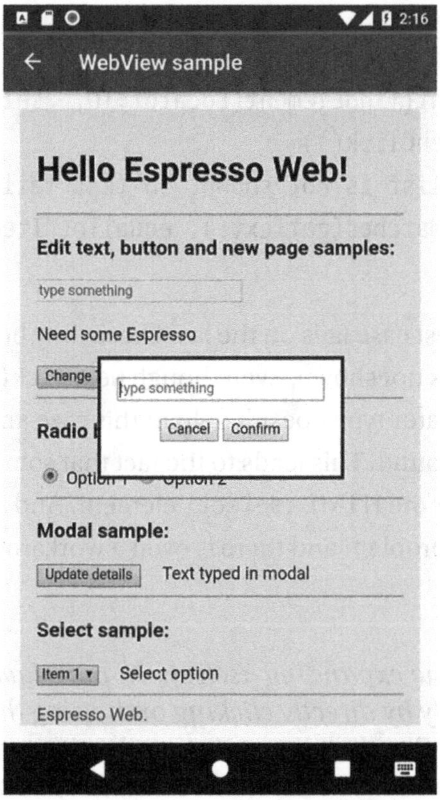

Figure 6-7. *The HTML <dialog> shown inside the Android web view client*

The next test case is about testing the interaction with the HTML <select> component. This turns out to be a problematic topic. To begin, the following test case was implemented.

chapter6.WebViewTest.failsToClickSelectDropDown().

```
@Test
fun failsToClickSelectDropDown() {
    openDrawer()
    onView(allOf(withId(R.id.design_menu_item_text),
            withText(R.string.settings_title))).perform(click())
    onData(instanceOf(PreferenceActivity.Header::class.java))
            .inAdapterView(withId(android.R.id.list))
            .atPosition(3)
            .perform(click())
```

```
onWebView()
        // Supposed to click on select.
        .withElement(findElement(Locator.ID, "selection_id"))
        .perform(webClick())
        // Select list is not shown, so test fails.
        .check(webMatches(getText(), equalTo("Item 3")))
}
```

The thing is that this test case fails on the last check only because the HTML <select> component list is not shown, even though webClick() was sent to the found element. Changing the locator type doesn't help in this case and it is not needed because the element was found. This leads to the fact that something is wrong with the webClick() action only for the HTML <select> element. And after a bit of research, it turned out to be a known problem and there is even a workaround to make it work with the additional button:

> *Browsers do not allow expanding <select> in pure JavaScript, that control can be expanded only by directly clicking on it using the mouse. The "select. click()" won't work. But there is a solution. We imitate expanded <select> control by creating another select with multiple options being displayed at once, this can be done by setting the "size" parameter. That multiselect will be positioned absolutely over the old single-option select control, and the old one will be hidden using style's visibility. That way the layout is kept the same, and the new control is displayed seamlessly. The new control looks only little differently, but that shouldn't be a problem, see it for yourself in screenshots below.*

`https://code.google.com/archive/p/expandselect/`

But there is a workaround from the testing side, without introducing UI components on the web page. Being on the screen with the web view shown, we can expand <select> by sending a ViewActions.pressKey(KeyEvent.KEYCODE_SPACE) event when it is focused. Just as if you do it via the browser. To move focus to the <select> element, we send as many tab actions as needed to navigate to the desired UI element— ViewActions.pressKey(KeyEvent.KEYCODE_TAB). Unfortunately, tests should sleep for a short amount of time, so the sent action can be applied in the web view. This is how it is done with our sample application.

chapter6.WebViewTest.verifiesSelectDropDown().

```
@Test
fun verifiesSelectDropDown() {
    openDrawer()
    onView(allOf(withId(R.id.design_menu_item_text),
            withText(R.string.settings_title))).perform(click())
    onData(instanceOf(PreferenceActivity.Header::class.java))
            .inAdapterView(withId(android.R.id.list))
            .atPosition(3)
            .perform(click())
    // Send TAB keys as many times as needed to reach the "select".
    Thread.sleep(300)
    onView(withId(R.id.web_view)).perform(pressKey(KeyEvent.KEYCODE_TAB))
    Thread.sleep(300)
    onView(withId(R.id.web_view)).perform(pressKey(KeyEvent.KEYCODE_TAB))
    Thread.sleep(300)
    onView(withId(R.id.web_view)).perform(pressKey(KeyEvent.KEYCODE_TAB))
    Thread.sleep(300)
    onView(withId(R.id.web_view)).perform(pressKey(KeyEvent.KEYCODE_TAB))
    Thread.sleep(300)
    onView(withId(R.id.web_view)).perform(pressKey(KeyEvent.KEYCODE_TAB))
    Thread.sleep(300)
    onView(withId(R.id.web_view)).perform(pressKey(KeyEvent.KEYCODE_TAB))
    Thread.sleep(300)
    // Send SPACE key to expand "select".
    onView(withId(R.id.web_view)).perform(pressKey(KeyEvent.KEYCODE_SPACE))
    /**
     * At this point android platform popup is shown.
     * Use Espresso native methods to select item from the list.
     */
    onView(withText("Item 3")).click()
```

```
onWebView()
        // Check that text from select list is set into the label.
        .withElement(findElement(Locator.ID, "selection_result"))
        .check(webMatches(getText(), equalTo("Item 3")))
}
```

This test case is fully functional but doesn't look good. By adding an additional expand function to ViewInteraction, we can clean up our test code.

Test Case chapter6.WebViewTest.verifiesSelectDropDown().

```
/**
 * Expand function for web view test case.
 * It contains a Thread.sleep() each time key event is sent.
 *
 * @param key - keycode from {@link KeyEvent}
 * @param milliseconds - milliseconds to sleep
 * @param count - amount of times {@link KeyEvent} should be executed
 */
fun ViewInteraction.pressKeyAndSleep(key: Int, milliseconds: Long, count:
Int = 1): ViewInteraction {
    for (i in 1..count) {
        /**
         * Having Thread.sleep() in tests is a bad practice.
         * Here we are using it just to solve specific issue and nothing more.
         */
        Thread.sleep(milliseconds)
        perform(ViewActions.pressKey(key))
    }
    return this
}
```

The verifiesSelectDropDown() test case becomes much more readable.

Test Case chapter6.WebViewTest.verifiesSelectDropDown().

```kotlin
@Test
fun verifiesSelectDropDown() {
    openDrawer()
    onView(allOf(withId(R.id.design_menu_item_text),
            withText(R.string.settings_title))).perform(click())
    onData(instanceOf(PreferenceActivity.Header::class.java))
            .inAdapterView(withId(android.R.id.list))
            .atPosition(3)
            .perform(click())
    onView(withId(R.id.web_view))
            // Send TAB keys as many times as needed to reach the "select".
            .pressKeyAndSleep(KeyEvent.KEYCODE_TAB, 500, 6)
            // Send SPACE key to expand "select".
            .perform(ViewActions.pressKey(KeyEvent.KEYCODE_SPACE))
    /**
     * At this point android platform popup is shown.
     * Use Espresso native methods to select item from the list.
     */
    onView(withText("Item 3")).click()
    onWebView()
            // Check that text from select list is set into the label.
            .withElement(findElement(Locator.ID, "selection_result"))
            .check(webMatches(getText(), equalTo("Item 3")))
}
```

A small note about the <select> drop-down. It is presented to the user as a native platform popup that can be interacted with via the Espresso methods, as shown in Figure 6-8.

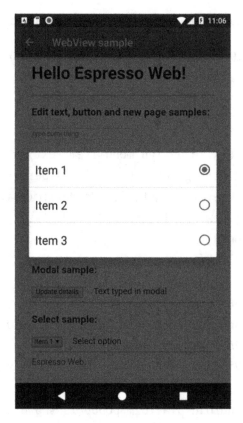

Figure 6-8. *HTML <select> drop-down options shown inside the Android web view client*

The last test case in the WebViewTest.kt class contains the rest of the Locator type's usage samples.

Test Case chapter6.WebViewTest.showsOtherLocatorsSample().

```
@Test
fun showsOtherLocatorsSample() {
    openDrawer()
    onView(allOf(withId(R.id.design_menu_item_text),
            withText(R.string.settings_title))).perform(click())
    onData(instanceOf(PreferenceActivity.Header::class.java))
            .inAdapterView(withId(android.R.id.list))
            .atPosition(3)
            .perform(click())
```

```
onWebView()
        // Find element by Locator.NAME
        .withElement(findElement(Locator.NAME, "text_input"))
        .perform(webScrollIntoView())
        // Find element by Locator.LINK_TEXT
        .withElement(findElement(Locator.LINK_TEXT, "Espresso Web."))
        .perform(webScrollIntoView())
        // Find element by Locator.PARTIAL_LINK_TEXT
        .withElement(findElement(Locator.PARTIAL_LINK_TEXT, "Espresso"))
        .perform(webScrollIntoView())
        // Find element by Locator.CLASS_NAME
        .withElement(findElement(Locator.CLASS_NAME, "header"))
        .check(webMatches(webScrollIntoView(), `is`(true)))
}
```

This test case shows how the webScrollIntoView() action can be used as a parameter to the WebAssertion.webMatches() method. This approach provides a more readable error description when the element we operate on is not found.

EXERCISE 18

Writing Web View Tests

1. Open the web_form.html page in the web browser and analyze the page structure. Search the elements by XPATH and CSS selectors.

2. Update the selectsRadioButtonWithCss() test so that the radio button with "Option 2" label is selected.

3. Write a test that finds all the elements by their XPATHs only.

4. Write a test that finds all the elements by their CSS locators only.

Summary

Espresso-Web is a nice addition to the Espresso APIs. It allows you to test hybrid applications with WebView components. Yes, it is not perfect and can't be used for purely web application testing, but it does its job quite well in an Espresso-like manner.

CHAPTER 7

Accessibility Testing

Most mobile applications are developed with established assumptions about the users or user types. In software testing, the term *user personas* reflects such user types, including their possible usage flows and how the application might help them in their daily activities. Despite the fact that user personas are created during the early stages of the software development lifecycle, they may not consider people with disabilities.

Around 300 million people around the world have a visual impairment and use mobile applications with the help of specific accessibility tools installed on their mobile devices.

Android Accessibility Tools

There are three tool types available on the Android platform for people with visual impairments:

- TalkBack—The preinstalled screen reader application that allows users to interact with Android applications without visual access to the screen. Users with visual impairments may rely on TalkBack to use your app.

- *BrailleBack*—An accessibility service that helps users with visual impairments use Braille devices. Working in combination with the TalkBack app, it provides a combined Braille and speech experience.

- *Voice Access*—Lets users control their Android devices with voice commands. Voice Access is available on devices running Android 5.0 (API level 21) and higher.

© Denys Zelenchuk 2019
D. Zelenchuk, *Android Espresso Revealed*, https://doi.org/10.1007/978-1-4842-4315-2_7

As you can see, BrailleBack relies on TalkBack, which reads back each interactive element available on the active screen to the user. In order to make Android applications accessible to users with visual impairments, developers should follow accessibility guidelines. Among them:

- *Label UI elements*—Many screen readers, such as TalkBack, rely on this service to properly explain the function of a particular control. For example, for UI objects such as `ImageView` and `ImageButton` objects, the `android:contentDescription` parameter is set to specify its purpose. For `EditText` objects, `android:hint` is used.

- *Group content*—Just as the visual UI is grouped into understandable components like lists with list items, so the screen reader content should also be grouped in a logical way. Instead of being presented as separate elements, items should be read back as a single announcement—a TO-DO item with a title, a description, and a checkbox state.

- *Create an easy-to-follow navigation*—Applications should support keyboards navigation and navigation gestures. Avoid having UI elements fade out or disappear after a certain amount of time.

- *Make touch targets large*—By providing larger touch targets, you make it substantially easier for users to navigate your app. In general, according to the guidelines, the touchable area of focusable item should be a minimum of 48dpx48dp.

- *Provide adequate color contrast*—People with poor vision or those who use devices with dimmed displays have difficulty reading information on the screen. By providing increased contrast ratios between the foreground and background colors in your app, you make it easier for users to navigate within and between screens.

Testing Application Accessibility

The Espresso testing framework supports writing automated accessibility tests that evaluate the accessibility of your application. In order to start writing accessibility tests, add the following dependencies to the `build.gradle` file.

Android Testing Support Library Accessibility Dependencies in the build.gradle File Inside the App Module.

```
androidTestImplementation "com.android.support.test.espresso:espresso-
accessibility:3.0.2"
androidTestImplementation "com.google.android.apps.common.testing.
accessibility.framework:accessibility-test-framework:2.1"
```

AndroidX Test library Accessibility Dependencies in the build.gradle file Inside the App Module.

```
androidTestImplementation 'androidx.test.espresso:espresso-
accessibility:3.1.0'
androidTestImplementation "com.google.android.apps.common.testing.
accessibility.framework:accessibility-test-framework:2.1"
```

After adding these dependencies, you have to enable accessibility checks, as shown in this sample:

```
companion object {

    @BeforeClass
    @JvmStatic
    fun setAccessibilityPrefs() {
        AccessibilityChecks.enable()
    }
}
```

Note   AccessibilityChecks should be enabled only once per test class, otherwise, the test will fail. Therefore, the @BeforeClass annotation should be used with methods in which checks are enabled. In Kotlin, the method annotated with the @BeforeClass annotation should be declared in the class companion object.

With AccessibilityChecks.enable() set, checks are enabled each time the Espresso ViewAction is called on the UI element, including its descendants. Such approach limits accessibility testing to UI test coverage.

To cover more UI elements within the test run, set setRunChecksFromRootView(true), which enables you to validate the entire view hierarchy.

Companion Object in chapter7.AccessibilityTest.kt Class.

```
@BeforeClass
@JvmStatic
fun setAccessibilityPrefs() {
    AccessibilityChecks.enable().setRunChecksFromRootView(true)
}
```

Unfortunately, it is not possible to set accessibility checks on each test method or test class, or to disable it after a test run.

There can be cases when an accessibility issue is known but has not been resolved. With the help of AccessibilityValidator implemented in com.google.android.apps. common.testing.accessibility.framework, you can suppress it:

```
@BeforeClass
@JvmStatic
fun setAccessibilityPrefs() {
    AccessibilityChecks.enable()
            .setRunChecksFromRootView(true)
            .setSuppressingResultMatcher(AccessibilityCheckResultUtils.
            matchesViews(
                    hasSibling(withId(R.id.menu_filter)))))
}
```

In a similar way, you can suppress multiple accessibility issues with the help of the anyOf() matcher, as shown here:

```
@BeforeClass
@JvmStatic
fun setAccessibilityPrefs() {
    AccessibilityChecks.enable()
            .setRunChecksFromRootView(true)
            .setSuppressingResultMatcher(AccessibilityCheckResultUtils.
            matchesViews(anyOf(
                    hasSibling(withId(R.id.menu_filter)),
                    withChild(withChild(withId(android.support.design.R.id.
                    snackbar_text))))))
}
```

By the way, you may notice accessibility issues with the native Android UI elements like snackbar. Suppressing them sometimes is not an easy task. In the previous code sample, the `withChild()` view matcher was used twice to locate the snackbar root layout and suppress the accessibility issue for it.

You can also keep tests running even with accessibility issues, by providing a `false` value to the `setThrowExceptionForErrors()` method:

```
@BeforeClass
@JvmStatic
fun setAccessibilityPrefs() {
    AccessibilityChecks.enable()
            .setRunChecksFromRootView(true)
            .setSuppressingResultMatcher(AccessibilityCheckResultUtils.
            matchesViews(anyOf(
                    hasSibling(withId(R.id.menu_filter)),
                    withChild(withChild(withId(android.support.design.R.id.
                    snackbar_text))))))
            .setThrowExceptionForErrors(false)
}
```

In this case, all the issues will be redirected to the `logcat` log, where logs with I are informative and shown in black, W are warnings and are in blue, and E are errors and are in red. See Figure 7-1.

```
2018-10-10 23:46:56.000 19364-19364/com.example.android.architecture.blueprints.todoapp.mock I/AccessibilityValidator:
    LinearLayout{id=2131296388, res-name=noTasks, visibility=VISIBLE, width=342, height=198, has-focus=false, has-focusable=false,
    has-window-focus=true, is-clickable=false, is-enabled=true, is-focused=false, is-focusable=false, is-layout-requested=false,
    is-selected=false, layout-params=android.widget.RelativeLayout$LayoutParams@e2a761, tag=null, root-is-layout-requested=false,
    has-input-connection=false, x=369.0, y=693.0, child-count=3}:    Non-clickable View has speakable text: "You have no TO-DOs!".
2018-10-10 23:46:56.003 19364-19364/com.example.android.architecture.blueprints.todoapp.mock W/AccessibilityValidator:
    RelativeLayout{id=2131296478, res-name=tasksContainer, visibility=VISIBLE, width=1080, height=1584, has-focus=true,
    has-focusable=true, has-window-focus=true, is-clickable=true, is-enabled=true, is-focused=true, is-focusable=true,
    is-layout-requested=false, is-selected=false, layout-params=android.view.ViewGroup$LayoutParams@5870286, tag=null,
    root-is-layout-requested=false, has-input-connection=false, x=0.0, y=0.0, child-count=2}: Clickable view's speakable text: "You
    have no TO-DOs!" is identical to that of 1 other clickable view(s)
2018-10-10 23:46:56.018 19364-19364/com.example.android.architecture.blueprints.todoapp.mock E/AccessibilityValidator:
    OverflowMenuButton{id=-1, desc=More options, visibility=VISIBLE, width=105, height=126, has-focus=false, has-focusable=false,
    has-window-focus=true, is-clickable=true, is-enabled=true, is-focused=false, is-focusable=true, is-layout-requested=false,
    is-selected=false, layout-params=android.support.v7.widget.ActionMenuView$LayoutParams@6e51747, tag=null,
    root-is-layout-requested=false, has-input-connection=false, x=127.0, y=10.0}: View falls below the minimum recommended size for
    touch targets. Minimum touch target width is 48dp. Actual width is 40dp.
```

Figure 7-1. *Accessibility logcat logs when setThrowExceptionForErrors(false) is set*

This is how the accessibility issue stacktrace looks like after a test fails:

```
com.google.android.apps.common.testing.accessibility.framework.integrations.
AccessibilityViewCheckException: There was 1 accessibility error:
OverflowMenuButton{id=-1, desc=More options, visibility=VISIBLE, width=105,
height=126, has-focus=false, has-focusable=false, has-window-focus=false,
is-clickable=true, is-enabled=true, is-focused=false, is-focusable=true,
is-layout-requested=false, is-selected=false, layout-params=android.
support.v7.widget.ActionMenuView$LayoutParams@48cbb74, tag=null, root-is-
layout-requested=true, has-input-connection=false, x=127.0, y=10.0}: View
falls below the minimum recommended size for touch targets. Minimum touch
target width is 48dp. Actual width is 40dp.
at com.google.android.apps.common.testing.accessibility.framework.
integrations.espresso.AccessibilityValidator.processResults(AccessibilityVa
lidator.java:187)...
```

You may notice that the header parts in both cases are identical.

In addition to automated accessibility testing, Google developers also provide a possibility to test manually using the Accessibility Scanner application (https://play. google.com/store/apps/details?id=com.google.android.apps.accessibility. auditor).

This application allows you to check for accessibility issues types and better understand errors shown in your Espresso accessibility test reports or inside the logcat logs based on the visual representation.

Figure 7-2 shows the accessibility scanner setup process.

Figure 7-2. *Start using the Accessibility scanner flow*

Figure 7-3 shows a couple of accessibility analysis examples with accessibility issues in the sample TO-DO application.

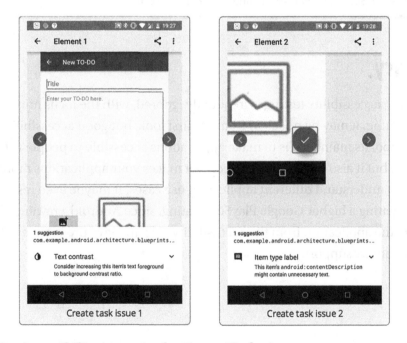

Figure 7-3. *Accessibility issues in the Create Task view*

EXERCISE 19

Executing Accessibility Tests

1. Install the Accessibility Scanner application and enable accessibility checks. Launch the sample TO-DO application and perform the accessibility checks across the application. Observe the issue types.

2. Run tests from the `AccessibilityTest.kt` class with the `AccessibilityChecks.enable()` option only. Observe the test results.

3. Run tests from the `AccessibilityTest.kt` class with the `setRunChecksFromRootView(true)` option. Observe the test results.

4. Suppress some accessibility failures, as shown in the `AccessibilityTest.kt` class's `setAccessibilityPrefs()` method, and run the tests again. Observe the test results.

5. Add the `setThrowExceptionForErrors(false)` parameter and run the tests. Observe the test results and device `logcat` logs.

Summary

Unfortunately, accessibility testing is frequently ignored, with the focus mostly on functional testing. It may be not clear from the first look, but good accessibility support is important too. Its main goal is to make applications accessible to people with visual impairments, but it also has nice side effects—it makes your applications more testable and helps you understand different application use cases. It maybe even result in your application getting a higher Google PlayStore rating, since Android-crawling algorithms may analyze the application from the accessibility side and give preference to those with proper accessibility support.

CHAPTER 8

Espresso and UI Automator: the Perfect Tandem

Espresso is a perfect and fast test automation framework, but it has one important limitation—we are allowed to operate only inside our test application context. This means that it is not possible to automate tests for the following use cases:

- Clicking application push notifications

- Accessing system settings

- Navigating from another app to the app being tested and vice versa

The reason for such a limitation lies in the nature of the Android Test instrumentation. Since during an Espresso test run, the application being tested and the test application processes are spawned, we are not allowed to interact with other applications installed on the mobile device, like the notification bar, camera, or system settings applications. But it is possible to access them using the UI Automator. The UI testing framework is suitable for cross-app functional UI testing.

Note   The UI Automator test framework supports Android 4.3 (API level 18) and higher.

© Denys Zelenchuk 2019
D. Zelenchuk, *Android Espresso Revealed*, https://doi.org/10.1007/978-1-4842-4315-2_8

The key features of the UI Automator include the following:

- A `uiautomatorviewer` to inspect the layout hierarchy. Starting with Android Studio 2.3, this was replaced by a monitor tool.

- An API to retrieve device state information and perform operations on it. The examples are pressing the device home or back button, changing device rotation, opening notifications, and taking a screenshot.

- APIs that support cross-application UI testing.

We will focus a bit on the UI Automator APIs:

- *By*—By is a utility class that enables the creation of BySelectors in a concise manner. Its primary function is to provide static factory methods for constructing BySelectors using a shortened syntax. For example, you would use `findObject(By.text("foo"))` rather than `findObject(new BySelector().text("foo"))` to select UI elements with the text value `"foo"`.

- *BySelector*—A BySelector specifies criteria for matching UI elements during a call to `findObject(BySelector)`.

- *Configurator*—Allows you to set key parameters for running UI Automator tests. The new settings take effect immediately and can be changed any time during the test run.

- *UiCollection*—Used to enumerate a container's UI elements for the purpose of counting or targeting a subelement by a child's text or description.

- *UiObject*—A `UiObject` is a representation of a view. It is not in any way directly bound to a view as an object reference. A `UiObject` contains information to help it locate a matching view at runtime based on the `UiSelector` properties specified in its constructor. Once you create an instance of a `UiObject`, it can be reused for different views that match the selector criteria.

- *UiObject2*—A UiObject2 represents a UI element. Unlike UiObject, it is bound to a particular view instance and can become stale if the underlying view object is destroyed. As a result, it may be necessary to call findObject(BySelector) to obtain a new UiObject2 instance if the UI changes significantly.

- *UiScrollable*—UiScrollable is a UiCollection and provides support for searching for items in scrollable layout elements. This class can be used with horizontally or vertically scrollable controls.

- *UiSelector*—Specifies the elements in the layout hierarchy for tests to target, filtered by properties such as text value, content-description, class name, and state information. You can also target an element by its location in a layout hierarchy.

In addition to this list of APIs, we should be familiar with the following framework class:

- *Until*—The Until class provides factory methods for constructing common conditions.

Note   The UI Automator testing framework is an instrumentation-based API and works with the AndroidJUnitRunnertest runner. This fact allows us to use Espresso together with UI Automator code in the same test.

Starting with UI Automator

To start using UI Automator, we should first set the dependency in the build.gradle file, as follows.

UI Automator Android Testing Support Library Dependency in the build.gradle File.

```
    androidTestImplementation 'com.android.support.test.
uiautomator:uiautomator-v18:2.1.3'
```

And set the AndroidX Test library dependency as well.

UI Automator AndroidX Test Library Dependency in the build.gradle File.

```
androidTestImplementation 'androidx.test.uiautomator:uiautomator:2.2.0'
```

Let's analyze the UI Automator from an Espresso perspective, which we are already familiar with, and try to figure out how different they are. We will also consider the UI Automator's strengths and weakness:

- Handling application transitions:

    - Espresso—Handles window transitions automatically.

    - UI Automator—Doesn't support automatic window transitions, i.e., switching between activities or fragments. You should explicitly use waitings.

- Locating UI elements:

    - Espresso—Core Espresso `onView()` and `onData()` methods together with view matchers or data matchers are used to locate the UI element.

    - UI Automator—Similar to Espresso, UI Automator has its own core `UiDevice` class. It contains such methods as `hasObject(BySelector)`, `findObject(BySelector)`, and `findObjects(BySelector)` that are used to search for an element or check its presence in the application UI.

- Waitings:

    - Espresso—The `IdlingResource` and third-party `ConditionWatcher` classes can be used as waiting mechanisms, including both networks related and element presence waitings. Both waiters should be implemented for each specific case.

    - UI Automator—Unlike Espresso, UI Automator has defined `wait()` and `performActionAndWait()` methods in the `UiDevice` class. Waitings can be easily tweaked by providing custom `SearchCondition` or `EventCondition` parameters.

- UI/view actions:

    - Espresso—Supports a wide range of view actions with the possibility to define your own. It's able to interact only with the application being tested.

- UI Automator—As mentioned, the UI Automator can interact with any application on the device. But the degree of action is very limited.

- Device controls:

  - Espresso—No support.

  - UI Automator—Provides a long list of device control methods starting from the device home button click to orientation control.

- Reporting:

  - Espresso—Supports much richer test failure reports and makes it easy to analyze test failures.

  - UI Automator—Usually returns nondescriptive stacktraces upon failure, which should be analyzed to realize what went wrong.

Based on these differences, you can see that in combination, these two form a very powerful feature set that covers almost all the needs in the Android test automation.

To more easily understand the UI Automator framework, we can describe its features using verbs:

- `UiDevice().find`—Shows UI Automator find methods.

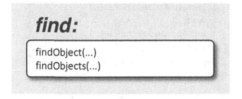

- `UiDevice().act`—Consolidates all actions that can be done with the device, from pressing the back device button to a shell command execution.

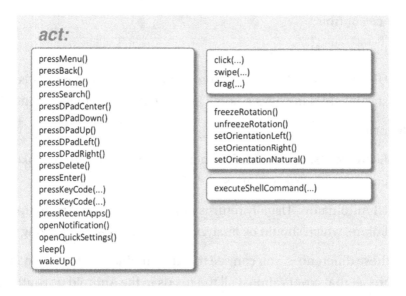

- `UiDevice().wait`—Waits for a certain condition to be fulfilled.

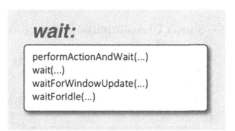

- `UiDevice().watch`—Represents a group of methods used to create and control condition watchers.

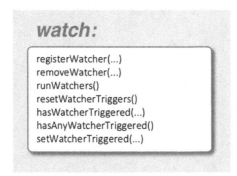

- `UiDevice().get`—Retrieves device or application parameters.

- `UiDevice().set`—Enables or disables layout hierarchy compression.

In the following sections, we will see how most of these `UiDevice` methods can be used when Espresso for Android cannot handle the issue.

Finding and Acting on UI Elements

The main UI Automator functionality is locating UI elements and performing actions on them. If we talk about UI Automator usage in combination with Espresso, then it can be used to navigate through third-party or system applications, take screenshots or, for example, execute shell commands. But, of course, the UI Automator can act as a standalone test automation framework.

As was described, the UI element search is done by the `findObject()` and `findObjects()` methods. The `findObject()` method takes instances of the following classes as parameters that specify criteria for matching UI elements in the hierarchy:

- `UiSelector()`

- `BySelector()`

The conceptual difference between them is in the way that search criteria specified by each selector is applied. To understand this, we will first look at the `UiSelector` sample tests implemented in the `UiAutomatorUiSelectorTest.kt` test class.

chapter8.UiAutomatorUiSelectorTest.uiSelectorSample().

```kotlin
private val instrumentation = InstrumentationRegistry.getInstrumentation()
private val uiDevice: UiDevice = UiDevice.getInstance(instrumentation)
private val fourSecondsTimeout = 4000L

@get:Rule
var activityTestRule = ActivityTestRule(TasksActivity::class.java)

/**
 * Creates two TO-DO items, marks first as done and verifies its text.
 */
@Test
fun uiSelectorSample() {
    // Add first To-Do item.
    uiDevice.findObject(
            UiSelector().resourceId(
                    "com.example.android.architecture.blueprints.todoapp.
                    mock:id/fab_add_task"))
            .click()
    uiDevice.findObject(UiSelector().resourceId(
            "com.example.android.architecture.blueprints.todoapp.mock:id/
            add_task_title"))
            .text = "item 1"
    uiDevice.findObject(UiSelector().resourceId(
            "com.example.android.architecture.blueprints.todoapp.mock:id/
            fab_edit_task_done"))
            .click()
```

```
uiDevice.findObject(UiSelector().text("TO-DO saved")).waitUntilGone
(fourSecondsTimeout)

// Add second To-Do item.
uiDevice.findObject(UiSelector().resourceId(
        "com.example.android.architecture.blueprints.todoapp.mock:id/
        fab_add_task"))
        .click()
uiDevice.findObject(UiSelector().resourceId(
        "com.example.android.architecture.blueprints.todoapp.mock:id/
        add_task_title"))
        .text = "item 2"
uiDevice.findObject(UiSelector().resourceId(
        "com.example.android.architecture.blueprints.todoapp.mock:id/
        fab_edit_task_done"))
        .click()
uiDevice.findObject(UiSelector().text("TO-DO saved")).waitUntilGone
(fourSecondsTimeout)

// Mark first To-Do item as done, click on it and validate text.
uiDevice.findObject(UiSelector().className(RecyclerView::class.java.name)
        .childSelector(UiSelector().checkable(true)))
        .click()
uiDevice.findObject(UiSelector().className(RecyclerView::class.java.name)
        .childSelector(UiSelector().className(LinearLayout::class.
        java)).instance(0))
        .click()
val detailViewTitle = uiDevice.findObject(UiSelector().resourceId(
        "com.example.android.architecture.blueprints.todoapp.mock:id/
        task_detail_title"))
assertTrue("To-Do \"item 1\" is not shown.", detailViewTitle.exists())
assertTrue("To-Do \"item 1\" is not shown.", detailViewTitle.text.
equals("item 1"))
}
```

As you can see, the UI Automator test contains an `ActivityTestRule` rule to start the application main `TasksActivity`. After that, the UI Automator code takes over the test execution and performs the UI interactions. All the `resourceId` values were taken from the `monitor` tool after dumping the application layout.

Also notice that the test code is barely readable because of the `uiDevice.findObject(UiSelector)` method calls on each test step. But there is a simple fix-since `uiDevice.findObject(UiSelector)` returns an `UiObject` instance that locates a matching view at runtime, it can be declared in advance and later reused for different views that match the selection criteria.

This is how the test method will look after simplification.

chapter8. UiAutomatorUiSelectorTest.uiSelectorSampleSimplified().

```
/**
 * Shows how interactsWithToDoInRecyclerViewUiSelector() test can be
   simplified
 * by declaring UiObject elements in advance.
 */
@Test
fun uiSelectorSampleSimplified() {

    // Declare UiObject instances that will be used later in test.
    val fabAddTask = uiDevice.findObject(UiSelector().resourceId(
            "com.example.android.architecture.blueprints.todoapp.
            mock:id/fab_add_task"))
    val taskTitle = uiDevice.findObject(UiSelector().resourceId(
            "com.example.android.architecture.blueprints.todoapp.
            mock:id/add_task_title"))
    val fabDone = uiDevice.findObject(UiSelector().resourceId(
            "com.example.android.architecture.blueprints.todoapp.
            mock:id/fab_edit_task_done"))
    val todoSavedText = uiDevice.findObject(UiSelector().text("TO-DO
    saved"))
    val taskDetailsTitle = uiDevice.findObject(UiSelector().resourceId(
            "com.example.android.architecture.blueprints.todoapp.
            mock:id/task_detail_title"))
```

```
val firstTodoCheckbox = uiDevice.findObject(UiSelector()
        .className(RecyclerView::class.java.name)
        .childSelector(UiSelector().checkable(true)).instance(0))
val firstTodoItem = uiDevice.findObject(UiSelector().
className(RecyclerView::class.java.name)
        .childSelector(UiSelector().className(LinearLayout::class.
        java)).instance(0))

// Add first To-Do item.
fabAddTask.click()
taskTitle.text = "item 1"
fabDone.click()
todoSavedText.waitUntilGone(fourSecondsTimeout)

// Add second To-Do item.
fabAddTask.click()
taskTitle.text = "item 2"
fabDone.click()
todoSavedText.waitUntilGone(fourSecondsTimeout)

// Mark first To-Do item as done, click on it and validate text.
firstTodoCheckbox.click()
firstTodoItem.click()
assertTrue("To-Do \"item 1\" is not shown.", taskDetailsTitle.exists())
assertTrue("To-Do \"item 1\" title was wrong.", taskDetailsTitle.
text.equals("item 1"))
}
```

This test method looks much nicer and is more readable. As a side effect, you receive easily maintainable code, so whenever element properties like id or class are changed, it will be enough to update them once in the declaration instead of changing them across the test code.

Let's move forward to the BySelector test samples implemented in the UiAutomatorBySelectorTest.kt class. The bySelectorSample() test demonstrates how the same test scenario automated in the UiAutomatorUiSelectorTest.kt class can be tested using BySelector and UiObject2.

chapter8.UiAutomatorBySelectorTest.bySelectorSample().

```kotlin
private val instrumentation = InstrumentationRegistry.getInstrumentation()
private val uiDevice: UiDevice = UiDevice.getInstance(instrumentation)
private val twoSeconds = 2000L
private val fourSeconds = 4000L
private val applicationPackage = "com.example.android.architecture.
blueprints.todoapp.mock"

@get:Rule
var activityTestRule = ActivityTestRule(TasksActivity::class.java)

/**
 * Creates two To-Do items, marks first as done and verifies its text.
 */
@Test
fun bySelectorSample() {
    // Add first To-Do item.
    uiDevice.wait(
            Until.findObject(By.res(applicationPackage, "fab_add_task")),
            twoSeconds)
            .clickAndWait(Until.newWindow(), twoSeconds)
    uiDevice.findObject(By.res(applicationPackage, "add_task_title")).
    text = "item 1"
    uiDevice.findObject(By.res(applicationPackage, "fab_edit_task_done"))
            .clickAndWait(Until.newWindow(), twoSeconds)
    uiDevice.wait(Until.gone(By.text("TO-DO saved")), fourSeconds)

    // Add second To-Do item.
    uiDevice.wait(Until.findObject(By.res(applicationPackage, "fab_add_
    task")), twoSeconds)
            .clickAndWait(Until.newWindow(), twoSeconds)
    uiDevice.findObject(By.res(applicationPackage, "add_task_title")).
    text = "item 2"
    uiDevice.findObject(By.res(applicationPackage, "fab_edit_task_done"))
            .clickAndWait(Until.newWindow(), twoSeconds)
    uiDevice.wait(Until.gone(By.text("TO-DO saved")), fourSeconds)
```

```
// Mark first To-Do item as done, click on it and validate text.
val todoList = uiDevice.findObject(By.clazz(RecyclerView::class.java))
todoList.children[0]
        .findObject(By.checkable(true))
        .click()
todoList.children[0]
        .click()
assertTrue("To-Do \"item 1\" is not shown.", uiDevice.hasObject(By.
text("item 1")))
}
```

The test code with BySelector may initially look more readable, but there is one drawback—BySelector() is applied and executed during a call to UiDevice. findObject(BySelector), reducing the flexibility in test code writing. That means the following line cannot be declared as a variable at the beginning of the test method and later reused.

chapter8.UiAutomatorBySelectorTest.bySelectorSample(): Clicking Add Task Floating Action Button.

```
uiDevice.findObject(By.res(applicationPackage, "fab_edit_task_done")).click()
```

What we still can do is extract the selector itself, as follows.

chapter8.UiAutomatorBySelectorTest.bySelectorSample(): Finding and Clicking Done Floating Action Button.

```
val fabDone = By.res(applicationPackage, "fab_edit_task_done")
uiDevice.findObject(fabDone).click()
```

The possible test method improvements are shown in the following code.

chapter8.UiAutomatorBySelectorTest.bySelectorSampleWithFindObjects().

```
@Test
fun bySelectorSampleWithFindObjects() {
    val fabAddTask = By.res(applicationPackage, "fab_add_task")
    val taskTitle = By.res(applicationPackage, "add_task_title")
    val fabDone = By.res(applicationPackage, "fab_edit_task_done")
```

```kotlin
    val todoSavedText = By.text("TO-DO saved")
    val checkBox = By.checkable(true)
    val toDoRecyclerView = By.clazz(RecyclerView::class.java)

    // Add first To-Do item.
    uiDevice.waitForWindowUpdate(uiDevice.currentPackageName, twoSeconds)
    uiDevice.wait(Until.findObject(fabAddTask), twoSeconds)
            .clickAndWait(Until.newWindow(), twoSeconds)
    uiDevice.findObject(taskTitle).text = "item 1"
    uiDevice.findObject(fabDone)
            .clickAndWait(Until.newWindow(), twoSeconds)
    uiDevice.wait(Until.gone(todoSavedText), fourSeconds)

    // Add second To-Do item.
    uiDevice.wait(Until.findObject(fabAddTask), twoSeconds)
            .clickAndWait(Until.newWindow(), twoSeconds)
    uiDevice.findObject(taskTitle).text = "item 2"
    uiDevice.findObject(fabDone)
            .clickAndWait(Until.newWindow(), twoSeconds)
    uiDevice.wait(Until.gone(todoSavedText), fourSeconds)

    // Mark first To-Do item as done, click on it and validate text.
    // Showcases findObjects() method use.
    val todoListItems = uiDevice.findObjects(toDoRecyclerView)
    todoListItems[0].findObject(checkBox).click()
    todoListItems[0].click()
    assertTrue("To-Do \"item 1\" is not shown.", uiDevice.hasObject(By.
    text("item 1")))
}
```

The last method also has a findObjects(BySelector) sample. In our specific case, we use this method to get the list of TO-DO items and then navigate through its items based on the position in the list.

This should be it about finding and acting on elements using the UI Automator. Of course, we haven't covered all the possible search criteria and actions, but the examples we discuss should be a good basis for you to move forward.

Waiting for UI Elements

In such test frameworks like UI Automator—where automated tests interact with multiple applications and where we don't have much control over network requests execution, application transitions, or animations—it is important to have proper waiting mechanisms that will allow us to write more reliable test code.

UI Automator waitings are presented by three types:

- *Waiting for* EventCondition—A condition that depends on an event or series of events having occurred.

- *Waiting for* SearchCondition—A condition that is satisfied by searching for UI elements.

- *Waiting for* UiObject2Condition—A condition that is satisfied when a UiObject2 is in a particular state.

All the conditions are implemented in the android.support.test.uiautomator. Until.java class in the Android Testing Support library or in androidx.test. uiautomator inside the AndroidX Test library.

The previous section contains some waiting examples and you probably noticed them. Waiting for an EventCondition was used in the following line and is responsible for finding the Add Task floating action button, clicking it, and then waiting for a new window to be presented to the user.

chapter8.UiAutomatorUiWatcherTest.kt: Instantiating UiWatcher Object.

```
uiDevice.wait(
        Until.findObject(By.res(applicationPackage, "fab_add_task")),
        twoSeconds)
        .clickAndWait(Until.newWindow(), twoSeconds)
```

Here, EventCondition is a change from the current window to a new one. It is used only as a parameter to the clickAndWait(EventCondition, Timeout) method. Here is are the EventConditions:

- newWindow()—Returns a condition that depends on a new window having appeared.

- scrollFinished()—Returns a condition that depends on a scroll having reached the end in the given direction.

SearchCondition is responsible for locating elements in the layout and represents the second waitings group:

- gone()—Returns a link SearchCondition that is satisfied when no elements matching the selector can be found.

- hasObject()—Returns a link SearchCondition that is satisfied when at least one element matching the selector can be found.

- findObject()—Returns a SearchCondition that is satisfied when at least one element matching the selector can be found. The condition will return the first matching element.

- findObjects()—Returns a link SearchCondition that is satisfied when at least one element matching the selector can be found. The condition will return all matching elements.

We already used the gone() method while waiting for snackbar with the TO-DO saved text gone in the create TO-DO flow, as shown here:

```
uiDevice.wait(Until.gone(By.text("TO-DO saved"), twoSeconds)
```

Here is an example of hasObject():

```
uiDevice.wait(Until.hasObject(By.text("TO-DO saved"), twoSeconds)
```

And the last type is UiObject2Condition. It waits for the specific UI object state or property:

- checkable()—Returns a condition that depends on a UiObject2 checkable state.

- checked()—Returns a condition that depends on a UiObject2 checked state.

- clickable()—Returns a condition that depends on a UiObject2 clickable state.

- enabled()—Returns a condition that depends on a link UiObject2 enabled state.

- focusable()—Returns a condition that depends on a link UiObject2 focusable state.

- `focused()`—Returns a condition that depends on a `UiObject2`'s focused state.

- `longClickable()`—Returns a condition that depends on a `UiObject2`'s long clickable state.

- `scrollable()`—Returns a condition that depends on a `UiObject2`'s scrollable state.

- `selected()`—Returns a condition that depends on a `UiObject2`'s selected state.

- `descMatches()`—Returns a condition that is satisfied when the object's content description matches the given regex.

- `descEquals()`—Returns a condition that is satisfied when the object's content description exactly matches the given string.

- `descContains()`—Returns a condition that is satisfied when the object's content description contains the given string.

- `descStartsWith()`—Returns a condition that is satisfied when the object's content description starts with the given string.

- `descEndsWith()`—Returns a condition that is satisfied when the object's content description ends with the given string.

- `textMatches()`—Returns a condition that is satisfied when the object's text value matches the given regex.

- `textNotEquals()`—Returns a condition that is satisfied when the object's text value does not match the given string.

- `textEquals()`—Returns a condition that is satisfied when the object's text value exactly matches the given string.

- `textContains()`—Returns a condition that is satisfied when the object's text value contains the given string.

- `textStartsWith()`—Returns a condition that is satisfied when the object's text value starts with the given string.

- `textEndsWith()`—Returns a condition that is satisfied when the object's text value ends with the given string.

The list is big enough and covers most used elements properties. They are similar to Espresso's ViewMatchers, which we are already familiar with.

Waiting for UiObject2Condition can be demonstrated by the following line of code, which searches for the first element inside the TO-DO recycler view list, locates the checkbox element in it, and waits until it is checked.

Waiting for UiObject2Condition Sample.

```
uiDevice.findObject(By.clazz(RecyclerView::class.java)).children[0]
        .findObject(By.clickable(true))
        .wait(Until.checked(true), twoSeconds)
```

Considering what we've covered so far, we can admit that UI Automator is a powerful test framework that can be used as a standalone test automation tool. But wait, we haven't yet unleashed its full power. Let's move to the next section and see what it prepared for us.

Watching for Conditions

There is one not widely known UI Automator feature that can add big value to your automated tests. The UiWatcher class represents a conditional watcher on the target device being tested. It contains only one method:

- checkForCondition()-Custom handler that is automatically called when the testing framework is unable to find a match using the UiSelector.

The checkForCondition() method is called automatically when UI Automator framework is in the process of matching a UiSelector and it is unable to match any element based on the specified criteria in the selector. When this happens, the callback will perform retries for a predetermined time, waiting for the display to update and show the desired widget. While the framework is in this state, it will call registered watchers' checkForCondition(). This gives the registered watchers a chance to look at the display and see if there is a recognized condition that can be handled. In doing so, this allows the current test to continue.

The possible use cases where UiWatcher can be useful can be handling one-time popups like low battery level dialogs, application feedback dialogs, advertisements, and permission granting for third-party applications. The beauty of this approach is that

UiWatcher should not be part of the test method but can be registered once per test class or per test package and act only when there is a need.

In order to control the UiWatcher states, there is list of methods in the UiDevice class:

- registerWatcher()—Registers a UiWatcher to run automatically when the testing framework is unable to find a match using a UiSelector.

- removeWatcher()—Removes a previously registered UiWatcher.

- resetWatcherTriggers()—Resets a UiWatcher that has been triggered. If a UiWatcher runs and its checkForCondition() call returns true, then the UiWatcher is considered triggered.

- runWatchers()—This method forces all registered watchers to run.

As an example, the TO-DO application's Statistics screen shows a dialog that must be dismissed. Open the UiAutomatorUiWatcherTest.kt class to see the details.

chapter8.UiAutomatorUiWatcherTest.kt.

```
@RunWith(AndroidJUnit4::class)
class UiAutomatorUiWatcherTest {

    @get:Rule
    var activityTestRule = ActivityTestRule(TasksActivity::class.java)

    @Before
    // Register dialog watcher.
    fun before() = registerStatisticsDialogWatcher()

    @After
    fun after() = uiDevice.removeWatcher("StatisticsDialog")

    @Test
    fun dismissesStatisticsDialogUsingWatcher() {
        val toolbar =
                "com.example.android.architecture.blueprints.todoapp.
                mock:id/toolbar"
        val menuDrawer =
                "com.example.android.architecture.blueprints.todoapp.
                mock:id/design_navigation_view"
```

```
// Open menu drawer.
uiDevice.findObject(
        UiSelector().resourceId(toolbar))
        .getChild(UiSelector().className(ImageButton::class.java.
        name))
        .click()

// Open Statistics section.
uiDevice.findObject(
        UiSelector()
                .resourceId(menuDrawer)
                .childSelector(
                        UiSelector()
                                .className(LinearLayoutCompat::
                                class.java.name).instance(1)))
        .click()

/**
 * Locate Statistics label based on the view id.
 * At this moment watcher kicks in and dismissed dialog by clicking
   on OK button.
 */
val statistics: UiObject = uiDevice.findObject(UiSelector()
        .resourceId("com.example.android.architecture.blueprints.
        todoapp.mock:id/statistics"))

// Assert expected text is shown.
assertTrue("Expected statistics label: \"You have no tasks.\" but
got: ${statistics.text}",
        statistics.text == "You have no tasks.")
}

/**
 * Register Statistics dialog watcher that will monitor dialog
   presence.
 * Dialog will be dismissed when appeared by clicking on OK button.
 */
```

```kotlin
private fun registerStatisticsDialogWatcher() {
    uiDevice.registerWatcher("StatisticsDialog", statisticsDialogWatcher)

    // Run registered watcher.
    uiDevice.runWatchers()
}

/**
 * Remove previously registered Statistics dialog.
 */
private fun removeStatisticsDialogWatcher() {
    uiDevice.removeWatcher("StatisticsDialog")
}

companion object {
    private val instrumentation = InstrumentationRegistry.
    getInstrumentation()
    private val uiDevice: UiDevice = UiDevice.
    getInstance(instrumentation)

    val statisticsDialogWatcher = UiWatcher {
        val okDialogButton = uiDevice.findObject(By.res("android:id/
        button1"))
        if (null != okDialogButton) {
            okDialogButton.click()
            return@UiWatcher true
        }
        false
    }
}
}
```

If we break it down, we will see that the UiWatcher instance is created first.

chapter8.UiAutomatorUiWatcherTest.kt: Instantiating UiWatcher Object.

```kotlin
companion object {
        private val instrumentation = InstrumentationRegistry.
        getInstrumentation()
        private val uiDevice: UiDevice = UiDevice.getInstance(instrumentation)

        val statisticsDialogWatcher = UiWatcher {
            val okButton = uiDevice.findObject(By.res("android:id/button1"))
            if (null != okButton) {
                okButton.click()
                return@UiWatcher true
            }
            false
        }
}
```

Then, from the setUp() method that will be executed before each test run, we call registerStatisticsDialogWatcher() to register the watcher and run it.

chapter8.UiAutomatorUiWatcherTest.kt: Registering and Running UiWatcher.

```kotlin
@Before
// Register dialog watcher.
fun before() = registerStatisticsDialogWatcher()

/**
 * Register Statistics dialog watcher that will monitor dialog presence.
 * Dialog will be dismissed when appeared by clicking on OK button.
 */
private fun registerStatisticsDialogWatcher() {
    uiDevice.registerWatcher("StatisticsDialog", statisticsDialogWatcher)

    // Run registered watcher.
    uiDevice.runWatchers()
}
```

At this point, everything is ready for running the dismissesStatisticsDialogUsing Watcher() test. The test starts the application, opens the menu drawer, and navigates to the Statistics section, where the AlertDialog is popping up. Then the UI Automator

framework tries to locate the Statistics text but can't. The `UiWatcher` mechanism starts
to check if there is something on the screen that was expected to be cached by the
running watcher. In our case, it is the `AlertDialog` OK button, which is clicked from
inside the watcher.

In general, it is worth trying to use `UiWatcher` in automated tests, which can enrich
test automation tooling and make test more legible.

Combining Espresso and UI Automator in Tests

At this point it should be clear enough how to use the UI Automator test framework as a
standalone test automation tool and it is a time to reveal the full power of Android test
automation using both Espresso and UI Automator inside a single test. To demonstrate
this, we will automate the use case where the TO-DO application sends the notification,
which, after clicked, opens `TasksActivity` (i.e., tasks list screen) to the user. The first
part of the test is automated using Espresso, starting from the moment when we click
Notification, the UI Automator will be used. At the end, the Espresso code will be used
again to verify the state of the application.

Let's take a look at the test itself.

chapter8.EspressoUiAutomatorTest.clickNotificationOpenMainPage().

```
private val instrumentation = InstrumentationRegistry.getInstrumentation()
private val uiDevice: UiDevice = UiDevice.getInstance(instrumentation)
private val twoSeconds = 2000L

@get:Rule
var activityTestRule = ActivityTestRule(TasksActivity::class.java)

 /**
 * Clicks notification triggered by application under test and
 * verifies that TasksActivity is shown.
 */
@Test
fun clickNotificationOpensTasksActivity() {
    openDrawer()
    onView(allOf(withId(R.id.design_menu_item_text),
            withText(R.string.settings_title))).perform(click())
```

```
onData(CoreMatchers.instanceOf(PreferenceActivity.Header::class.java))
        .inAdapterView(withId(android.R.id.list))
        .atPosition(1)
        .onChildView(withId(android.R.id.title))
        .check(matches(withText("Notifications")))
        .perform(click())

// Click on Send notification item
onData(withKey("notifications_send"))
        .inAdapterView(allOf(
                withId(android.R.id.list),
                withParent(withId(android.R.id.list_container))))
        .check(matches(isDisplayed()))
        .perform(click())

// Perform UI Automator actions.
uiDevice.openNotification()

// Click notification by text and wait for application to appear.
uiDevice.findObject(By.text("My notification"))
        .clickAndWait(Until.newWindow(), twoSeconds)

// Verify application layout with Espresso
onView(withId(R.id.noTasksIcon)).check(matches(isDisplayed()))
}
```

If the notification is delayed, we can wait for it using the wait() method. This case is covered by the second test method in the same class. The TO-DO application sends a notification with a small delay and the test handles it by waiting for the notification object.

chapter8.EspressoUiAutomatorTest: Clicking on Delayed Notification By Its Text.

```
// Wait and click delayed notification by text.
uiDevice.findObject(By.res("com.android.systemui:id/notification_stack_
scroller"))
        .wait(Until.findObject(By.text("My notification")), 8000)
    .clickAndWait(Until.newWindow(), twoSeconds)
```

As you can see, with both frameworks, we can cover most of the use cases we need, starting from testing an application using Espresso to more complicated cases like interacting with notifications, opening system settings, and dealing with other third-party applications using UI Automator.

EXERCISE 20

Implementing a Practice Test Using Espresso and UI Automator

1. Implement a test using the UI Automator `UiSelector` that creates and then modifies the TO-DO item.

2. Implement a test using the UI Automator `BySelector` that creates two TO-DO items, marks one as done, filters out the active TO-DO item, and verifies it.

3. Implement a test that opens a contextual menu in the TO-DO list toolbar and clicks on the share button. Modify the existing `UiWatcher` to wait for Gmail application icon/text shown in the application chooser and click on it from inside the `UiWatcher`.

4. Implement a test that uses Espresso and the UI Automator code and automates the process described in Step 3.

Summary

Depending on its goal, an Android UI test may target different applications: instrumented applications, third-party applications, or both. In the case of third-party or mixed applications, the testing is performed using the UI Automator framework, which is a powerful testing tool that allows wider test coverage compared to pure Espresso tests. Combining Espresso and the UI Automator framework creates UI tests that are powerful enough to cover most of the use cases we can imagine.

CHAPTER 9

Dealing with Runtime System Actions and Permissions

Nowadays, most Android applications support multiple locales, and many request different system permissions, for example permission to access the device camera, location permissions, and permission to write to external storage.

With the evolution of the Android platform, the approach to application permissions has changed in favor of user privacy. Starting from API level 23, application permissions are asked during application runtime and upon user requests. Such permissions are represented by a system popup or system dialog and are not the part of the application being tested. Moreover, these permissions can be revoked by the users any time from the application settings. Of course, the mentioned application states should be handled properly before or during UI tests are run.

This chapter explains the different ways we can deal with system actions like permission request dialogs and describes the possible solutions for changing the Android emulator system language programmatically.

© Denys Zelenchuk 2019
D. Zelenchuk, *Android Espresso Revealed*, https://doi.org/10.1007/978-1-4842-4315-2_9

Changing the Emulator System Language Programmatically

Up to API level 27, Android provided a possibility to set the system locale by sending the intent via an adb command or directly from the test code. This could be achieved because CustomLocale.apk was preinstalled on emulators and was able to handle the sent intent. An example of adb shell am command is the following:

```
adb shell am broadcast -a com.android.intent.action.SET_LOCALE --es \
        com.android.intent.extra.LOCALE "en_US" com.android.customlocale2
```

However, starting with API level 28, the CustomLocale.apk application was removed from the emulator image, which required another solution. After a closer look at the Android emulator release notes (https://developer.android.com/studio/releases/emulator), the solution was clear. Starting with Android emulator version 27.2.9 (from May 2018), you can load a QuickBoot snapshot without restarting the emulator. The emulator release notes page explains how to do this manually with the help of the emulator Extended Controls window inside the Settings section. See Figure 9-1.

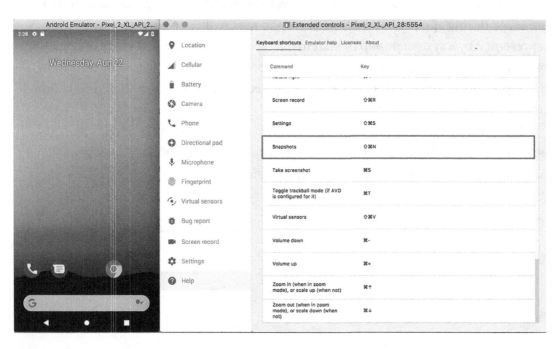

Figure 9-1. *Emulator extended controls*

When the snapshot view appears, you put the device into the desired state and click the TAKE SNAPSHOT button. The new snapshot with an automatically generated name is taken and shown in the snapshot list. See Figure 9-2.

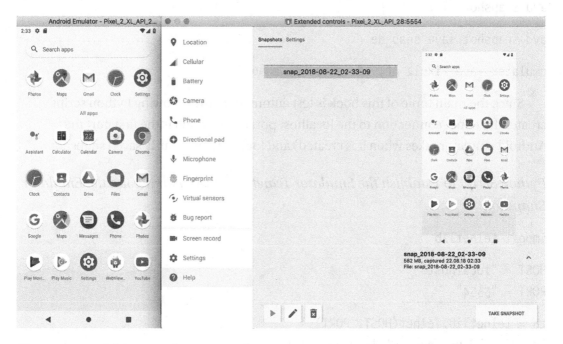

Figure 9-2. *Taking emulator snapshots*

Note   Renaming the snapshot in the emulator Extended Controls window will not rename it globally, but just creates the alias. The actual snapshot name will remain unchanged.

The same can be done by communicating with the Android emulator via the `telnet` console command (more information about the emulator `telnet` command can be found at `https://developer.android.com/studio/run/emulator-console`). In the following code examples, you can see how to establish the telnet session with a running emulator, list existing snapshots, take the snapshot, and load it during emulator runtime.

Sample Script to Save and Load the Emulator Snapshot.

```
telnet localhost 5554

avd snapshot list

avd snapshot save snap_de

emulator -avd Pixel2_API_28 -snapshot snap_de
```

Since the main topic of this book is test automation, the following Python script creates the telnet connection to the localhost port 5554 (which is the first port the Android emulator takes when it is created) and loads the previously saved snapshot.

Python Script to Establish the Emulator Telnet Connection and Load the Emulator Snapshot.

```
import telnetlib

HOST = "localhost"
PORT = "5554"

tn = telnetlib.Telnet(HOST, PORT)
tn.write(b"avd snapshot load name\n")
tn.write(b"exit\n")
```

Alternatively, you can do the same thing using the expect scripting utility (for MacOS and UNIX users only).

Expect Utility Script to Establish the Emulator Telnet Connection and Load the Emulator Snapshot.

```
#!/usr/bin/expect

set timeout 15
spawn telnet localhost 5554
expect "OK"
send "avd snapshot load snap_de\r"
expect "OK"
send "exit\r"
```

To install the expect utility on your computer, use these commands:

- Mac: `brew install expect`

- UNIX/Linux: `yum install expect`

In general, the current snapshot approach works not only for setting emulator language but also gives us the ability to have different snapshots for many use cases, which you can come up with by your own.

EXERCISE 21

Using the Emulator Snapshot Functionality

1. Launch an emulator and save a couple of emulator snapshots with the help of emulator Extended Controls window. Load the snapshots manually.

2. Launch an emulator using the console commands. Connect the telnet session to the emulator and save a couple of emulator snapshots. Load the snapshots from the console.

3. Create a Python script with emulator telnet commands and run it. Observe the result.

4. Install the expect utility on your computer, and then create and execute the script with the expect telnet commands. Observe the results.

Handling Runtime Permissions

Another burning topic in Android test automation related to system popups are runtime permissions. Appropriate permission should be requested by the Android application when it requires resources or information outside of its sandbox. The application declares permissions in the AndroidManifest.xml file and then requests that the user approve each permission at runtime (on Android 6.0 and higher).

When the user triggers a piece of code that requires additional permissions, the prompt shown by the system describes the permission group your app needs access to, not the specific permission.

In order to showcase this functionality, our sample application requests permission when we are adding an image to the TO-DO item. Try it out.

Enabling Permissions Using the GrantPermissionRule

Now let's take a look at the RuntimePermissionTest.kt class, which contains the GrantPermissionRule sample. The GrantPermissionRule rule grants runtime permissions on Android M (API 23) and above. This rule is used when a test requires a runtime permission to do its work. When applied to a test class, this rule attempts to grant all requested runtime permissions. The requested permissions will then be granted on the device and will take immediate effect.

Clicking on the camera icon in the sample TO-DO application triggers the Camera permission prompt to be shown to the user. The prompt belongs to the different application package, called com.andriod.packageinstaller, which Espresso cannot interact with. So, in order to reduce external dependencies and keep our Espresso tests hermetic, GrantPermissionRule can be used to start the test with the already granted permission.

chapter9.RuntimePermissionsTest.kt.

```kotlin
@RunWith(AndroidJUnit4::class)
class RuntimePermissionsTest {

    /**
     * Manifest.permission.CAMERA permission will be granted before the
     * test run.
     */
    @get:Rule
    var mRuntimePermissionRule = GrantPermissionRule
            .grant(Manifest.permission.CAMERA)

    /**
     * Provided activity will be launched before each test.
     */
    @get:Rule
    var activityTestRule = ActivityTestRule(TasksActivity::class.java)

    @Test
    fun takesCameraPicture() {
        val toDoTitle = TestData.getToDoTitle()
        val toDoDescription = TestData.getToDoDescription()
```

```
// Adding new TO-DO.
onView(withId(R.id.fab_add_task)).perform(click())
onView(withId(R.id.add_task_title))
        .perform(typeText(toDoTitle), closeSoftKeyboard())
onView(withId(R.id.add_task_description))
        .perform(typeText(toDoDescription), closeSoftKeyboard())

// Clicking on camera button to trigger the permission dialog.
onView(withId(R.id.makePhoto)).perform(click())
onView(withId(R.id.picture)).perform(click())
waitForElement(onView(withId(R.id.fab_edit_task_done))).
perform(click())

// verifying new TO-DO with title is shown in the TO-DO list.
onView(withText(toDoTitle)).check(matches(isDisplayed()))
    }
}
```

This current approach works well, but it has its pros and cons. The positive aspects are:

- UI tests remain hermetic and do not require interactions with other system services.

- Permission is granted for each test case inside the test class.

However, there are also some negative moments:

- It is not possible to test different runtime permission use cases like getting permission after denial or trying to use the feature without permission granted.

- There is no way to revoke a permission after it is granted. Attempting to do so will crash the instrumentation process.

In general, using GrantPermissionRule is a nice way to grant runtime permissions and avoid permission dialogs from showing up and blocking the application UI. From the other side, as was stated, it limits us in terms of covering multiple runtime permission requests use cases that are also part of the application that should be tested.

Handling Runtime Permissions Using UI Automator

Another way to handle runtime permissions is to use the UI Automator test framework functionality together with Espresso. Since it allows us to interact with any application, we are able to perform UI actions on permission dialogs as well.

First, let's consider the possible use cases. In total, there can be at least three use cases where the runtime permission dialog is involved:

- Camera permissions granted the first time the permission dialog is shown to the user.

- Camera permission denied by the user during the first occurrence, but then the user realizes that she needs such functionality and enables it when the permission dialog is presented a second time.

- Permission is denied two times. The second denial was made with the Don't Ask Again checkbox checked. The user tries to use the Camera feature again, but now she must manually enable it from the application permission settings.

And just to be clear, there is an application code-behind all four use cases, which in the case of using `GrantPermissionRule`, are not covered by automated tests and require manual testing.

Second, we may face an issue using only `AndroidJUnitRunner` for permission tests. The thing is that each test requires a clean application state without granted permissions. Therefore, the option with the Android Test Orchestrator described in Chapter 1 should be used with `testInstrumentationRunnerArguments clearPackageData: 'true'` `parameter (see app/build.gradle file for more details)`. It ensures that each test will be run within its own invocation, including the cleaned application permissions state.

Third, we have to inspect all areas we will navigate to with the Monitor tool, making the UI dump and collect identifiers from elements used in defined use cases.

Figure 9-3 shows the Grant Camera Permission dialog, used when a TO-DO item is created with an attached image.

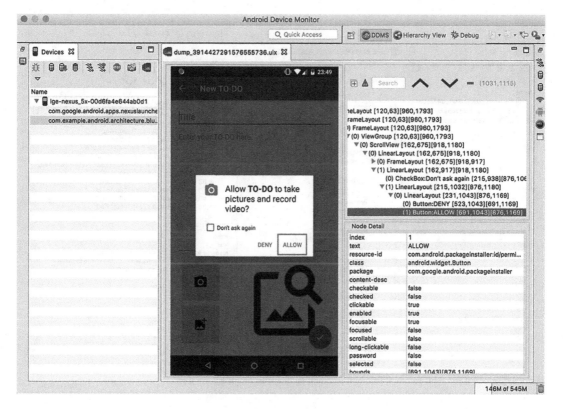

Figure 9-3. *Dumping the TO-DO application UI with Camera Permission dialog*

Figure 9-4 demonstrates the inspection of the TO-DO application settings page in the system's settings application.

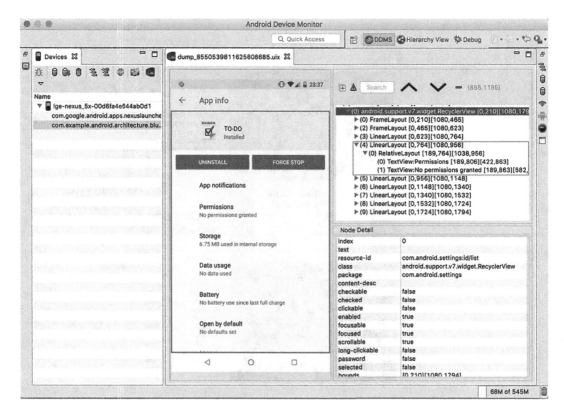

Figure 9-4. *UI dump of the TO-DO application on the settings page*

Figure 9-5 shows the inspection of the TO-DO application permissions settings page inside the system's settings application.

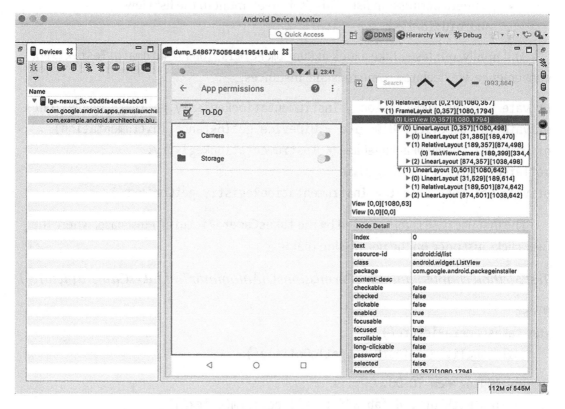

Figure 9-5. *UI dump of the TO-DO application in the settings app permissions page*

This is the list of UI elements we should collect and which tests will operate on (referenced device Nexus 5X, operation system Android 8.1.0):

- Allow button—com.android.packageinstaller:id/permission_allow_button

- Deny button —com.android.packageinstaller:id/permission_deny_button

- Don't Ask Again checkbox—com.android.packageinstaller:id/do_not_ask_checkbox

- Permissions list item—Fourth item in the recycler view `com.android.settings:id/list`

- Camera permission list item—Zeroth element in the list view `android:id/list`

And finally, our tests. Take a look at `RuntimePermissionsUiAutomatorTest.kt`. For convenience, we declared some reusable instances:

```
private val instrumentation = InstrumentationRegistry.getInstrumentation()
private val uiDevice: UiDevice = UiDevice.getInstance(instrumentation)
private val todoAppPackageName = InstrumentationRegistry.
getTargetContext().packageName
private val testContext = InstrumentationRegistry.getContext()
```

The first use case is represented by the `takesCameraPicture()` test case, where the user clicks just once on the permission dialog.

Test Method chapter9.RuntimePermissionsUiAutomatorTest.takesCameraPicture().

```
@Test
fun takesCameraPicture() {
    val toDoTitle = TestData.getToDoTitle()

    // Adding new TO-DO.
    onView(withId(R.id.fab_add_task)).perform(click())
    onView(withId(R.id.add_task_title))
            .perform(typeText(toDoTitle), closeSoftKeyboard())

    // Clicking on camera button to trigger the permission dialog.
    onView(withId(R.id.makePhoto)).perform(click())

    // UI Automator - click permission dialog ALLOW button.
    uiDevice.findObject(By.res("com.android.packageinstaller:id/permission_
allow_button")).click()

    onView(withId(R.id.picture)).perform(click())
    waitForElement(onView(withId(R.id.fab_edit_task_done))).perform(click())

    // verifying new TO-DO with title is shown in the TO-DO list.
    onView(withText(toDoTitle)).check(matches(isDisplayed()))
}
```

The second use case is covered by the deniesAndGrantsPermission() test.

Test Method chapter9.RuntimePermissionsUiAutomatorTest.
deniesAndGrantsPermission().

```
@Test
fun deniesAndGrantsPermission() {
    val toDoTitle = TestData.getToDoTitle()

    onView(withId(R.id.fab_add_task)).perform(click())
    onView(withId(R.id.add_task_title))
            .perform(typeText(toDoTitle), closeSoftKeyboard())
    onView(withId(R.id.makePhoto)).perform(click())

    // UI Automator - click permission dialog DENY button.
    uiDevice.findObject(By.res("com.android.packageinstaller:id/permission_
    deny_button")).click()

    onView(withId(R.id.makePhoto)).perform(click())
    onView(withId(R.id.snackbar_action)).perform(click())

    uiDevice.findObject(By.res("com.android.packageinstaller:id/permission_
    allow_button")).click()

    onView(withId(R.id.picture)).perform(click())
    waitForElement(onView(withId(R.id.fab_edit_task_done))).perform(click())

    onView(withText(toDoTitle)).check(matches(isDisplayed()))
}
```

In the third use case, it gets a bit more complicated since we have to interact with the settings application. Here goes the test.

Test Method chapter9.RuntimePermissionsUiAutomatorTest.
deniesAndGrantsPermissionFromSettings().

```
@Test
fun deniesAndGrantsPermissionFromSettings() {
    val toDoTitle = TestData.getToDoTitle()

    onView(withId(R.id.fab_add_task)).perform(click())
    onView(withId(R.id.makePhoto)).perform(click())
```

```
uiDevice
        .findObject(By.res("com.android.packageinstaller:id/permission_
        deny_button"))
        .click()

onView(withId(R.id.makePhoto)).perform(click())
onView(withId(R.id.snackbar_action)).perform(click())

// UI Automator - click on permission dialog checkbox and DENY button
uiDevice
        .findObject(By.res("com.android.packageinstaller:id/do_not_ask_
        checkbox"))
        .click()
uiDevice
        .findObject(By.res("com.android.packageinstaller:id/permission_
        deny_button"))
        .click()

// Clicking camera button to trigger permission dialog.
onView(withId(R.id.makePhoto)).perform(click())
onView(withId(R.id.snackbar_text))
        .check(matches(allOf(isDisplayed(), withText("Camera
        unavailable"))))

sendApplicationSettingsIntent()
enableCameraPermission()
launchBackToDoApplication()

onView(withId(R.id.fab_add_task)).perform(click())
onView(withId(R.id.add_task_title))
        .perform(typeText(toDoTitle), closeSoftKeyboard())
onView(withId(R.id.makePhoto)).perform(click())
onView(withId(R.id.picture)).perform(click())
waitForElement(onView(withId(R.id.fab_edit_task_done))).
perform(click())
onView(withText(toDoTitle)).check(matches(isDisplayed()))
}
```

Where sendApplicationSettingsIntent() is responsible for creating and firing an intent to show the TO-DO application settings page.

Sends Intent to Open the TO-DO Application Settings chapter9.RuntimePermissions UiAutomatorTest.sendApplicationSettingsIntent().

```
private fun sendApplicationSettingsIntent() {
    // Create intent to open To-Do application settings.
    val intent = Intent()
    intent.action = Settings.ACTION_APPLICATION_DETAILS_SETTINGS
    val uri = Uri.fromParts("package", todoAppPackageName, null)
    intent.data = uri
    intent.addFlags(Intent.FLAG_ACTIVITY_CLEAR_TASK)
    testContext.startActivity(intent)
}
```

Then enableCameraPermission() contains the code to open the application's permission settings and click on the camera permission item (see Figures 9-4 and 9-5).

Enables Camera Permission in the TO-DO application settings chapter9. RuntimePermissionsUiAutomatorTest.enableCameraPermission().

```
private fun enableCameraPermission() {
    // Wait for application Settings to appear
    uiDevice.wait(Until.hasObject(By.pkg("com.android.settings")), 5000)

    // Click on Permissions item.
    uiDevice.findObject(By.res("com.android.settings:id/list"))
            .children[3].clickAndWait(Until.newWindow(), 2000)

    // CLick on Camera item and wait for checked toggle state.
    uiDevice.findObject(By.res("android:id/list"))
            .children[0].click()
    uiDevice.findObject(By.res("android:id/list"))
            .children[0].wait(Until.checked(true), 1000)
}
```

Finally, launchBackToDoApplication() sends an intent to launch the sample application.

Sends Intent to Open the TO-DO Application chapter9.RuntimePermissions
UiAutomatorTest.launchBackToDoApplication().

```
private fun launchBackToDoApplication() {
    // Create intent to open To-Do application.
    val intent = testContext.packageManager.getLaunchIntentForPackage(todoA
    ppPackageName)
    InstrumentationRegistry.getContext().startActivity(intent)
}
```

After running tests from RuntimePermissionsUiAutomatorTest, we can see in
Figure 9-6 that the runtime looks good—36 seconds for three tests that interact with
third-party applications.

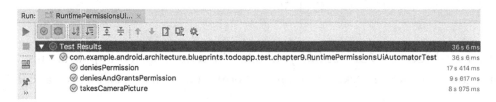

Figure 9-6. *RuntimePermissionsUiAutomatorTest.kt tests runtime*

EXERCISE 22

Using Runtime Permissions

1. Delete GrantPermissionRule from RuntimePermissionsTest.kt and
   run a test. Observe the results. Revert the GrantPermissionRule deletion
   and run the test again. Observe the results.

2. Run all tests implemented in the RuntimePermissionsUiAutomatorTest.
   kt class. Remove any Android Test Orchestrator dependencies from the
   application build.gradle file and run the test again. Observe the results.
   Revert to the original file.

3. Write a test that opens the TO-DO application settings and enables camera
   permission. Then open the TO-DO application and proceed with task creation.

Summary

This chapter showed how to change the Android emulator system language at runtime and described different ways of handling runtime permissions in UI tests. It should be clear that multi-language support is a must-have for modern Android applications. This requires thorough testing and enabling the test environment to switch emulator system languages easily is an essential part of this test infrastructure.

Having an easy and reliable way to set runtime permissions is a crucial and sensitive topic for the end users. It impacts user satisfaction and should be thoroughly tested. Applications should handle different permission flows properly and without mistakes. Of course, it is up to you to select which testing approach works best for your specific case—using the GrantPermissionRule or fully automating the permission granting with the UI Automator framework. With the knowledge from this chapter, you can do that easily.

CHAPTER 10

Android Test Automation Tooling

This chapter contains information about the tools provided by the Android platform that are used in test automation. We will discuss topics about setting up virtual or physical devices for test automation, figure out how the Espresso Test Recorder can help us when writing automated tests, and learn how to run automated tests in the Firebase Test Lab.

Setting Up a Virtual or Physical Device for Test Automation

A properly configured virtual or physical device is a must-have for reliable tests. Here is a list of device properties that may affect test execution and produce flakiness in your tests:

- System animations

- Touch and hold delay

- Virtual keyboard appearance

Let's start with system animations. Unfortunately, Espresso cannot handle system animations, which may lead to flaky tests. This is one of Espresso's major limitations. On the other hand, animations should be tested manually and disabling them in automated tests doesn't harm us. The Android operation system has three system animation types:

- *Window animation scale*—Sets the window animation playback speed so you can check its performance at different speeds. A lower scale results in a faster speed.

© Denys Zelenchuk 2019
D. Zelenchuk, *Android Espresso Revealed*, https://doi.org/10.1007/978-1-4842-4315-2_10

- *Transition animation scale*—Sets the transition animation playback speed so you can check its performance at different speeds. A lower scale results in a faster speed.

- *Animation duration scale*—Sets the animation's duration.

These animation properties are available from the Settings ➤ System ➤ Developer option, inside the Drawing section, as shown in Figure 10-1.

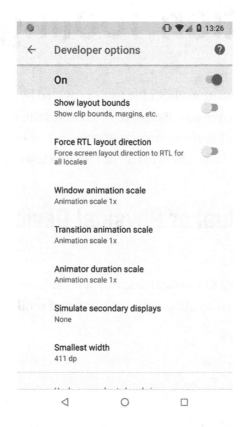

Figure 10-1. *System animation properties in the device developer options*

And of course, we want all animations to be disabled automatically. This is achievable in two ways. We can execute the following shell commands before the test runs or when the device starts.

Shell Commands to Set System Animation Properties.

```
adb shell settings put global animator_duration_scale 0.0
adb shell settings put global transition_animation_scale 0.0
adb shell settings put global window_animation_scale 0.0
```

The second option is to execute the same commands, but using a UiDevice instance before the test runs.

Setting System Animation Properties in the @BeforeClass Method.

```
companion object {

    @BeforeClass
    @JvmStatic
    fun setDevicePreferencies() {
        val uiDevice = UiDevice.getInstance(InstrumentationRegistry.
        getInstrumentation())
        uiDevice.executeShellCommand("settings put global animator_
        duration_scale 0.0")
        uiDevice.executeShellCommand("settings put global transition_
        animation_scale 0.0")
        uiDevice.executeShellCommand("settings put global window_animation_
        scale 0.0")
    }
}
```

In this example, we used the @BeforeClass annotation to execute it once for the whole test class.

The second device property that can bring flakiness is the Touch and Hold Delay. You can find it in the System ➤ Accessibility section, as shown in Figure 10-2.

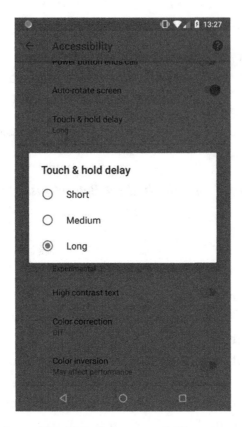

Figure 10-2. *The Touch and Hold Delay accessibility property*

This property is responsible for setting the time used by the system to differentiate between click and long click actions. If a click's touch time exceeds the Touch and Hold Delay limit, it's interpreted as a long click. This is visible if you tap and hold the toolbar icon to see its content description. On some real devices, when this delay value is short, a single click may become a long click, which causes the automated UI test to fail. To avoid this, we can modify the Touch and Hold Delay value. The first option for doing so is to execute the following shell command (the delay value is in milliseconds):

```
adb shell settings put secure long_press_timeout 1500
```

The second option is run from inside the @BeforeClass method, as follows.

Setting Touch and Hold Delay in the @BeforeClass Method.

```
companion object {

    @BeforeClass
    @JvmStatic
```

```
fun setDevicePreferencies() {
    val uiDevice = UiDevice.getInstance(InstrumentationRegistry.
    getInstrumentation())
    uiDevice.executeShellCommand("settings put secure long_press_
    timeout 1500")
}
}
```

By the way, the default Short value is set to 500 milliseconds, Medium is set to 1000 milliseconds, and Long is set to 1500 milliseconds.

Let's now discuss the final device property that can cause flakiness in our tests—the virtual keyboard appearance. At first look, the virtual keyboard seems not related at all to test flakiness but there is one thing we have to keep in mind—Espresso for Android operates only in our application under the test context and it is not allowed to interact with any third-party applications.

Guess what? The virtual keyboard doesn't belong to our application. So, there may be cases when mobile device performance becomes slow and the ViewActions. closeSoftKeyboard() method is not executed fast enough. At that point, if the tests need to click on UI elements that are hidden behind the virtual keyboard (which is supposed to be closed, but is still in the process of closing), they accidentally click on the keyboard instead. The following exception is thrown:

```
java.lang.SecurityException: Injecting to another application requires
INJECT_EVENTS permission
```

To avoid this issue, we can manually disable the virtual keyboard appearance on the virtual device. Unfortunately, there is no nice way to do this on real devices unless you connect physical keyboards to them. To disable a virtual keyboard, navigate to Settings ➤ System ➤ Languages & Input ➤ Physical keyboard and disable the Show Virtual Keyboard option. Or, again, this can be done via the shell:

```
adb shell settings put secure show_ime_with_hard_keyboard 0
```

You can also execute the same command from inside the test, as follows.

Disabling a Virtual Keyboard in the @BeforeClass Method.

```kotlin
companion object {

    @BeforeClass
    @JvmStatic
    fun setDevicePreferencies() {
        val uiDevice = UiDevice.getInstance(InstrumentationRegistry.
        getInstrumentation())
        uiDevice.executeShellCommand("settings put secure show_ime_with_
        hard_keyboard 0")
    }
}
```

After combining all the mentioned commands, here is what we get.

chapter10.devicesetup.DeviceSetupTest.kt.

```kotlin
companion object {

    @BeforeClass
    @JvmStatic
    fun setDevicePreferences() {
        val uiDevice = UiDevice.getInstance(InstrumentationRegistry.
        getInstrumentation())
        uiDevice.executeShellCommand("settings put global animator_
        duration_scale 0.0")
        uiDevice.executeShellCommand("settings put global transition_
        animation_scale 0.0")
        uiDevice.executeShellCommand("settings put global window_animation_
        scale 0.0")
        uiDevice.executeShellCommand("settings put secure long_press_
        timeout 1500")
        uiDevice.executeShellCommand("settings put secure show_ime_with_
        hard_keyboard 0")
    }
}
```

It does not matter which approach you use to set test devices in a test friendly state; they will definitely make your automated tests more reliable and less flaky.

EXERCISE 23

Configuring a Device for Test Automation

1. Create an Android emulator and observe the default values for System Animations, Virtual Keyboard, and Touch and Hold Delay in the accessibility menu. Run the test implemented in `chapter10.DeviceSetupTest.kt`. After the test runs, observe the same properties' values and compare the results.

2. Set the default emulator or device system animations, Virtual Keyboard, and Touch and Hold Delay states. Execute all shell commands manually from the terminal. Observe the mentioned properties afterward.

3. Create a shell script with all the shell commands from this paragraph that executes them on the connected device.

Using the Espresso Test Recorder Tool

The Espresso authors were probably inspired by the Selenium IDE test recorder and decided to add this same capability into Espresso as well. The Espresso Test Recorder tool allows inexperienced users to create Espresso UI tests with less effort. It became available and stable in Android Studio version 2.3.

The Test Recorder tool is integrated into Android Studio IDE and available from the Run ➤ Record Espresso Test menu, as shown in Figure 10-3.

Figure 10-3. *Record Espresso Test option in the Android Studio Run menu*

Before starting, you should have a test device connected or a virtual device created in advance. After recording is triggered, you are asked to select a target device. After the application is built, it will be deployed to the target device and will run in debug mode. See Figure 10-4.

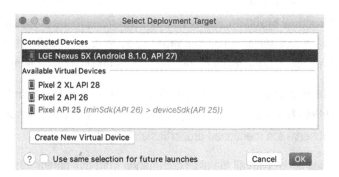

Figure 10-4. *Target device selection dialog*

While recording is ongoing, application interactions will be tracked and shown inside recorder view. Figure 10-5 demonstrates adding a new TO-DO flow in the sample application.

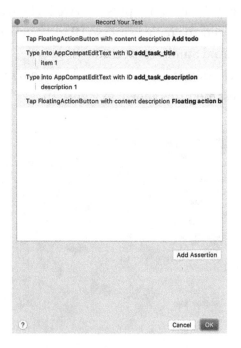

Figure 10-5. *Espresso Test Recorder window*

The Add Assertion button allows you to add an assertion of the following types (see Figure 10-6):

- Text is—Equivalent to check(matches(withText()))

- Exists—Equivalent to check(matches(isDisplayed()))

- Does not exist—Equivalent to check(doesNotExist())

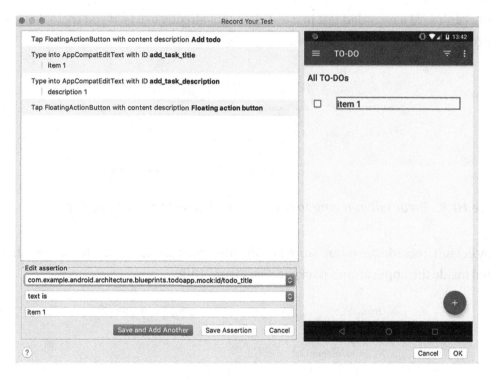

Figure 10-6. *Adding assertions to the Espresso Test Recorder*

After you are done with the recording and you click the OK button, you will be asked to provide the name of the test class and select the test class language (Java or Kotlin). See Figure 10-7.

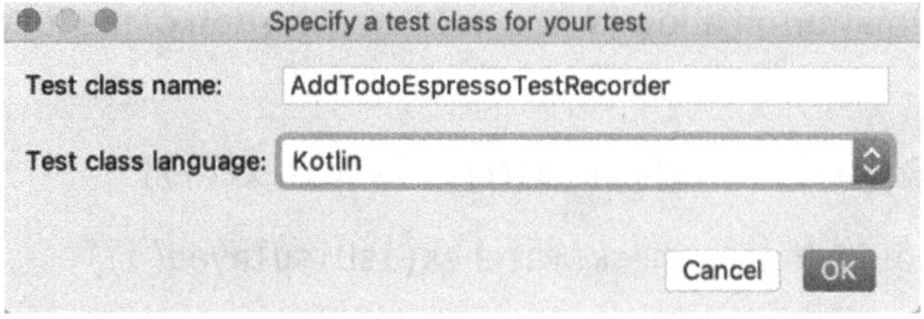

Figure 10-7. *Saving the recorded test in a test class file*

You can't save a recorded test in a test class that already exists. If you try to do this, the error in Figure 10-8 will be shown.

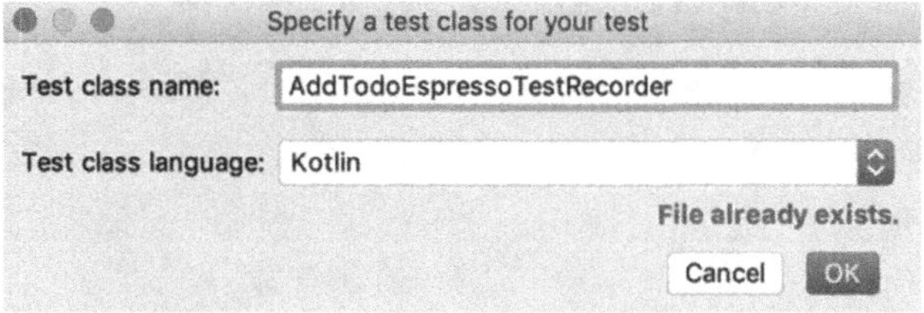

Figure 10-8. *Error when trying to save a recorded test into an existing file*

By default, recorded tests are stored inside the `tasks` package, which is automatically created inside the application's package. See Figure 10-9.

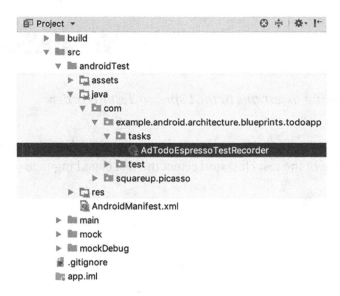

Figure 10-9. *Path where recorded tests are saved*

The Espresso Test Recorder can be tweaked from inside Android Studio preferences. You can observe that with the default depth values (Max UI depth = 3, ScrollView detection = 5, and Assertion depth = 3), the test recorder and the application are quite slow. If you lowering them to 1 or 2, they become much more responsive. See Figure 10-10.

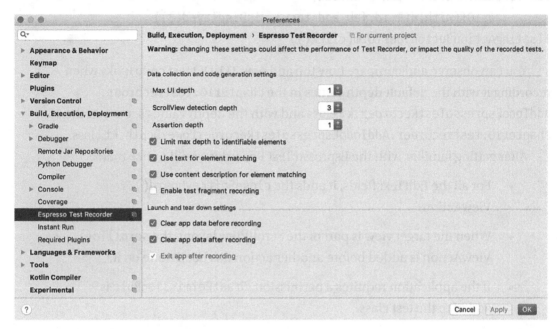

Figure 10-10. *Espresso Test Recorder preferences*

Next, you can see how clicking on the Add TO-DO floating action button is recorded with the default depth values.

Click Add TO-DO Button Code Generated by Recorder with Default Depth Values.

```
val floatingActionButton = onView(
        allOf(withId(R.id.fab_add_task), withContentDescription("Add todo"),
            childAtPosition(
                    allOf(withId(R.id.coordinatorLayout),
                            childAtPosition(
                                    withClassName(`is`("android.widget.
                                    LinearLayout")),
                                    1)),
                    1),
            isDisplayed()))
floatingActionButton.perform(click())
```

Here is an example of the same action, but with the Max UI depth set to 1.

Click Add TO-DO Button Code Generated by Recorder with Depth Values set to 1.

```
val floatingActionButton = onView(
        allOf(withId(R.id.fab_add_task), isDisplayed()))
floatingActionButton.perform(click())
```

You can observe and compare how the add new TO-DO test code looks when recording it with the default depth values in the `chapter10.testrecorder.` `AddTodoEspressoTestRecorder.kt` class and with the depth values set to 1 in the `chapter10.testrecorder.AddTodoEspressoTestRecorderLowerDepth.kt` class.

After getting familiar with the Espresso Test Recorder, you'll notice that:

- For all the EditText fields, it adds the `closeSoftKeyboard()` ViewAction.

- When the target view is part of the ScrollView layout, the `scrollTo()` ViewAction is added before another action has been done on it.

- If the application requires a permission, `GrantPermissionRule` is added to the test class.

In general, the Espresso Test Recorder may be a good way to start with Espresso itself, but it has some drawbacks as well:

- Application speed while recording is slow (even slower with higher depth values, but lowering the depth value can lead to failed tests).

- Generated code can be massive and hard to read.

- It has limited assertion support.

- Automatically generated tests usually require additional customization.

- There is no support for application delays caused by network requests, so you should manually create and register an `IdlingResource`.

- WebView layouts are not supported.

EXERCISE 24

Using the Espresso Test Recorder

1. Record a test that adds and edits a new TO-DO with assertions. Save the test class in the Kotlin language. Observe the generated code. Run the recorded test.

2. Open Android Studio Preferences ➤ Espresso Test Recorder and lower the Max UI depth and Assertion Depth to 1. Record the test described in Step 1. Observe the generated code and compare it to the code from Step 1. Run the recorded test.

3. Record a test that triggers the Camera permission dialog. Observe the generated code. Run the recorded test.

Running Espresso Tests in the Firebase Test Lab from Android Studio

It is widely known that the Android platform, by its nature, has significant device fragmentation. To deal with this, you may have a wide range of mobile devices based on the usage statistics. But this is quite costly, taking into account the fact that you have to maintain it. Even if this is a must-have in manual testing, in test automation we tend to use Android emulators, custom device labs, or third-party services. Third-party services did provide such a possibility for mobile developers but they were not standardized and were costly. Then Google decided to bring its own device-testing solution into the Android ecosystem. It's called the Firebase Test Lab. It allows developers to run automated tests on real devices or emulators without the need to maintain them.

Let's look at how to start using Firebase and what benefits it brings. First, starting from `https://firebase.google.com/`, you should navigate to the Firebase console and log in with your Google account (see Figure 10-11).

| ▲ Firebase | Products | Use Cases | Pricing | Do > | Q Search | GO TO CONSOLE ⋮ ● |

Figure 10-11. *The Firebase toolbar*

There you will notice that you will already have a couple of sample projects to play with and the possibility to add your own by clicking on Add Project. See Figure 10-12.

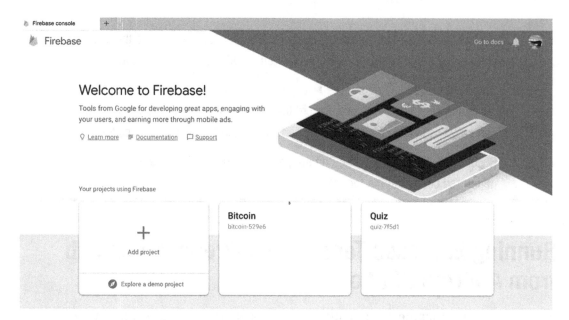

Figure 10-12. *The Firebase welcome desktop*

After clicking Add Project, you will be asked to provide the project name and select other parameters related to the service location. When the project name is provided, the project will automatically receive its project ID, which is a unique identifier for your Firebase project. See Figure 10-13.

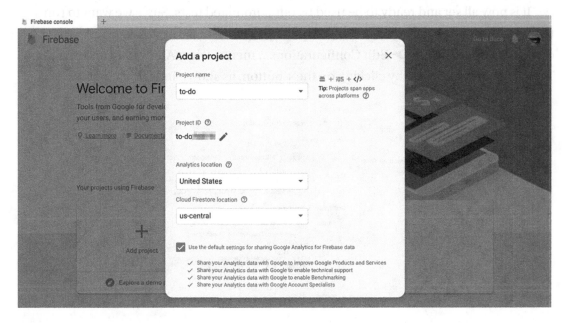

Figure 10-13. *Firebase, Add a Project*

After you are done with it, you will land on the Project Overview screen. From there, you can navigate to the Test Lab, as shown in Figure 10-14.

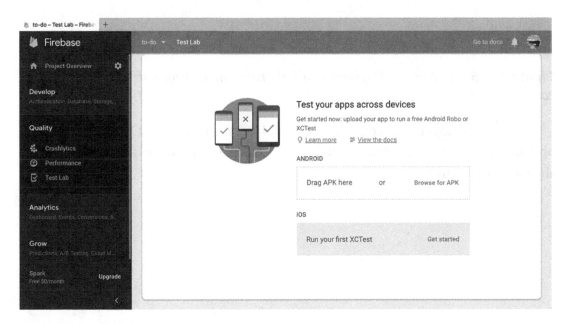

Figure 10-14. *The Firebase Test Lab initial state*

It is now all set and ready to be used by our automated tests. Since we want to run them via Android Studio, we have to set up the proper test configuration from there. To do this, we open the Run ➤ Edit Configurations... menu, select Android Instrumentation Tests, and add a new one by clicking on the + button, as shown in Figure 10-15.

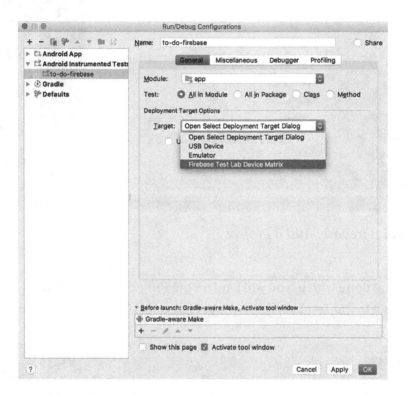

Figure 10-15. *Adding the Firebase Test Lab instrumentation test configuration*

In the Deployment Target options, we should set the Firebase Test Lab Device Matrix option as a target and then sign in with the same Google account into the Firebase, as shown in Figure 10-16.

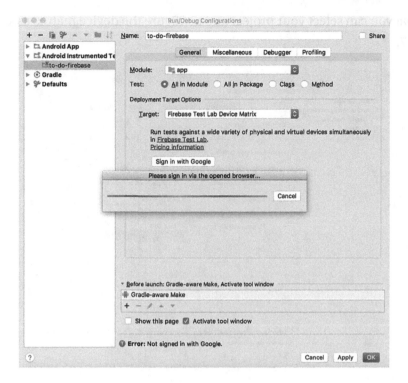

Figure 10-16. *Logging in to the Firebase Test Lab*

After that you can select your project and configure the device matrix, as shown in Figure 10-17.

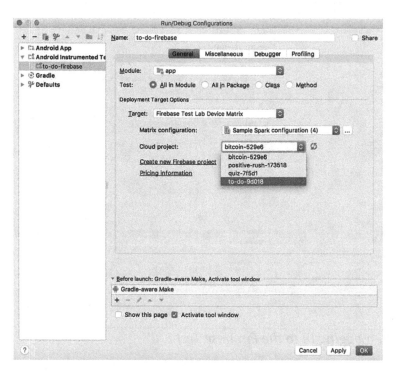

Figure 10-17. *Selecting the Firebase Test Lab project*

Figure 10-18 shows how the device matrix dialog looks.

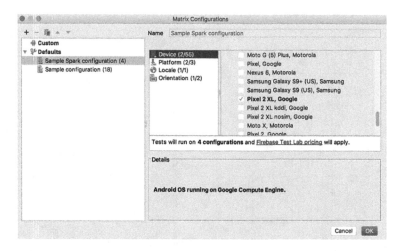

Figure 10-18. *Selecting the Firebase Test Lab device matrix*

It's worth mentioning that, for our sample project, we used the Spark pricing plan, which is free and has its limitations. You get 10 tests per day on virtual devices and five tests per day on real devices.

When all is ready, we can select and run the test using the Firebase test configuration, as shown in Figure 10-19.

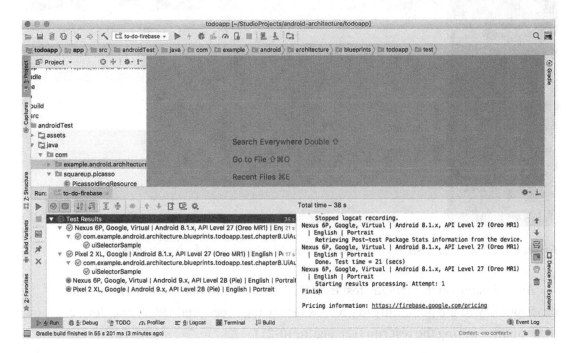

***Figure 10-19.** Running tests in the Firebase Test Lab inside Android Studio*

When the test execution is finished, we can return to the Firebase Test Lab console and observe the test results from the last run, as shown in Figure 10-20.

Figure 10-20.   *Test results overview in the Firebase Test Lab console*

After clicking on the specific test execution, you will land at the detail test run description with the possibility to preview device logs, recorded video, and device performance during the test run (see Figure 10-21).

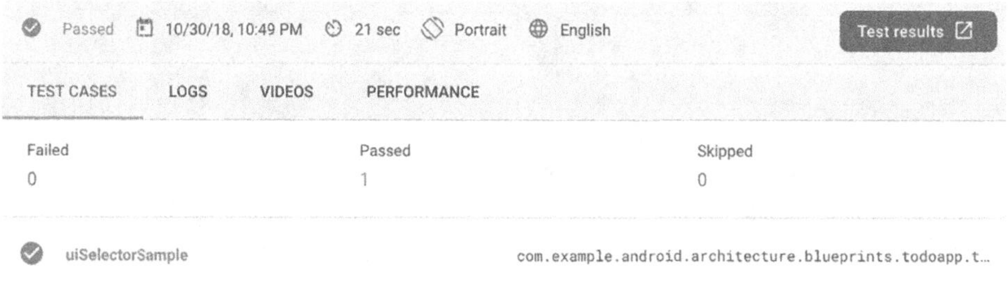

Figure 10-21.   *Detailed test case overview in the Firebase Test Lab console*

EXERCISE 25

Running Espresso and UI Automator Tests in the Firebase Test Lab

1. Configure your Firebase account, open the Firebase console, and set up the project.

2. In the Android Studio IDE, add a new Android Instrumentation Test configuration and connect to the project created in Step 1.

3. Run the tests and observe the results locally and inside the Firebase Test Lab console.

CHAPTER 11

The Screen Object Design Pattern in Android UI Tests

The Screen Object Design Pattern in mobile UI tests is equivalent to the well known Page Object Design Pattern in web tests, which is the abstraction layer representing an interface that allows its users to operate page elements or validate the page state. Since Page Object takes its name from the web page, it is hard to name a mobile application View or Screen, which is represented to the users as a page. This chapter demonstrates how the Screen Object Design Pattern can be applied to Android UI tests using Kotlin. You will learn to create a screen object that represents a single Android application activity or fragment (i.e., a screen) and then use these objects or their methods in tests that represent real user flows.

Pros and Cons of the Screen Object Design Pattern in Android Test Projects

When a screen object is defined, it contains a set of methods that are used in tests and represent the screen functionality or specific screen state validation. From the test execution side, this eliminates the need to write step-by-step test instructions in favor of calling those methods.

Pros

Let's look at the benefits to this approach:

- Logical test steps separation
- More readable tests
- Easy-to-build user flows

231

© Denys Zelenchuk 2019
D. Zelenchuk, *Android Espresso Revealed*, https://doi.org/10.1007/978-1-4842-4315-2_11

- Easily maintainable tests
- Code reuse

Logical Test Steps Separation

A test step refers to the functional user action that sometimes may consist of multiple test interactions with the application being tested. For example, adding new TO-DO to the sample TO-DO application consists of three actions: typing title, typing a description, and clicking the Done button.

More Readable Tests

Based on these logical steps, after all the screens are defined, we will end up having a set of these steps that have easy-to-understand names. So, even inexperienced test engineers can easily understand the test flow's logic.

Easy-to-Build User Flows

The user flow here is the set of chained test methods that can represent one screen or navigate from one screen to another, thereby replicating the end user behavior. They are super useful to understand the end user flow's test coverage.

Easily Maintainable Tests

Since all the screen elements declarations are located in one class, it reduces the amount of maintenance effort when there is application refactoring. Imagine a situation in which the login button is identified by its ID. This button is used in multiple tests and is clicked by the Espresso `onView(withId(R.id.loginButton)).perform(click())` code. Then the ID of the button changes, which leads to updating all the code lines where it is used. Having, let's say, a `LoginScreen` class that contains a Login button declaration and implements the login method makes the change done only in one place—the `LoginScreen`.

Code Reuse

This point is very similar to the previous one, because of the fact that view elements are encapsulated in the screen or their methods and usually are not accessible by other screens. That means they can be reused in multiple test flows by calling screen methods that contain screen elements.

Cons

Here are some cons to using the Screen Object Design Pattern:

- There is no clear way to handle views used across different screens

- The same action may open different screens depending on the navigation stack

- Too detailed screen methods lead to long tests

Handling Views Across Different Screens

As mentioned, there is no clear way to handle views or view groups used across different screens. Android mobile applications have shared and reusable components across many application screens and this impacts and challenges this test design pattern. Here we are talking about such views as menu drawers or tab bars. Figure 11-1 shows two of the TO-DO application screenshots.

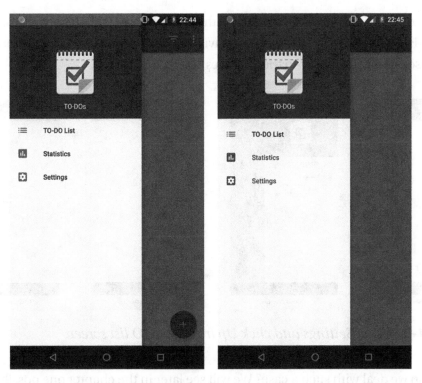

Figure 11-1. *Menu drawer opened from the TO-DOs list screen (left side) and from the Statistics screen (right side)*

233

Both of them have the same menu drawer component. Now where should this menu drawer component be declared? Should it belong to each screen duplicating the test source code? We will see later how this case can be handled.

Same Action Opening Different Screens

Recall that the same action may open different screens depending on the navigation stack. In Android applications, depending on the activity navigation stack or on the application logic, the same action on one screen may have a different end result based on the navigation flow prior to the current application state. A good example of such a case is the TO-DO application Back or Up button click navigation from the Settings section. Let's try two flows:

1.   Open the Settings section from the TO-DO list screen. From the Settings screen, click the Up button.

2.   Open the Settings section from the Statistics screen. From the Settings screen, click the Up button.

As you can see in Figures 11-2 and 11-3, the Up button is used in both cases, but the end result is different. In the first case, we navigate back to the TO-DO list screen. In the second case, we navigate back to the Statistics screen.

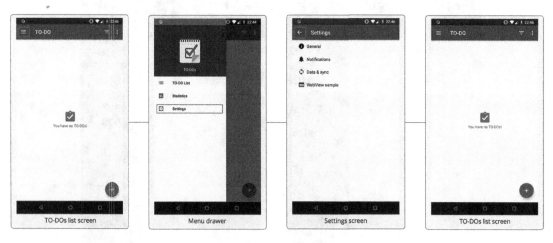

Figure 11-2. *Open Settings and click Up from TO-DO list screen*

How do we deal with such a case? We will see later in the chapter one possible solution.

Figure 11-3. *Open Settings and click Up from the Statistics screen*

Detailed Screen Methods Lead to Long Tests

Sometimes test engineers tend to be too detailed when creating screen classes and their methods. They try to wrap almost each single action or verification into a method, dramatically increasing the number of steps inside each test. We should try to always find a golden middle—on the one side having the proper logical split without making screen methods too small and detailed; and on the another side we should not put a lot of screen actions or verifications into a small number of methods.

Applying the Screen Object Design Pattern

It is a time to switch to the example. First, we will look at how a single TO-DO application screen can be implemented, including its visual representation. Figure 11-4 breaks down the New TO-DO screen into functional sections.

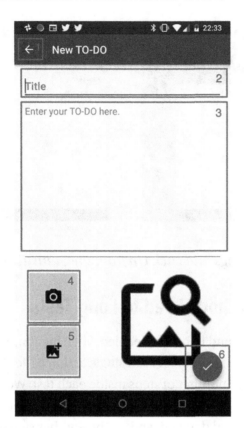

Figure 11-4. *The New TO-DO screen broken into functional screen object elements*

As Figure 11-4 shows, the New TO-DO screen contains six functional or actionable elements. Each of these elements represents a single method in the AddEditToDoScreen. For example, the typeToDoTitle method will look the following way:

```
class AddEditToDoScreen {

    private val addToDoTitleEditText = onView(withId(R.id.add_task_title))

    fun typeToDoTitle(title: String): AddEditToDoScreen {
        addToDoTitleEditText.perform(typeText(title), closeSoftKeyboard())
        return this
    }
}
```

Performing an action on elements two and three will keep users on the same screen; therefore, their methods will return the same AddEditToDoScreen instance.

In a similar way, methods for other elements are created. The rest of them redirect the user to different application screens. This is the example of a method that clicks the Done floating action button that returns a ToDoListScreen instance:

```
class AddEditToDoScreen {

    private val doneFabButton = onView(withId(R.id.fab_edit_task_done))

    fun clickDoneFabButton(): ToDoListScreen {
        doneFabButton.perform(click())
        return ToDoListScreen()
    }
}
```

Here, the clickDoneFabButton() method returns an instance of ToDoListScreen according to the application flow. We should also include verification methods that validate the screen in a specific state and system back action.

And one more thing—single screen actions may be too detailed for the test step and logically may be grouped into a set of screen actions. A good example is when adding new TO-DO flows that consist of three actions: typing a title, typing a description, and clicking a floating action button. Let's look at the final ToDoListScreen implementation state.

chapter11.screens.AddEditToDoScreen.kt.

```
class AddEditToDoScreen : BaseScreen() {

    private val addToDoDescriptionEditText = onView(withId(R.id.add_task_
    description))
    private val addToDoTitleEditText = onView(withId(R.id.add_task_title))
    private val doneFabButton = onView(withId(R.id.fab_edit_task_done))
    private val emptyToDoSnackbar = onView(withText(R.string.empty_task_
    message))
    private val upButton = onView(allOf(
            instanceOf(ImageButton::class.java),
            withParent(withId(R.id.toolbar))))

    fun typeToDoTitle(title: String): AddEditToDoScreen {
        addToDoTitleEditText.perform(typeText(title), closeSoftKeyboard())
```

```
        return this
    }

    fun typeToDoDescription(description: String): AddEditToDoScreen {
        addToDoDescriptionEditText.perform(typeText(description),
        closeSoftKeyboard())
        return this
    }

    /**
     * Represents adding new to-do flow
     */
    fun addNewToDo(taskItem: TodoItem): ToDoListScreen {
        typeToDoTitle(taskItem.title)
        typeToDoDescription(taskItem.description)
        clickDoneFabButton()
        return ToDoListScreen()
    }

    fun addEmptyToDo(): AddEditToDoScreen {
        clickDoneFabButton()
        return this
    }

    fun clickDoneFabButton(): ToDoListScreen {
        doneFabButton.perform(click())
        return ToDoListScreen()
    }

    fun clickUpButton(): ToDoListScreen {
        hamburgerUpButton.perform(click())
        return ToDoListScreen()
    }

    fun clickBackButton(): ToDoListScreen {
        Espresso.pressBack()
        return ToDoListScreen()
    }
```

```
    fun verifySnackbarForEmptyToDo(): AddEditToDoScreen {
        emptyToDoSnackbar.check(matches(withEffectiveVisibility(Visibility.
        VISIBLE)))
        return this
    }
}
```

In this code snippet, you can see that the AddEditToDoScreen class extends the BaseScreen class, which can contain common screen elements like the Up button ViewInteraction in our case.

In this same way, other applications screens can be created. When this is done, we can start writing UI tests. To tell the truth, it now becomes really easy—test steps are chained based on the logical functional flows.

chapter11.tests.AddToDoTest.kt.

```
/**
 * Validates TO-DOs creation flows using Screen Object Pattern.
 */
class AddToDoTest : BaseTest() {

    @Test
    fun addsNewTodo() {
        ToDoListScreen()
                .clickAddFabButton()
                .addNewToDo(todoItem)
                .verifyToDoIsDisplayed(todoItem)
    }

    @Test
    fun addsNewTodoWithoutDescription() {
        ToDoListScreen()
                .clickAddFabButton()
                .typeToDoTitle(todoItem.title)
                .clickDoneFabButton()
                .verifyToDoIsDisplayed(todoItem)
    }
```

```kotlin
@Test
fun triesToAddEmptyToDo() {
    ToDoListScreen()
            .clickAddFabButton()
            .addEmptyToDo()
            .verifySnackbarForEmptyToDo()
}

companion object {
    private var todoItem = TodoItem()

    @Before
    fun setUp() {
        todoItem = TodoItem.new
    }
}
}
```

Returning to the advantages of the Screen Object Design Pattern, we can see that all of them are covered:

- *Logical test steps separation*—Achieved by splitting actions per screen and creating functional flows like the addNewToDo(...) method.

- *More readable tests*—With the current implementation, it is clear from the test where we start and what exact actions are performed.

- *Easy-to-build user flows*—Having a set of screens returning their public results makes writing test cases easy.

- *Easily maintainable tests*—Achieved by isolating element declaration inside the screen class. So, there is no need to update them in multiple places after the application is refactored.

- *Code reuse*—As you can see, the screen methods can be reused by any test without the need to replicate the same or similar code.

We also covered one negative point:

- *Too detailed screen methods lead to long tests*—This issue should be solved by creating functional flows as was shown by the addNewToDo(...) method. Instead of writing many steps belonging to the same screen, we group them into one method. Keep in mind that functional flows ideally should be isolated per screen; otherwise, it will be hard to understand test steps or analyze test failures.

Now we will analyze the case shown in Figure 11-1 where the menu drawer view was used across different TO-DO application screens (ToDoListScreen, StatisticsScreen, etc.). In this situation, we have two options—we can duplicate the code in each screen (which we don't want) or we can create the new class similar to the screen but that will represent the common view. Since it doesn't represent the screen itself, we will call it MenuDrawerView. In the example application, it is implemented inside the BaseScreen class.

chapter11.screens.BaseScreen.MenuDrawerView inner class.

```
/**
 * Base screen that shares common functionality for main application
   settings
 * like TO-DO list screen and Statistics screen.
 */
open class BaseScreen {

    private val hamburgerButton = onView(allOf(
            instanceOf(ImageButton::class.java),
            withParent(withId(R.id.toolbar))))

    fun openMenu(): MenuDrawerView {
        hamburgerButton.perform(click())
        return MenuDrawerView()
    }

    inner class MenuDrawerView {
        private val todoListMenuItem = onView(allOf(
                withId(R.id.design_menu_item_text),
                withText(R.string.list_title)))
        private val statisticsMenuItem = onView(allOf(
```

```kotlin
                withId(R.id.design_menu_item_text),
                withText(R.string.statistics_title)))
        private val settingsMenuItem = onView(allOf(
                withId(R.id.design_menu_item_text),
                withText(R.string.settings_title)))
        private val todoMenuLogo = onView(withId(R.id.headerTodoLogo))
        private val todoMenuText = onView(withId(R.id.headerTodoText))

        fun clickTodoListMenuItem(): ToDoListScreen {
            todoListMenuItem.perform(click())
            return ToDoListScreen()
        }

        fun clickStatisticsMenuItem(): StatisticsScreen {
            statisticsMenuItem.perform(click())
            return StatisticsScreen()
        }

        fun clickSettingsMenuItem(): SettingsScreen {
            settingsMenuItem.perform(click())
            return SettingsScreen()
        }

        fun verifyMenuLayout(): MenuDrawerView {
            todoMenuText.check(matches(allOf(
                    isDisplayed(),
                    withText(R.string.navigation_view_header_title))))
            statisticsMenuItem.check(matches(isDisplayed()))
            todoListMenuItem.check(matches(isDisplayed()))
            return this
        }
    }
}
```

Now we address the last problematic moment we mentioned—the same action may open different screens depending on the navigation stack shown in Figures 11-2 and 11-3. Here we will use simplest solution and add multiple methods with the same functionality. The only difference is in the type of returned screen.

chapter11.screens.SettingsScreen.kt.

```kotlin
class SettingsScreen {

    private val upButton = onView(allOf(
            instanceOf(AppCompatImageButton::class.java),
            withParent(withId(R.id.action_bar))))

    fun navigateUpToToDoListScreen(): ToDoListScreen {
        upButton.perform(click())
        return ToDoListScreen()
    }

    fun navigateUpToStatisticsScreen(): StatisticsScreen {
        upButton.perform(click())
        return StatisticsScreen()
    }
}
```

Here is the test case implementation.

chapter11.tests.SettingsTest.verifiesUpNavigation().

```kotlin
/**
 * Validates TO-DOs application Settings functionality.
 */
class SettingsTest : BaseTest() {

    /**
     * Validates application UP button navigation from Settings screen.
     */
    @Test
    fun verifiesUpNavigation() {
        ToDoListScreen()
                .openMenu()
                .clickSettingsMenuItem()
                .navigateUpToToDoListScreen()
                .verifyToDoListScreenInitialState()
                .openMenu()
                .clickStatisticsMenuItem()
```

```
            .dismissAlertDialog()
            .openMenu()
            .clickSettingsMenuItem()
            .navigateUpToStatisticsScreen()
            .verifyStatisticsScreenInitialState()
    }
}
```

EXERCISE 26

Writing Tests Using the Screen Object Design Pattern

1. Create screen classes for all the application activities and fragments.

2. Write at least one test per created screen.

CHAPTER 12

Testing Robot Pattern with Espresso and Kotlin

The next test automation pattern we discuss is the Testing Robot Pattern, which in fact is not much different than the Screen Object Pattern. The main idea behind it is similar— you separate the test implementation from the business logic. This pattern was created by Jake Wharton and was first presented in May, 2016.

Separating the What from the How

The concept of the Testing Robot Pattern is to separate what we are testing (the high-level representation of real-user application interactions or flows) from how we perform the testing (the low-level implementation of interactions performed by automated tests). Figure 12-1 shows examples of the what and how.

© Denys Zelenchuk 2019
D. Zelenchuk, *Android Espresso Revealed*, https://doi.org/10.1007/978-1-4842-4315-2_12

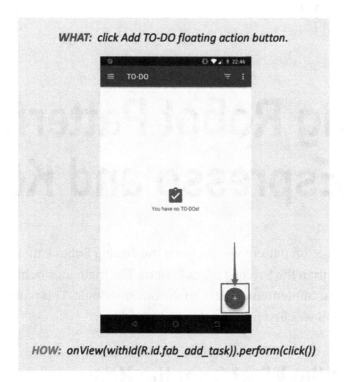

Figure 12-1. *Separating the what from the how when testing*

The idea is to create a robot with as many "what" methods as there is screen functionality represented by the robot. Let's start with basic samples and move to the final Espresso Testing Robots implementation. First, we look at the Builder Pattern (where each class method returns the same class instance), which is very similar to the Screen Object Pattern we discussed in Chapter 11. It's the initial step on the way to the Testing Robot Pattern. Here is the `BuilderToDoListRobot.kt` class, which represents the Builder Pattern applied to the TO-DO list screen.

chapter12.robots.BuilderToDoListRobot.kt Represents the Builder Pattern.

```
/**
 * Builder Pattern applied to TO-DO list screen.
 */
class BuilderToDoListRobot {

    fun addToDo() {
        onView(withId(R.id.fab_add_task)).perform(click())
    }
```

```kotlin
fun showCompleted(): BuilderToDoListRobot {
    onView(withId(R.id.menu_filter)).perform(click())
    onView(allOf(withId(R.id.title), withText("Completed"))).
    perform(click())
    return this
}

fun showActive(): BuilderToDoListRobot {
    onView(withId(R.id.menu_filter)).perform(click())
    onView(allOf(withId(R.id.title), withText("Active"))).
    perform(click())
    return this
}

fun verifyToDoShown(withTitle: String): BuilderToDoListRobot {
    onView(withText(withTitle)).check(matches(isDisplayed()))
    return this
}

fun verifyToDoNotShown(withTitle: String): BuilderToDoListRobot {
    onView(withText(withTitle)).check(matches(not(isDisplayed())))
    return this
}

fun markCompleted(toDoTitle: String): BuilderToDoListRobot {
    onView(allOf(withId(R.id.todo_complete), hasSibling(withText(toDoTi
    tle)))).perform(click())
    return this
}

fun checkDefaultLayout(): BuilderToDoListRobot {
    onView(withId(R.id.noTasksMain)).check(matches(isDisplayed()))
    onView(withId(R.id.noTasksIcon)).check(matches(isDisplayed()))
    return this
}
}
```

In a similar way, the `BuilderAddEditToDoRobot.kt` class is implemented. The test case that uses the Builder Pattern is shown next.

chapter12.RobotsTest.robotChecksToDoStateChangeBuilder() Showcases the Builder Pattern.

```
@Test
fun robotChecksToDoStateChangeBuilder() {
    BuilderToDoListRobot()
            .checkDefaultLayout()
            .addToDo()
    BuilderAddEditToDoRobot()
            .title(toDoTitle)
            .description(toDoDescription)
            .done()
    BuilderToDoListRobot()
            .verifyToDoShown(toDoTitle)
            .markCompleted(toDoTitle)
            .showActive()
            .verifyToDoNotShown(toDoTitle)
            .showCompleted()
            .verifyToDoShown(toDoTitle)
}
```

You can see that the `BuilderToDoListRobot.kt` test class functions represent the "how" and the test case steps show us the "what". Notice the clear screen separation— each time we start the test or go to a different screen (i.e., an Activity or Fragment), we create a new class instance. This approach works, but it is far from the final Robot Pattern implementation.

The next step is to use the Kotlin language advantages to simplify the Builder Pattern implementation. To understand how this is done, we must refer to the `chapter12.ToDoListRobot.kt` file, where the `ToDoListRobot` class together with `toDoList()` function are declared.

Declared in chapter12.robots.ToDoListRobot.kt.

```
/**
 * Extension function that takes ToDoListRobot class function(s)
 * as a parameter, executes this function(s), and returns a
* ToDoListRobot instance.
 */
fun toDoList(func: ToDoListRobot.() -> Unit) = ToDoListRobot().apply { func() }
```

1.   Here, toDoList(func: ToDoListRobot.() -> Unit) is an extension function that accepts the ToDoListRobot function func as a parameter. Based on the Unit type, you can guess that the func function returns nothing.

2.   The apply { func() } function in the ToDoListRobot().apply { func() } expression executes the provided functions inside the apply() function block as if they are called from inside the ToDoListRobot class. This is possible due to the nature of the apply() function, which according to Kotlin documentation:

```
/**
 * Calls the specified function [block] with `this` value as its receiver
   and returns `this` value.
 */
```

Where this in the current case is the ToDoListRobot class.

In this same way, we implement a similar function for the AddEditToDoRobot class:

```
fun addEditToDo(func: AddEditToDoRobot.() -> Unit) = AddEditToDoRobot().
apply { func() }
```

Now let's see how two static functions transform the previously discussed test case.

Test Case Where Robot Constructors Are Replaced by Extension Functions. chapter12.RobotsTest.robotChecksToDoStateChangeRobotsSeparation().

```
@Test
fun robotChecksToDoStateChangeRobotsSeparation() {
    toDoList {
        checkDefaultLayout()
        addToDo()
    }
    addEditToDo {
        title(toDoTitle)
        description(toDoDescription)
        done()
    }
    toDoList {
        verifyToDoShown(toDoTitle)
        markCompleted(toDoTitle)
        showActive()
        verifyToDoNotShown(toDoTitle)
        showCompleted()
        verifyToDoShown(toDoTitle)
    }
}
```

As you can see, we no longer need the constructors. Instead, we call the static functions toDoList{ } and addEditTodo{ }, which act on behalf of the ToDoListRobot and AddEditToDoRobot classes.

In the next step, the functions that return new robots are modified. In the test case we work with, it is the addToDo() and done() functions. So, it becomes almost equivalent to the toDoList{ } and addEditTodo{ } static functions:

```
infix fun addToDo(func: AddEditToDoRobot.() -> Unit): AddEditToDoRobot {
    onView(withId(R.id.fab_add_task)).perform(click())
    return AddEditToDoRobot().apply(func)
}
```

The test case is changed into the following.

Test Case Where Robots Transition Functions Act Similarly to toDoList{ } and
addEditTodo{ }. chapter12 .RobotsTest.robotChecksToDoStateChange().

```
@Test
fun robotChecksToDoStateChange() {
    toDoList {
        checkDefaultLayout()
    }.addToDo {
        title(toDoTitle)
        description(toDoDescription)
    }.done {
        verifyToDoShown(toDoTitle)
        markCompleted(toDoTitle)
        showActive()
        verifyToDoNotShown(toDoTitle)
        showCompleted()
        verifyToDoShown(toDoTitle)
    }
}
```

The last thing we have to do to make the Testing Robot Pattern better is to use
Kotlin's infix function notation for functions that return new robots. The infix notation
allows us to call a function without using the period and brackets:

```
infix fun addTask(func: AddEditToDoRobot.() -> Unit): AddEditToDoRobot {
    onView(withId(R.id.fab_add_task)).perform(click())
    return AddEditToDoRobot().apply(func)
}
```

This is how the final test case looks.

Test Case Where Robots Transition Functions Act Similarly to toDoList{ } and addEditTodo{ }. chapter12 .RobotsTest.robotChecksToDoStateChange().

```
@Test
fun robotChecksToDoStateChangeInfix() {
    toDoList {
        checkDefaultLayout()
    } addToDo {
        title(toDoTitle)
        description(toDoDescription)
    } done {
        verifyToDoShown(toDoTitle)
        markCompleted(toDoTitle)
        showActive()
        verifyToDoNotShown(toDoTitle)
        showCompleted()
        verifyToDoShown(toDoTitle)
    }
}
```

At this point, we have a clear separation of what we are testing from the how we do the test. The test case in this chapter represents the business logic of what should be tested. This keeps the test structure short, logical, and without technical implementation details.

To improve it even more, we can use Kotlin's inner classes to represent smaller view groups, like filtering or menus belonging to the same robot. Take a look at the example shown in Figure 12-2.

As shown in Figure 12-2, the TO-DO list screen is split into three parts:

1. The main functional area is represented by the ToDoListRobotWithInnerClasses class.

2. A filter view group called ToDoListFilter is declared as an inner class.

3. A menu view group called ToDoListMenu is declared as an inner class.

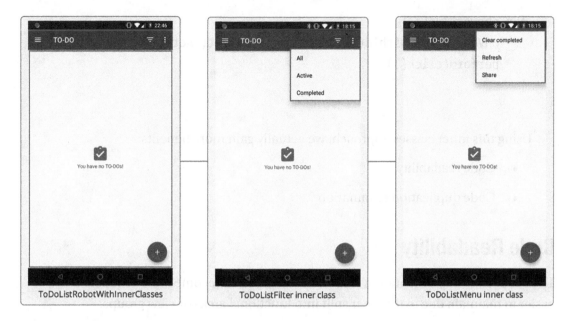

Figure 12-2. *Adding inner classes inside a robot class*

For convenience, we added Espresso actions that trigger view groups to appear inside inner classes constructors.

Inner Class Inside the TasksListRobotWithInnerClasses Class.

```
fun toDoListFilter(func: ToDoListFilter.() -> Unit) = ToDoListFilter().
apply { func() }
inner class ToDoListFilter {
    init {
        onView(withId(R.id.menu_filter)).perform(click())
    }

    fun showAll() {
        onView(allOf(withId(R.id.title), withText("All"))).perform(click())
    }

    fun showCompleted() {
        onView(allOf(withId(R.id.title), withText("Completed"))).perform(click())
    }
```

```
   fun showActive() {
       onView(allOf(withId(R.id.title), withText("Active"))).
       perform(click())
   }
}
```

Using this inner classes approach, we actually gain more benefits:

- Code readability

- Code duplication elimination

Code Readability

The robot class implementation and the test code both become more readable and easier to maintain due to the clear split into functional areas or view groups.

Code Duplication Elimination

Inner class constructors can execute the steps needed to trigger functionality, such as clicking the Filter toolbar icon to show all possible filtering options and then navigate through the options.

EXERCISE 27

Writing Tests Using the Screen Testing Robots Pattern

1. Create robots for the Settings and Statistics screen.

2. Think about the menu drawer and implement a solution that will best fit its functionality. Write a test that involves the menu drawer navigation.

CHAPTER 13

Supervised Monkey Tests with Espresso and UI Automator

Application stability is a top application quality indicator. Poor stability leads to low user ratings in Android PlayStore, which in turn lowers the application's overall rating and reduces the downloads. In order to keep applications stable, the Android platform provides a tool called monkeyrunner (https://developer.android.com/studio/test/monkeyrunner) to test the application from the stability side.

Unfortunately, monkeyrunner is not integrated into Espresso or the UI Automator framework, which makes it almost useless for applications that require user login or for specific application states that monkey tests should start from. Moreover, it is impossible to collect valuable test results without implementing custom tests, which results in parsing solutions.

Taking this information into account, it is clear that monkey-like tests must be much smarter and easier to control. This chapter explains how to implement your own supervised monkey tests.

The Monkeyrunner Issue and Solution

Let's take a closer look at what makes monkeyrunner so unusable:

- With monkeyrunner, tests are not part of the project codebase and are not controlled by Espresso or the UI Automator test framework.

- It is not the part of androidx or android.support library.

© Denys Zelenchuk 2019
D. Zelenchuk, *Android Espresso Revealed*, https://doi.org/10.1007/978-1-4842-4315-2_13

- It is a standalone tool with its own issues and need for maintenance.

- It is hard to fetch and process test results.

- It was written in the Python programming language, which makes it harder to integrate with existing UI tests.

This list of monkeyrunner cons forces us to implement our own solution. Luckily, we don't need to do much to have it in place. The idea is to write monkey tests in a native test framework like Espresso or UI Automator, or both. This introduces the following advantages:

- Monkey tests become part of the UI tests' codebase, which means they are fully owned and controlled by you.

- You can use UI tests in combination with monkey tests (for example, you can use a UI test to log in and afterward start the monkey tests).

- It's easy to fetch and process test results, using the existing reporting infrastructure.

- Monkey tests can be supervised, which means if you leave the application, you can identify it and launch the application.

- Different UI events or gestures can be implemented when needed.

Monkey Tests for Instrumented and Third-Party Applications

As mentioned, the monkeyrunner tool does not satisfy our requirements for monkey tests; therefore, in this section, we will implement our own supervised monkey tests.

Identifying Monkey Tests Operational Area

We have tools that we will use to write monkey tests. Now we have to think about the concept of how and where these monkey tests should operate. Figure 13-1 defines the areas where the monkey test should perform its actions.

Figure 13-1. *Device screen areas. Red represents areas that should be ignored and blue shows the areas of interest.*

According to the official Android documentation, the top and the bottom bars are called the navigation bar (see Figure 13-2) and status bar (see Figure 13-3).

Figure 13-2. *Navigation bar*

Figure 13-3. *Status bar*

Our first task is to identify the dimensions of the navigation and status bar and calculate the coordinates of the area we want our monkey tests to operate on. The ScreenDimensions class contains all the methods that perform this calculation. On top of this, it also generates random coordinates for monkey actions in our areas of interest. To fully understand how these calculations are performed, Figure 13-4 shows the device screen coordinates system.

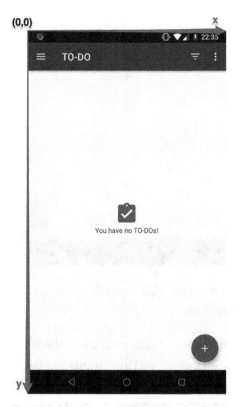

Figure 13-4. *Android screen coordinates system*

In short, the elements height calculation is determined from the top down, starting from the (0, 0) coordinate. Now it should be clear that to calculate the zero coordinate of the desired area, we need to know the height of the status bar. The same goes for the bottom-right corner, but in this case, we also need the height of the navigation bar. All of these calculations are done in the ScreenDimensions.kt class.

chapter13.ScreenDimensions.kt Class Keeps All the Functions That Calculate Screen Dimensions and Generates Random Coordinates.

```
/**
 * Calculates screen dimensions, navigation, status and action bars
   dimensions.
 * Generates random coordinates for monkey clicks.
 */
object ScreenDimensions {

    private val heightWithoutNavigationBar: Int
    private var width = 0
    private val uiDevice = UiDevice.getInstance(InstrumentationRegistry.
    getInstrumentation())
    private val appContext = InstrumentationRegistry.getInstrumentation().
    targetContext
    private val navBarResourceId =
            appContext.resources.getIdentifier("navigation_bar_height",
            "dimen", "android")
    private val statusBarResourceId =
            appContext.resources.getIdentifier("status_bar_height",
            "dimen", "android")

    init {
        width = uiDevice.displayWidth
        heightWithoutNavigationBar = uiDevice.displayHeight -
        ScreenDimensions.navigationBarHeight
    }

    /**
     * Calculate navigation bar height.
     */
    val navigationBarHeight : Int get() {
        return if (navBarResourceId > 0) {
            appContext.resources.getDimensionPixelSize(navBarResourceId)
        } else {
            0
        }
```

```
    }
    /**
     * Calculate status bar height.
     */
    val statusBarHeight: Int get() {
        return if (statusBarResourceId > 0) {
            appContext.resources.getDimensionPixelSize(statusBarResourceId)
        } else {
            0
        }
    }

    val randomY: Int
        get()  = (statusBarHeight..heightWithoutNavigationBar).random()

    val randomX: Int
        get() = (0..width).random()

    private fun IntRange.random() =
            Random().nextInt((endInclusive + 1) - start) +  start
}
```

As you can see, we are using the UiDevice instance to get the device screen's width and height and using the application context to get the navigation bar and status bar height based on their resource identifiers.

Defining the Monkey Test Actions

The next step is to define the actions that our monkey tests will perform:

- *Click action*—This action should indicate a click on random coordinates (randomX, randomY) inside the area of interest marked off in Figure 13-1. The UiDevice.click(int x, int y) action will be used for this purpose.

- *Drag (or swipe)*—Drag and swipe actions should be executed based on randomly defined start (startX, startY) and end (endX, endY) coordinates. We use the UiDevice.drag(int startX, int startY, int endX, int endY, int steps) action here. The steps parameter is the number of steps for the swipe action. Each step execution is throttled to five milliseconds per step, so for 100 steps, the swipe will take around 0.5 seconds to complete.

- *Click system back button*—The UiDevice.pressBack() action will be used to simulate a short press on the system's back button.

- *Launch application*—Here we will have different approaches to launching an application based on the application being tested. For a debug application, we need access to the source code, so we will use ActivityTestRule from the android.support library project and the ActivityScenario.launch(Activity.class) function from the androidx.test library. For third-party applications, we have another way of launching applications using the package name, which will be discussed later.

- *Relaunch application in case monkey tests left it*—Basically we reuse the implementation from the previous point. This allows the monkey tests to leave the application and will make the tests more closely emulate real use case scenarios, when mobile users leave an application after a certain amount of time and then launch the application again.

Now we move to the implementation of all the mentioned actions, which can be seen in the chapter13.Monkey.kt file.

chapter13.Monkey.kt.

```
/**
 * Class that keeps Monkey tests logic and main actions.
 */
object Monkey {

    private val uiDevice = UiDevice.getInstance(InstrumentationRegistry.
    getInstrumentation())
    private val appContext = InstrumentationRegistry.getInstrumentation().
    targetContext
    private val toDoAppPackageName = appContext.packageName
    private const val numberOfSteps = 10
```

```kotlin
// Random integer value used by modulus operator (%) to decide which
action should be performed.
private const val dragNow = 7
private const val pressNowBack = 13

// Variable that will keep action description for logging/exception
building purpose.
private var monkeyAction = ""

/**
 * Drags from start to end coordinate.
 *
 * @param startX - start x coordinate
 * @param startY - start y coordinate
 * @param endX - end x coordinate
 * @param endY - end y coordinate
 */
private fun drag(startX: Int, startY: Int, endX: Int, endY: Int) {
    uiDevice.drag(
            startX,
            startY,
            endX,
            endY,
            numberOfSteps)
}

/**
 * Runs monkey tests for provided package.
 *
 * @param actionsCount - number of events to execute during monkey tests.
 * @param packageName - package name that should be tested. If not
   provided TO-DO application is tested.
 */
fun run(actionsCount: Int, packageName: String = toDoAppPackageName) {

    loop@ for (i in 0..actionsCount) {
```

```kotlin
        if (PackageInfo.shouldRelaunchTheApp(monkeyAction, packageName)) {
            relaunchApp(packageName)
        }

        val randomX = ScreenDimensions.randomX
        val randomY = ScreenDimensions.randomY

        when {
            i % dragNow == 0 -> {
                val randomX2 = ScreenDimensions.randomX
                val randomY2 = ScreenDimensions.randomY
                monkeyAction = String.format(
                        "drag from: %d - %d to: %d - %d", randomX,
                        randomY, randomX2, randomY2
                )
                drag(randomX, randomY, randomX2, randomY2)
                continue@loop
            }
            i % pressNowBack == 0 -> {
                monkeyAction = "press back system button"
                uiDevice.pressBack()
                continue@loop
            }
            else -> {
                monkeyAction = "click coordinate x:$randomX y:$randomY"
                uiDevice.click(randomX, randomY)
                continue@loop
            }
        }
    }
}

/**
 * Launches the application by its package name.
 * In case package name is equal to the TO-DO application
   package  ActivityScenario.launch() is used.
 *
```

```
    * @param packageName - name of the package to relaunch
    */
   private fun relaunchApp(packageName: String) {

       if (packageName == toDoAppPackageName) {
           ActivityScenario.launch(TasksActivity::class.java)
       } else {
           PackageInfo.launchPackage(packageName)
       }
   }
}
```

This implementation of the monkey actions looks clear and easy extendable. Even this number of actions is enough to perform good monkey tests. But it is also easy to extend it, which we can do by introducing one more action inside the when {} block.

The dragNow and pressNowBack constants are defined in a way to minimize cases where both expressions actionCount % dragNow or actionCount % pressNowBack return 0 (zero). You can of course change them to values suitable for your needs.

One of the important roles that logic plays in monkey tests is handled by this condition:

```
if (PackageInfo.shouldRelaunchTheApp(monkeyAction, packageName)) {
       relaunchApp(packageName)
}
```

In short, this condition checks if the tests left the tested application or a crash occurred. If the monkey tests left an application, the relaunch mechanism is triggered. If an error occurred, an exception is created and thrown.

Implementing Package-Dependent Functionality

There are three monkey test functionalities that rely on the application package name that we would like to implement:

- Launching or relaunching the test application in case we are testing a third-party application.

- Checking if the test application process is in the error state.

- Creating a function that identifies the need to relaunch the test application.

All of these cases are implemented in the chapter13.PackageInfo.kt file, as shown here.

chapter13.PackageInfo.kt.

```
/**
 * Provides package helper methods.
 */
object PackageInfo {

    private val uiDevice = UiDevice.getInstance(InstrumentationRegistry.
    getInstrumentation())
    private val testContext = InstrumentationRegistry.getInstrumentation().
    context

    /**
     * Checks if there is a need to relaunch the application.
     *
     * @return true when application under test is not displayed to the user.
     */
    fun shouldRelaunchTheApp(monkeyAction: String, packageName: String):
    Boolean {
        if (!isAppInErrorState(monkeyAction, packageName)
                && uiDevice.currentPackageName != packageName) {
            return true
        }
        return false
    }

    /**
     * Launches application based on its package name.
     * @param packageName - the name of the package to launch.
     */
    fun launchPackage(packageName: String) {
        val intent = testContext
                .packageManager
                .getLaunchIntentForPackage(packageName)!!
        testContext.startActivity(intent)
```

```kotlin
        uiDevice.wait(Until.hasObject(By
            .pkg(packageName)),
            5000)
    }

    /**
     * Checks if target application process is in error state and throws an
     exception, otherwise returns true.
     *
     * @return false if application is in error state, otherwise throws
     exception and fails the test.
     */
    private fun isAppInErrorState(monkeyAction: String, packageName:
    String): Boolean {
        val manager = testContext.getSystemService(Context.ACTIVITY_
        SERVICE) as ActivityManager
        var errorDescription = ""

        // Get processes in error state, return false when list is null.
        manager.processesInErrorState?.forEach {

            val isTargetPackage = it.processName.contains(packageName)
            when {
                isTargetPackage && it.condition == CRASHED ->
                    errorDescription = "Application $packageName crashed
                    after $monkeyAction action"
                isTargetPackage && it.condition == NOT_RESPONDING ->
                    errorDescription = "Application $packageName not
                    responding after $monkeyAction action"
            }
            /** Build and throw new Espresso PerformException with proper
            description and stacktrace
             * At this point test is failed.
             */
            throw PerformException.Builder()
                    .withActionDescription(errorDescription)
                    .withCause(Throwable(it.stackTrace))
```

```
                .build()
        }
        return false
    }
}
```

Here, the shouldRelaunchTheApp() function validates two conditions. First, it determines if the test application is in an error state (CRASH or ANR). If it's not, then it checks if the tested application has been shown to the user and if not relaunches it. The launchPackage(packageName) function uses the test context to send the start activity intent to the system and, with the help of the UiDevice wait mechanism, waits for the application to start. The last function, called isAppInErrorState(monkeyAction, packageName), ensures that the tested application process is currently not in the error state. When an error state is identified, the Espresso PerformException function is created with additional information about the last monkey action performed and the exception stacktrace. This way we are using the Espresso error reporting mechanism and the fail monkey test.

Next are the actual monkey tests for the instrumented and third-party applications. The com.google.android.dialer package (Android Phone application) is used for the third-party example.

chapter13.MonkeyTest.kt.

```
/**
 * Test class that demonstrates supervised monkey tests.
 */
@RunWith(AndroidJUnit4::class)
class MonkeyTest {

    @get:Rule
    var grantPermissionRule: GrantPermissionRule = GrantPermissionRule.grant(
            Manifest.permission.CAMERA,
            Manifest.permission.WRITE_EXTERNAL_STORAGE)

    @get:Rule
    var screenshotWatcher = ScreenshotWatcher()

    /**
     * Monkey tests will be executed against TO-DO application.
```

```kotlin
 */
@Test
fun testsInstrumentedApp() {
    ActivityScenario.launch(TasksActivity::class.java)
    Monkey.run(200)
}

/**
 * Monkey tests will be executed against provided application package name.
 * This is the example of how to test 3rd party application.
 */
@Test
fun testsThirdPartyApp() {
    val packageName = "com.google.android.dialer"
    PackageInfo.launchPackage(packageName)
    Monkey.run(200, packageName)
}
}
```

While running these tests, we can see that the monkey actions are a bit slower than the monkeyrunner tests because of the need to check the application state during each test step. But we can neglect this issue, keeping in mind all the pros of having them implemented using Android native testing frameworks.

EXERCISE 28

Running Monkey Tests

1. Check out the master branch of the TO-DO application project and migrate it to AndroidX. After migration, execute Build ➤ Clean project. Run some tests. If there are failures, analyze and fix them by updating the proguard rules or updating dependences in the build.gradle file.

2. Implement a test class with a test that launches application activity using ActivityScenario.launch(Activity.class) in the @Before method and then runs the test.

Summary

Unfortunately, on the Android platform, monkey tests are not treated very important. The outdated `monkeyrunner` Python tool is supplied for this need instead of providing better support via native Android platform testing frameworks like UI Automator or Espresso. But even so, without too much effort, it is possible to run meaningful monkey tests that include easy ways to start and prepare the proper application under a test state, run supervised monkey tests, and report test results using the native testing frameworks functionality.

CHAPTER 14

AndroidX Test Library

A May 2018 Google I/O event announced the AndroidX open source project, which is used to develop, test, package, version, and release libraries within Android Jetpack. AndroidX replaces the Android Support Library. One of its major improvements is the fact that AndroidX packages are separately maintained and updated, so you can update AndroidX Libraries in your project independently.

Since Android Test Libraries are part of the Android Support Library, AndroidX also contains the AndroidX Test Library. Its beta version was announced at the Google I/O event in May 2018. During the Android DevSummit 2018 event, Google announced its stable 1.0 version. The AndroidX Test Library eliminates the need to maintain many different testing tools, with styles and APIs that are used on different test levels.

For your convenience, the second branch is called `androidx-espresso-revealed` with a TO-DO sample application project that was migrated to AndroidX. In order to use it, just switch the branch using the `git checkout androidx-espresso-revealed` command. You may need to clean the project using the Android Studio Build ➤ Clean option or even use File ➤ Invalidate Cashes / Restart... to avoid build issues.

AndroidX Test Compared to the Testing Support Library

The test pyramid in Figure 14-1 shows different test levels that were isolated from each other by the technology and the tools used to test them.

© Denys Zelenchuk 2019
D. Zelenchuk, *Android Espresso Revealed*, https://doi.org/10.1007/978-1-4842-4315-2_14

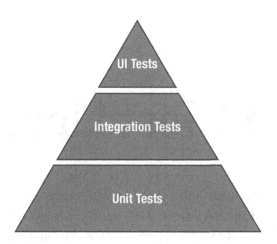

Figure 14-1. *Testing pyramid*

The problem was that tests from different levels were not portable; they were tied to the testing tools and the environment they were written on. With the AndroidX Test Library, this problem is resolved. Now you can use a single set of test libraries to write tests related to different test levels—unit, integration, and user interface (or end-to-end) tests.

As we are talking about UI end-to-end tests in this book, we will focus on the new features in the AndroidX Test Library compared to the Android Testing Support Library from the UI test perspective:

- `ApplicationProvider`– Provides the ability to retrieve the current application context in tests.

- `ActivityScenario` and `FragmentScenario`– `ActivityScenario` provides APIs to start and drive an activity's lifecycle state for testing. It works with arbitrary activities and works consistently across different versions of the Android framework. `FragmentScenario` provides an API to start and drive a fragment's lifecycle state for testing. It works with arbitrary fragments and works consistently across different versions of the Android framework.

- The new `Truth` Assertion Library—`Truth` is a fluent assertions library that can be used as an alternative to `JUnit`- or Hamcrest-based assertions when constructing the validation step for your tests.

- Migrated all other libraries and dependencies to `androidx.test`– All the dependencies from the `android.test.support` library were migrated to `androidx.test`.

Configuring Projects for AndroidX Test

In order to start using AndroidX Test in a newly created project, you have to follow nearly the same steps as with the android.support library:

1. To ensure you will have most recent AndroidX Test Libraries, add Google's Maven repository inside the build.gradle file as the following:

```
allprojects {
    repositories {
        jcenter()
        google()
    }
}
```

2. Add the AndroidX Test dependencies you need in the UI tests:

```
// Espresso UI Testing
androidTestImplementation "androidx.test.espresso:espresso-core:$rootProject.espressoVersion"
androidTestImplementation "androidx.test.espresso:espresso-contrib:$rootProject.espressoVersion"
androidTestImplementation "androidx.test.espresso:espresso-intents:$rootProject.espressoVersion"
androidTestImplementation "androidx.test.espresso.idling:idling-concurrent:$rootProject.espressoVersion"
androidTestImplementation "androidx.test.espresso:espresso-idling-resource:$rootProject.espressoVersion"
androidTestImplementation "androidx.test.espresso:espresso-web:$rootProject.espressoVersionAndroidX"
androidTestImplementation "androidx.test.espresso:espresso-accessibility:$rootProject.espressoVersion"
```

3. Add the AndroidX Test instrumentation runner:

```
testInstrumentationRunner 'androidx.test.runner.AndroidJUnitRunner'
```

4. To use the Android Test Orchestrator, add this line:

```
testOptions {
    execution 'ANDROIDX_TEST_ORCHESTRATOR'
}
```

This is enough to start writing UI tests, as we do in the sample TO-DO application.

Migrating to AndroidX

AndroidX migration is integrated into Android Studio IDE, so it is quite easy to migrate both main and test applications. To start the migration process, choose Refactor ➤ Migrate to AndroidX... from Android Studio menu. You can also right-click on the project inside the project view and select these menu options. See Figure 14-2.

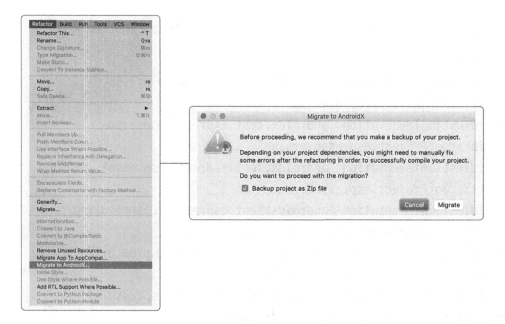

Figure 14-2. *The Migrate to AndroidX option in Android Studio*

Before the migration is initiated, you will be asked to back up your project just in case you have compile issues after the migration. You will be also warned about fixing migration errors manually depending on your project dependencies.

In a couple of minutes (depending on the project's complexity), the whole project will be migrated to the AndroidX Library. It's really simple and easy. After it's automatically triggered, the `gradle sync` task all seems to be good, as it shows BUILD SUCCESSFUL. But (there is always a but), during the first test run, the following issue occurred just after the test started.

Proguard Obfuscation Issue When Migrating to AndroidX.

```
Started running tests

java.lang.NoClassDefFoundError: Failed resolution of: Landroidx/test/
espresso/IdlingRegistry;
...
Caused by: java.lang.ClassNotFoundException: Didn't find class "androidx.
test.espresso.IdlingRegistry" on path: DexPathList[[zip file "/system/
framework/android.test.runner.jar", zip file "/system/framework/android.test.
mock.jar", zip file "/data/app/com.example.android.architecture.blueprints.
todoapp.mock.test-U-I7D8dt-qcnzY2buNTPzw==/base.apk", zip file "/data/app/com.
example.android.architecture.blueprints.todoapp.mock-JWNE8BTGptjn2ZWTifC78Q==/
base.apk"],nativeLibraryDirectories=[/data/app/com.example.android.
architecture.blueprints.todoapp.mock.test-U-I7D8dt-qcnzY2buNTPzw==/lib/
arm64, /data/app/com.example.android.architecture.blueprints.todoapp.mock-
JWNE8BTGptjn2ZWTifC78Q==/lib/arm64, /system/lib64, /vendor/lib64]]
...

Tests ran to completion.
```

It turns out that AndroidX migration doesn't care, for good or bad, about project proguard files, meaning that if there were some defined `proguard` rules for the `android.support` libraries, they are not touched. The following sample code contains an example of the not-migrated `android.support` library classes mentioned in the `proguard-rules.pro` TO-DO application.

Migrate to AndroidX… Doesn't Migrate Proguard Files.

```
-keep class android.support.v4.widget.DrawerLayout { *; }
-keep class android.support.test.espresso.IdlingResource { *; }
-keep class android.support.test.espresso.IdlingRegistry { *; }
```

As mentioned, manual migration error fixes would be necessary.

ActivityScenario in UI Tests

ActivityScenario provides APIs to start and drive the activity's lifecycle stage (for example, Stage.CREATED, Stage.RESUMED, Stage.DESTROYED, etc.) for testing. These APIs are more suitable to integration tests when each activity state can be tested quickly and easily. What is important for UI tests is the fact that they can be used instead of ActivityTestRule to launch the application under the test activity before each test run.

chapter14.ActivityScenarioTest.kt.

```
/**
 * Sample of ActivityScenario.launch(Activity.class) method usage.
 */
@RunWith(AndroidJUnit4::class)
class ActivityScenarioTest {

    @Before
    fun launchTasksActivity() {
        ActivityScenario.launch(TasksActivity::class.java)
    }

    @Test
    fun activityScenarioLaunchSample() {
        openContextualActionModeOverflowMenu()
        onView(allOf(withId(R.id.title), withText(R.string.refresh))).
        perform(click())
    }
}
```

As you can see, it doesn't differ much from a usage perspective. But you will not have an instance of ActivityTestRule and, as a result, cannot access the launched activity.

Using Truth Assertion Library in UI Tests

Although it was developed mostly for unit and integration tests, the Truth Assertion Library can provide benefits to UI tests as well. We used JUnit assertions in Chapter 8 to assert element presence on the screen in the UI automator tests. Let's take a look at the difference between basic JUnit and Truth assertions.

Table 14-1. *Basic JUnit and Truth Assertions Comparison*

JUnit	Truth
assertEquals(b, a)	assertThat(a).isEqualTo(b)
assertTrue(c)	assertThat(c).isTrue()
assertTrue(d.contains(a))	assertThat(d).contains(a)
assertTrue(d.contains(a) && d.contains(b)) assertTrue(d.contains(a) || d.contains(b) || d.contains(c))	assertThat(d). containsAllOf(a, b) assertThat(d). containsAnyOf(a, b, c)

To tell the truth, the Truth syntax is more readable, easier to write, and is similar to Hamcrest library methods, which we used while writing Espresso tests. Now moving to the test failure reporting part. It is important to have a meaningful and descriptive test failure stacktrace, so the failure analysis doesn't require much time and effort. The TruthTest.kt class contains two tests that fail to demonstrate the failure reporting by both JUnit and Truth and compare them afterward.

chapter14.TruthTest.kt. Both Tests Fail to Demonstrate the Stacktrace Difference Between JUnit and Truth Assertions.

```
@RunWith(AndroidJUnit4::class)
class TruthTest {

    private val uiDevice: UiDevice = UiDevice.getInstance(Instrumentation
    Registry.getInstrumentation())

    @Before
    fun launchTasksActivity() {
        ActivityScenario.launch(TasksActivity::class.java)
    }

    /**
     * Specifically fails the test using JUnit assertion.
     */
    @Test
    fun generatesJunitAssertionError() {
        val selector = uiDevice.findObject(UiSelector().resourceId(
```

```
            "com.example.android.architecture.blueprints.todoapp.
            mock:id/fab_add_task"))

    // JUnit assertion.
    assertFalse(
            "Element with selector $selector is present on the screen
            when it should not",
            selector.exists())
}

/**
 * Specifically fails the test using Truth assertion.
 */
@Test
fun generatesTruthAssertionError() {
    val selector = uiDevice.findObject(UiSelector().resourceId(
            "com.example.android.architecture.blueprints.todoapp.
            mock:id/fab_add_task"))

    // Truth assertion.
    assertThat(selector.exists()).isFalse()
}
}
```

Here is a sample error stacktrace from an old JUnit assertTrue(MESSAGE, CONDITION) method and one generated by the TruthTest.generatesJunitAssertionError() method implemented in the chapter's TO-DO sample.

JUnit Error Stacktrace Generated by Failure in the generatesJunitAssertionError() Test.

```
java.lang.AssertionError: Element with selector androidx.test.uiautomator.
UiObject@ce91768 is present on the screen when it should not
at org.junit.Assert.fail(Assert.java:88)
at org.junit.Assert.assertTrue(Assert.java:41)
at org.junit.Assert.assertFalse(Assert.java:64)
at com.example.android.architecture.blueprints.todoapp.test.chapter14.
TruthTest.generatesJunitAssertionError(TruthTest.kt:33)
at java.lang.reflect.Method.invoke(Native Method)
```

at org.junit.runners.model.FrameworkMethod$1.runReflectiveCall(Framework
Method.java:50)
at org.junit.internal.runners.model.ReflectiveCallable.
run(ReflectiveCallable.java:12)
at org.junit.runners.model.FrameworkMethod.invokeExplosively(Framework
Method.java:47)
at org.junit.internal.runners.statements.InvokeMethod.
evaluate(InvokeMethod.java:17)
at androidx.test.internal.runner.junit4.statement.RunBefores.
evaluate(RunBefores.java:80)
at org.junit.runners.ParentRunner.runLeaf(ParentRunner.java:325)
at org.junit.runners.BlockJUnit4ClassRunner.
runChild(BlockJUnit4ClassRunner.java:78)
at org.junit.runners.BlockJUnit4ClassRunner.
runChild(BlockJUnit4ClassRunner.java:57)
at org.junit.runners.ParentRunner$3.run(ParentRunner.java:290)
at org.junit.runners.ParentRunner$1.schedule(ParentRunner.java:71)
at org.junit.runners.ParentRunner.runChildren(ParentRunner.java:288)
at org.junit.runners.ParentRunner.access$000(ParentRunner.java:58)
at org.junit.runners.ParentRunner$2.evaluate(ParentRunner.java:268)
at org.junit.runners.ParentRunner.run(ParentRunner.java:363)
at androidx.test.ext.junit.runners.AndroidJUnit4.run(AndroidJUnit4.java:104)
at org.junit.runners.Suite.runChild(Suite.java:128)
at org.junit.runners.Suite.runChild(Suite.java:27)
at org.junit.runners.ParentRunner$3.run(ParentRunner.java:290)
at org.junit.runners.ParentRunner$1.schedule(ParentRunner.java:71)
at org.junit.runners.ParentRunner.runChildren(ParentRunner.java:288)
at org.junit.runners.ParentRunner.access$000(ParentRunner.java:58)
at org.junit.runners.ParentRunner$2.evaluate(ParentRunner.java:268)
at org.junit.runners.ParentRunner.run(ParentRunner.java:363)
at org.junit.runner.JUnitCore.run(JUnitCore.java:137)
at org.junit.runner.JUnitCore.run(JUnitCore.java:115)
at androidx.test.internal.runner.TestExecutor.execute(TestExecutor.java:56)
at androidx.test.runner.AndroidJUnitRunner.onStart(AndroidJUnitRunner.java:388)
at android.app.Instrumentation$InstrumentationThread.run(Instrumentation.
java:2145)

It is worth mentioning that the JUnit `assertTrue()` method accepts the error description message that's present in the first stacktrace line.

By contrast, here is the Truth `assertThat(CONDITION).isFalse()` sample error stacktrace.

Truth Error Stacktrace Generated by Failure in the generatesTruthAssertionError() Test.

```
expected to be false
at com.example.android.architecture.blueprints.todoapp.test.chapter14.
TruthTest.generatesTruthAssertionError(TruthTest.kt:41)
```

EXERCISE 29

Migrating to AndroidX

1. Check out the master branch of the TO-DO application project and migrate it to AndroidX. After the migration is complete, choose Build ➤ Clean Project. Run some tests. If there are failures, analyze and fix them by updating the `proguard` rules or updating dependences in the `build.gradle` file.

2. Implement a test class with a test that launches application activity using `ActivityScenario.launch(Activity.class)` in the `@Before` method and then runs the test.

3. Implement a test using an UI automator testing framework that will use the `JUnit` Assertion Library to validate the test results. Make the test fail and observe the stacktrace.

4. Implement a test using an UI automator testing framework that will use the `Truth` Assertion Library to validate the test results. Make the test fail and observe the stacktrace.

Summary

In general, AndroidX Test is a nice step forward. It brings alignment among different test types in terms of testing tools and dependencies used. The main weakness so far is that it targets unit and integration tests with only tiny improvements on UI tests. But more will certainly come for UI tests in time and hopefully with higher frequency than with the testing support library.

CHAPTER 15

Improving Productivity and Testing Unusual Components

This chapter contains code samples that were not covered in other chapters and Espresso testing tips that may increase your daily test writing productivity.

Creating Parameterized Tests

Sometimes we may have a need to write a single test that is applicable to many similar cases. For example, we might need a test that validates how the same EditText field behaves with different String values provided as input. In this case, the JUnit Parameterized custom runner can be used. It allows us to have one test inside a parameterized class (https://github.com/junit-team/junit4/wiki/parameterized-tests). The following example demonstrates a parameterized test class with a single parameter.

chapter15.parameterizedtest.ParameterizedTestSingleParameter.kt.

```
/**
 * Parameterized test with single parameter.
 */
@RunWith(value = Parameterized::class)
class ParameterizedTestSingleParameter(private val title: String) :
BaseTest() {
```

© Denys Zelenchuk 2019
D. Zelenchuk, *Android Espresso Revealed*, https://doi.org/10.1007/978-1-4842-4315-2_15

```kotlin
@Test
fun usesSingleParameters() {
    // Add new TO-DO.
    onView(withId(R.id.fab_add_task)).perform(click())
    onView(withId(R.id.add_task_title))
            .perform(typeText(title), closeSoftKeyboard())
    onView(withId(R.id.fab_edit_task_done)).perform(click())

    // Verify new TO-DO with title is shown in the TO-DO list.
    onView(withText(title)).check(matches(isDisplayed()))
}

companion object {
    @JvmStatic
    @Parameterized.Parameters
    fun data() = listOf(
            TodoItem().title,
            TodoItem().title,
            TodoItem().title)
}
}
```

During the test run, each instance of the ParameterizedTestSingleParameter class will be constructed using the provided title argument. So, in the end, we will have as many test runs as the number of parameters provided. In this case, it is three.

A parameterized test class with multiple test parameters can be created in a similar way, as follows.

chapter15.parameterizedtest.ParameterizedTestMultipleParameters.kt.

```kotlin
/**
 * Parameterized test with multiple parameters.
 */
@RunWith(value = Parameterized::class)
class ParameterizedTestMultipleParameters(
        private val title: String,
        private val description: String) : BaseTest() {
```

```kotlin
@Test
fun usesMultipleParameters() {
    // Add new TO-DO.
    onView(withId(R.id.fab_add_task)).perform(click())
    onView(withId(R.id.add_task_title))
            .perform(typeText(title), closeSoftKeyboard())
    onView(withId(R.id.add_task_description))
            .perform(typeText(description), closeSoftKeyboard())
    onView(withId(R.id.fab_edit_task_done)).perform(click())

    // Verify new TO-DO with title is shown in the TO-DO list.
    onView(withText(title)).check(matches(isDisplayed()))
}

companion object {
    @JvmStatic
    @Parameterized.Parameters
    fun data() = arrayOf(
            arrayOf("item 1", "description 1"),
            arrayOf("item 2", "description 2"),
            arrayOf("item 3", "description 3"))
}
}
```

Aggregating Tests into Test Suites

In order to run a set of tests that may belong or may test for a particular application functionality, they are best organized into test suites. The JUnit Suite Runner can be the right choice here. It allows you to manually build a suite containing tests from many test classes. Here is how it looks.

chapter15.testsuite.TestSuiteSample.kt

```kotlin
/**
 * Organizing test classes into a test suite.
 */
@RunWith(Suite::class)
```

```
@Suite.SuiteClasses(
        AddToDoTest::class,
        EditToDoTest::class,
        FilterToDoTest::class)
class TestSuiteSample
```

This way, you can organize tests into a logical structure depending on the tested functionality or on the test types, such as Smoke, Regression, etc.

Using AndroidStudio Live Templates in UI Tests

The code completion feature in many modern integrated development environments (IDEs) increased our code writing productivity quite a lot. But thanks to AndroidStudio, we have an even more powerful tool that can help us code even faster—live templates.

Live templates are predefined code snippets that can be inserted into code by typing their abbreviations. They can be added to AndroidStudio via Preferences ➤ Editor ➤ Live Templates. There are a set of predefined Live Templates groups and you can add your own group or your own live template. To do this, click the + button and select the proper option. After that, you provide an abbreviation name, template text (the code snippet that will be later inserted instead of the abbreviation), an optional description, and the proper context where your template will be available. In our case, the Kotlin and Java contexts were selected, as shown in Figure 15-1.

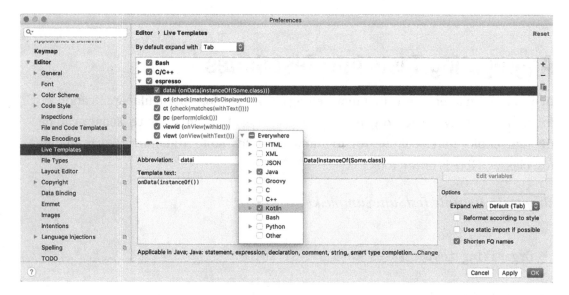

Figure 15-1. *Adding a live template*

The created templates can be used in specified contexts, by just typing the template abbreviation and clicking the Tab button, as shown in Figure 15-2.

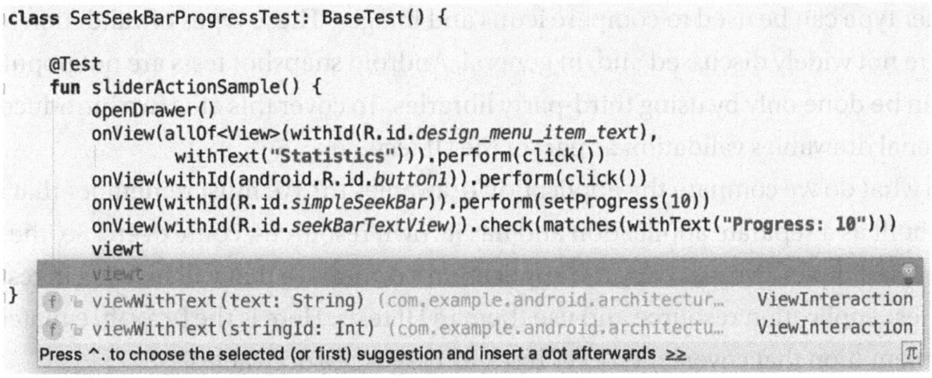

```
class SetSeekBarProgressTest: BaseTest() {

    @Test
    fun sliderActionSample() {
        openDrawer()
        onView(allOf<View>(withId(R.id.design_menu_item_text),
                withText("Statistics"))).perform(click())
        onView(withId(android.R.id.button1)).perform(click())
        onView(withId(R.id.simpleSeekBar)).perform(setProgress(10))
        onView(withId(R.id.seekBarTextView)).check(matches(withText("Progress: 10")))
        viewt
        viewt
}
    f  viewWithText(text: String) (com.example.android.architectur…   ViewInteraction
    f  viewWithText(stringId: Int) (com.example.android.architectu…    ViewInteraction
    Press ^. to choose the selected (or first) suggestion and insert a dot afterwards ≥≥        π
```

Figure 15-2. *Using a live template by typing the abbreviation and clicking Tab*

It is also easy to export predefined live templates when you switch your computer or want to share them. To do this, just open the File ➤ Export Settings … menu and select Live Templates, as shown in Figure 15-3.

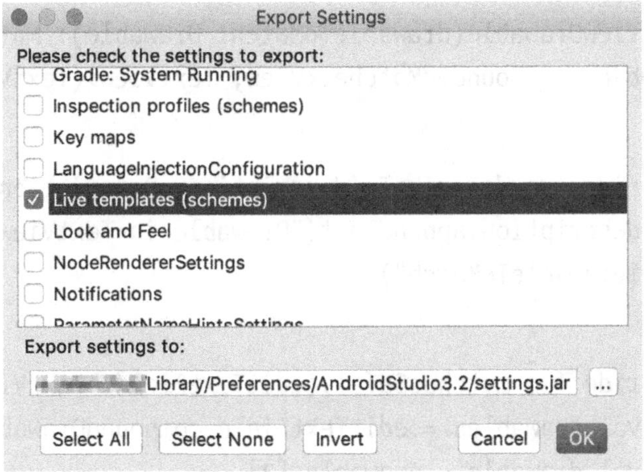

Figure 15-3. *Exporting live templates*

For your convenience, a small list of Espresso live templates was created and exported as a .jar file into the TO-DO application project in the following path: todoapp/book_assets/livetemplates.jar.

Espresso Drawable Matchers

Another custom matcher type that we must know about are the `Drawable` matchers. This matcher type can be used to compare icons and images. These types of validation in UI tests are not widely discussed and, in general, Android snapshot tests are not popular and can be done only by using third-party libraries. To cover this area, we introduce additional drawables validation as part of the UI tests.

So what do we compare the application drawables to? We must remember that a test is built as a separate application and has its own resources, context, etc. So, the solution is simple—we just copy the application's drawables that will be used in tests into a test application resource and use them in UI tests. Here is the `Drawable` matchers implementation that covers the `TextView` and `ImageView` drawables.

chapter15.drawablematchers.DrawableMatchers.kt.

```kotlin
/**
 * Contains TextView and ImageView Drawable matchers.
 */
class DrawableMatchers {

    fun withTextViewDrawable(drawableToMatch: Drawable): Matcher<View> {
        return object : BoundedMatcher<View, TextView>(TextView::class.
        java) {

            override fun describeTo(description: Description) {
                description.appendText("Drawable in TextView
                $drawableToMatch")
            }

            override fun matchesSafely(editTextField: TextView): Boolean {
                val drawables = editTextField.compoundDrawables
                val drawable = drawables[2]

                return isSameBitmap(drawableToMatch, drawable)
            }
        }
    }
}
```

```kotlin
fun withImageViewDrawable(expectedDrawable: Drawable?): Matcher<View> {
    return object : BoundedMatcher<View, ImageView>(ImageView::class.
    java) {
        override fun describeTo(description: Description) {
            description.appendText("Drawable in ImageView
            $expectedDrawable")
        }

        public override fun matchesSafely(imageView: ImageView) =
                isSameBitmap(imageView.drawable, expectedDrawable)
    }
}

fun isSameBitmap(drawable: Drawable?, expectedDrawable: Drawable?):
Boolean {
    var localDrawable = drawable
    var localExpectedDrawable = expectedDrawable

    // Return if null.
    if (localDrawable == null || localExpectedDrawable == null) {
        return false
    }

    // StateListDrawable lets you assign a number of graphic images to
    a single
    // Drawable and swap out the visible item by a string ID value.
    if (localDrawable is StateListDrawable
      && localExpectedDrawable is StateListDrawable) {
            localDrawable = localDrawable.current
            localExpectedDrawable = localExpectedDrawable.current
    }

    // BitmapDrawable - a Drawable that wraps a bitmap and can be
    tiled, stretched, or
    // aligned.
    if (localDrawable is BitmapDrawable) {
        val bitmap = localDrawable.bitmap
```

```
            val otherBitmap = (localExpectedDrawable as BitmapDrawable).
            bitmap
            return bitmap.sameAs(otherBitmap)
        }
        return false
    }
}
```

Here is its usage.

chapter15.drawablematchers.DrawableMatchersTest.kt.

```
/**
 * Demonstrates Drawable matchers usage.
 */
class DrawableMatchersTest : BaseTest() {

    @Test
    fun checkDrawableInMenuDrawer() {
        openDrawer()
        onView(withId(R.id.headerTodoLogo))
                .check(matches(DrawableMatchers()
                        .withImageViewDrawable(getMenuIconDrawable())))
    }

    private fun getMenuIconDrawable(): Drawable? {
        val drawableId = com.example.android.architecture.blueprints.
        todoapp.mock.test
                .R.drawable.test_logo
        return InstrumentationRegistry.getInstrumentation().context.
        getDrawable(drawableId)
    }
}
```

In this test, we are comparing the icon shown inside the TO-DO application drawer called logo.png name in main application drawables with the one stored in the test application drawable resources called test_logo.

> **Note**   It is not possible to import the `R.class` file from the main and test applications, so we have to explicitly provide the path to test the application `R.class`.

Setting SeekBar Progress in Espresso UI Tests

This section demonstrates how to set the `SeekBar` progress with a custom Espresso `ViewAction`. We know from Chapter 2 how to create a custom `ViewAction` and the `SeekBar` case is one of the simplest.

chapter15.setseekbarprogress.SeekBarViewActions.kt.

```kotlin
/**
 * ViewActions that operate on SeekBar
 */
object SeekBarViewActions {

    /**
     * Sets progress of a SeekBar.
     *
     * @param value - the progress value between min and max SeekBar value
     */
    fun setProgress(value: Int): ViewAction {
        return object : ViewAction {
            override fun getConstraints(): Matcher<View> {
                return isAssignableFrom(SeekBar::class.java)
            }

            override fun getDescription(): String {
                return ("Set slider progress to $value.")
            }
```

```
            override fun perform(uiController: UiController, view: View) {
                val seekBar = view as SeekBar
                seekBar.progress = value
            }
        }
    }
}
```

The usage in the test also looks simple, as follows.

chapter15.setseekbarprogress.SetSeekBarProgressTest.kt.

```
/**
 * Testing SeekBar change.
 */
class SetSeekBarProgressTest: BaseTest() {

    @Test
    fun sliderActionSample() {
        openDrawer()
        onView(allOf(withId(R.id.design_menu_item_text),
                withText(R.string.statistics_title))).perform(click())
        onView(withId(android.R.id.button1)).perform(click())
        onView(withId(R.id.simpleSeekBar)).perform(setProgress(10))
        onView(withId(R.id.seekBarTextView)).check(matches(withText
        ("Progress: 10")))
    }
}
```

APPENDIX A

Espresso-Web Cheat Sheet

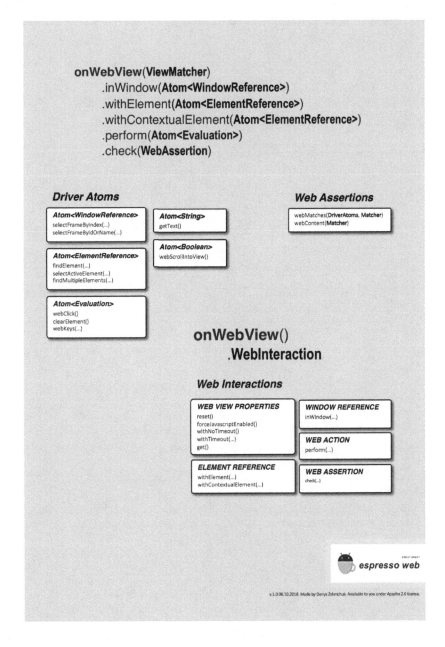

© Denys Zelenchuk 2019
D. Zelenchuk, *Android Espresso Revealed*, https://doi.org/10.1007/978-1-4842-4315-2

APPENDIX B

UI Automator Cheat Sheet

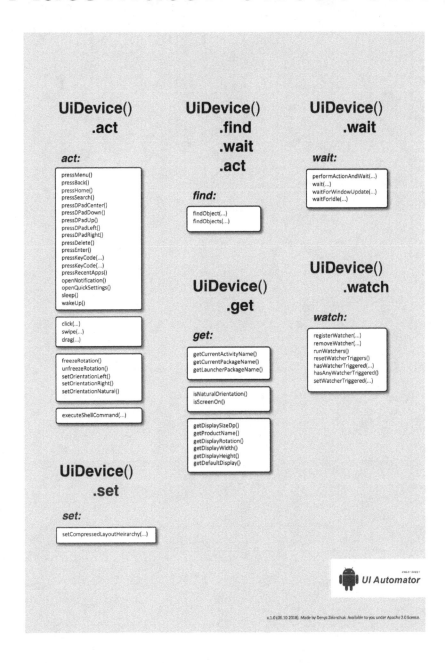

© Denys Zelenchuk 2019
D. Zelenchuk, *Android Espresso Revealed*, https://doi.org/10.1007/978-1-4842-4315-2

APPENDIX C

Apache License

Apache License

Version 2.0, January 2004

http://www.apache.org/licenses/

TERMS AND CONDITIONS FOR USE, REPRODUCTION, AND DISTRIBUTION

1. Definitions.

"License" shall mean the terms and conditions for use, reproduction, and distribution as defined by Sections 1 through 9 of this document.

"Licensor" shall mean the copyright owner or entity authorized by the copyright owner that is granting the License.

"Legal Entity" shall mean the union of the acting entity and all other entities that control, are controlled by, or are under common control with that entity. For the purposes of this definition, "control" means (i) the power, direct or indirect, to cause the direction or management of such entity, whether by contract or otherwise, or (ii) ownership of fifty percent (50%) or more of the outstanding shares, or (iii) beneficial ownership of such entity.

"You" (or "Your") shall mean an individual or Legal Entity exercising permissions granted by this License.

"Source" form shall mean the preferred form for making modifications, including but not limited to software source code, documentation source, and configuration files.

© Denys Zelenchuk 2019
D. Zelenchuk, *Android Espresso Revealed*, https://doi.org/10.1007/978-1-4842-4315-2

"Object" form shall mean any form resulting from mechanical transformation or translation of a Source form, including but not limited to compiled object code, generated documentation, and conversions to other media types.

"Work" shall mean the work of authorship, whether in Source or Object form, made available under the License, as indicated by a copyright notice that is included in or attached to the work (an example is provided in the Appendix below).

"Derivative Works" shall mean any work, whether in Source or Object form, that is based on (or derived from) the Work and for which the editorial revisions, annotations, elaborations, or other modifications represent, as a whole, an original work of authorship. For the purposes of this License, Derivative Works shall not include works that remain separable from, or merely link (or bind by name) to the interfaces of, the Work and Derivative Works thereof.

"Contribution" shall mean any work of authorship, including the original version of the Work and any modifications or additions to that Work or Derivative Works thereof, that is intentionally submitted to Licensor for inclusion in the Work by the copyright owner or by an individual or Legal Entity authorized to submit on behalf of the copyright owner. For the purposes of this definition, "submitted" means any form of electronic, verbal, or written communication sent to the Licensor or its representatives, including but not limited to communication on electronic mailing lists, source code control systems, and issue tracking systems that are managed by, or on behalf of, the Licensor for the purpose of discussing and improving the Work, but excluding communication that is conspicuously marked or otherwise designated in writing by the copyright owner as "Not a Contribution."

"Contributor" shall mean Licensor and any individual or Legal Entity on behalf of whom a Contribution has been received by Licensor and subsequently incorporated within the Work.

2. Grant of Copyright License. Subject to the terms and conditions of this License, each Contributor hereby grants to You a perpetual, worldwide, non-exclusive, no-charge, royalty-free, irrevocable copyright license to

reproduce, prepare Derivative Works of, publicly display, publicly perform, sublicense, and distribute the Work and such Derivative Works in Source or Object form.

3. Grant of Patent License. Subject to the terms and conditions of this License, each Contributor hereby grants to You a perpetual, worldwide, non-exclusive, no-charge, royalty-free, irrevocable (except as stated in this section) patent license to make, have made, use, offer to sell, sell, import, and otherwise transfer the Work, where such license applies only to those patent claims licensable by such Contributor that are necessarily infringed by their Contribution(s) alone or by combination of their Contribution(s) with the Work to which such Contribution(s) was submitted. If You institute patent litigation against any entity (including a cross-claim or counterclaim in a lawsuit) alleging that the Work or a Contribution incorporated within the Work constitutes direct or contributory patent infringement, then any patent licenses granted to You under this License for that Work shall terminate as of the date such litigation is filed.

4. Redistribution. You may reproduce and distribute copies of the Work or Derivative Works thereof in any medium, with or without modifications, and in Source or Object form, provided that You meet the following conditions:

You must give any other recipients of the Work or Derivative Works a copy of this License; and
You must cause any modified files to carry prominent notices stating that You changed the files; and
You must retain, in the Source form of any Derivative Works that You distribute, all copyright, patent, trademark, and attribution notices from the Source form of the Work, excluding those notices that do not pertain to any part of the Derivative Works; and
If the Work includes a "NOTICE" text file as part of its distribution, then any Derivative Works that You distribute must include a readable copy of the attribution notices contained within such NOTICE file, excluding those notices that do not pertain to any part of the Derivative Works, in at least one of the following places: within a NOTICE text file distributed as part of the Derivative Works; within the Source form or documentation, if

provided along with the Derivative Works; or, within a display generated by the Derivative Works, if and wherever such third-party notices normally appear. The contents of the NOTICE file are for informational purposes only and do not modify the License. You may add Your own attribution notices within Derivative Works that You distribute, alongside or as an addendum to the NOTICE text from the Work, provided that such additional attribution notices cannot be construed as modifying the License.

You may add Your own copyright statement to Your modifications and may provide additional or different license terms and conditions for use, reproduction, or distribution of Your modifications, or for any such Derivative Works as a whole, provided Your use, reproduction, and distribution of the Work otherwise complies with the conditions stated in this License.

5. Submission of Contributions. Unless You explicitly state otherwise, any Contribution intentionally submitted for inclusion in the Work by You to the Licensor shall be under the terms and conditions of this License, without any additional terms or conditions. Notwithstanding the above, nothing herein shall supersede or modify the terms of any separate license agreement you may have executed with Licensor regarding such Contributions.

6. Trademarks. This License does not grant permission to use the trade names, trademarks, service marks, or product names of the Licensor, except as required for reasonable and customary use in describing the origin of the Work and reproducing the content of the NOTICE file.

7. Disclaimer of Warranty. Unless required by applicable law or agreed to in writing, Licensor provides the Work (and each Contributor provides its Contributions) on an "AS IS" BASIS, WITHOUT WARRANTIES OR CONDITIONS OF ANY KIND, either express or implied, including, without limitation, any warranties or conditions of TITLE, NON-INFRINGEMENT, MERCHANTABILITY, or FITNESS FOR A PARTICULAR PURPOSE. You are solely responsible for determining the appropriateness of using or redistributing the Work and assume any risks associated with Your exercise of permissions under this License.

8. Limitation of Liability. In no event and under no legal theory, whether in tort (including negligence), contract, or otherwise, unless required by applicable law (such as deliberate and grossly negligent acts) or agreed to in writing, shall any Contributor be liable to You for damages, including any direct, indirect, special, incidental, or consequential damages of any character arising as a result of this License or out of the use or inability to use the Work (including but not limited to damages for loss of goodwill, work stoppage, computer failure or malfunction, or any and all other commercial damages or losses), even if such Contributor has been advised of the possibility of such damages.

9. Accepting Warranty or Additional Liability. While redistributing the Work or Derivative Works thereof, You may choose to offer, and charge a fee for, acceptance of support, warranty, indemnity, or other liability obligations and/or rights consistent with this License. However, in accepting such obligations, You may act only on Your own behalf and on Your sole responsibility, not on behalf of any other Contributor, and only if You agree to indemnify, defend, and hold each Contributor harmless for any liability incurred by, or claims asserted against, such Contributor by reason of your accepting any such warranty or additional liability.

END OF TERMS AND CONDITIONS

APPENDIX: HOW TO APPLY THE APACHE LICENSE TO YOUR WORK
To apply the Apache License to your work, attach the following boilerplate notice, with the fields enclosed by brackets "[]" replaced with your own identifying information. (Don't include the brackets!) The text should be enclosed in the appropriate comment syntax for the file format. We also recommend that a file or class name and description of purpose be included on the same "printed page" as the copyright notice for easier identification within third-party archives.

Copyright [yyyy] [name of copyright owner]

Licensed under the Apache License, Version 2.0 (the "License");
you may not use this file except in compliance with the License.
You may obtain a copy of the License at

    http://www.apache.org/licenses/LICENSE-2.0

APPENDIX C   APACHE LICENSE

Unless required by applicable law or agreed to in writing, software distributed under the License is distributed on an "AS IS" BASIS, WITHOUT WARRANTIES OR CONDITIONS OF ANY KIND, either express or implied. See the License for the specific language governing permissions and limitations under the License.

Index

A

© Denys Zelenchuk 2019

D. Zelenchuk, *Android Espresso Revealed*, https://doi.org/10.1007/978-1-4842-4315-2

Printed in the United States
By Bookmasters